Selection
for
Secondary Education

PETER GORDON

University of London Institute of Education

THE WOBURN PRESS

First published 1980 in Great Britain by
THE WOBURN PRESS
Gainsborough House, Gainsborough Road,
London, E11 1RS, England

and in the United States of America by
THE WOBURN PRESS
c/o Biblio Distribution Centre
81 Adams Drive, P.O. Box 327, Totowa, N.J. 07511

British Library Cataloguing in Publication Data

Gordon, Peter, *b. 1927*
  Selection for secondary education.
  1. High schools – England – Entrance requirements
  – History
  1. Title
  373.1′2′160942   LB1627

ISBN 0-7130-0157-7

Photoset in Times by Saildean Ltd
Reproduced from copy supplied
printed and bound in Great Britain
by Billing and Sons Limited
Guildford, London, Oxford, Worcester

Contents

Introduction

It is generally stated by educational historians that selection for secondary education is largely an issue of the present century, stemming from the provision of municipal 'grammar' schools after the 1902 Education Act. In fact, the movement can be traced back much further. The Schools Inquiry Commission, appointed in 1864 to consider the state of the endowed schools, revealed a disturbing picture. Recommendations for reform, put forward by the Commission, were to be effected by legislation in the shape of the Endowed Schools Act of 1869. The body charged with implementing change was the Endowed Schools Commission, later absorbed into the Charity Commission. It addressed itself, amongst other things, to a searching investigation into ways of providing education above elementary for able children of the poor in the absence of State intervention.

The first part of this book will be devoted to an analysis of attitudes towards the award of scholarships and exhibitions at the time, and to a consideration of some of the factors determining selection procedures and the chances of the poor obtaining a 'secondary' education, up to the end of the century. It will also indicate the extent to which the policies governing the award of free places at the municipal secondary schools favoured by the Board of Education after the 1902 Act were continuations of already existing practices.

Copious evidence is now available which provides useful information on the changing social composition of recipients of secondary education in the last three decades of the nineteenth century. This will be examined as well as its effect on the curriculum.

From the time of the 1907 Regulations for Secondary Schools which first established the system of free places, it was recognized that with the growing number of elementary school pupils attending the new secondary schools, the concept of a 'ladder of education' was no longer appropriate. Social and political attitudes were changing; and writers such as R. H. Tawney in his book *Secondary Education For All*, 1922, linked secondary education and

vii

social justice, and conceived of secondary education as a broad highway. Local selection procedures, as well as governmental edicts, had a crucial bearing on how far this was achieved. Although the political-administrative decisions have been described by some historians, the ways in which local education authorities carried out this task remain largely unexplored.

The study should end with the passing of the 1944 Education Act, which provided universal secondary schooling, but the post-war creation of the tripartite system – grammar, technical and modern schools – made selection still necessary. It was not until the Education Act of 1976 that the Secretary of State was given new powers to compel local authorities to end selection in their areas and establish comprehensive schools. The situation has changed again with the repeal of this Act in 1979: the debate has now been reopened on the form which secondary education should take.

This book then, is a survey of the history of selection from the earliest times. It is hoped that it will provide a perspective for considering some of the issues involved in the provision of secondary education in the last century as well as in the present.

Acknowledgements

During the writing of this book, I have received much support and help from a variety of sources. For permission to quote from papers in their possession, I wish to thank the National Trust, Hughenden Manor, Bucks., Lord Cairns, Lord Cranbrook, Sir William Gladstone, the Directors of the Goodwood Estate Company, the Marquess of Salisbury and Lord Cobham.

I am indebted to the staffs of the London Library, the Public Record Office, the Department of Education and Science Library and the University of London Institute of Education Library for their assistance in tracing relevant material. Equally I am grateful to the county record offices and university archive departments whose names are listed in the Bibliography. The Secretary of the Incorporated Association of Headmasters was also kind enough to make available for consultation the early Minute Books of the Association.

I would like to acknowledge the cheerful manner in which Valerie Gregory and Lynn Cairns carried out the translation of the manuscript into its typed form. My final debt of thanks is to David Gordon for his bibliographical assistance and to my wife Tessa for her advice and encouragement during the preparation of this work.

CHAPTER 1

The Need for Reform: The Endowed Schools before 1869*

The state of the endowed schools up to 1864

At the middle of the nineteenth century, the endowed schools of England, estimated at some 782 above the elementary stage, presented a picture of education in decay. Of these, 27 per cent were nominally classical, 23 per cent taught no Greek but Latin, and 43 per cent were non-classical.[1] Endowed schools had developed haphazardly: there was no differentiation between types of endowed schools, whose origins and prescription as to entrance qualifications and type of education provided varied according to the intentions of their pious founders and to the state of the endowment itself.

Many of the early schools contained a good proportion of poor boys who received their education and maintenance at the foundation's expense. One of the first examples of a good-class education for poor boys is the well-known one of Winchester College, founded by William Wykeham in 1382. There, the boys learned alongside fee-paying scholars, and sixty years later, Eton followed in conscious imitation. Entrants had to satisfy the authorities that they were 'poor and needy'.[2] The essential feature of these early foundations was the boarding facilities, which marked them off from the day schools. The foundation boys, as they were called, formed the backbone of the school.[3] It was inevitable that the Church should be the agent responsible, either directly or indirectly, for ensuring that endowments created for the

---

* A description of the different types of school mentioned in this book is given in the glossary.

1

provision of free education for those who needed it were correctly applied.

The Renaissance in England led to the establishment of grammar schools up and down the country, which were day schools providing the elements of Greek and Latin to their scholars.[4] By the sixteenth century, entry was based on aptitude and ability, rather than on ability to pay. Such people as Cranmer and Thomas Cromwell were products of this system. It was Cranmer who resisted the exclusion of the 'ploughman's son' from the cathedral school at Canterbury, stating that 'if the gentleman's son is apt to learning, let him be admitted: if not apt to learning, let the poor man's child, being apt, enter into his own.'[5]

Whilst most noble families continued the tradition of educating their sons and daughters within the precincts of their homes,[6] a number began to send them at first to the local grammar schools and later to the more exclusive establishments which catered for this demand in and around London.[7] The rise of the great public schools[8] dates from the eighteenth century, when the local character of the school gave place to that of a national one. The shift from a tentative middle class in the 1820s to a middle class whose days of struggle for recognition were behind them, led to a demand for more radical reform than would otherwise have been possible. The qualifications for admission were changed. Initially, the effect was to exclude the poor boy, and local preferences stipulated by the founder were swept away.[9] Later, the Clarendon Commission (1860-4), which investigated the leading public schools and recommended no major changes in their class structure, used the same arguments in defending this view as earlier headmasters had done:

> Speaking generally, it must be said that the difficulty of assigning a precise meaning to the word poverty, the doubt what class of persons, if any, at the present day really answers to the *pauperes at indigentes scholares* of the Lancastrian and Tudor periods, and the further doubt whether poverty is not after all best served by giving the widest encouragement to industry, coupled with the interest which every school has in collecting the best boys from the largest surface, have tended, and will continually tend, to render the qualification of indigence practically inoperative.[10]

This was seen in the growing proportion of non-foundationers to foundationers[11] and in the methods by which foundationers were obliged to pay sums of money.[12] Because of the emphasis on classics, it would be impossible for a boy to reach the required standard for entry as a foundationer without either coaching or attendance at a private school. The mood of the times was efficiency and value for money. The reforms of Arnold at Rugby (1827), Kennedy at Shrewsbury (1836), and Vaughan at Harrow (1844) were in line with this. Coupled with these new ideals was the necessity for exclusiveness. Arnold, for instance, doubled the fees for free scholars and Vaughan was ruthless with regard to local preference.[13]

The Public Schools Act, which was passed in the year that the Schools Inquiry Commission reported (1868), whilst preserving the social superiority of the public school, cleared up many abuses. 'By its provisions each school was required to submit a scheme for a new and more representative governing body. This body was given full powers with regard to school fees, the curriculum, and the appointment or dismissal of the headmaster. The latter was responsible to the governing body, but he had the right to appoint his assistant masters and they had no appeal to the governors from his decisions.'[14] Although schemes had to be submitted and approved by the Queen in Council, thereafter no Government supervision of public schools was contemplated; no inspections were to be carried out and each school was free to develop as it wished, within the bounds of the Act. A reluctance to move with the times marked off the public schools from those establishments below them. The Clarendon Commission, in its recommendations, was not prepared to encourage the establishment of modern departments in the schools under review though these had been such a success at the newer proprietary schools of Marlborough and Cheltenham.[15]

The outcome of the remodelling of the public schools, supported by the Clarendon findings, was their estrangement from the bulk of the grammar schools, from which many had themselves risen; the diminished prestige of the many endowed schools;[16] and a growing division in society. As one writer put it, 'the sons of manufacturers and professional men in the now populous industrial districts were in great measure cut off from early and intimate association with the sons of the poorer families in the neighbourhood of their homes.'[17]

The state of the endowed schools other than the leading ones was not conducive to complacency on the part of ambitious parents. The curriculum ranged from that of a full classical education to a merely elementary one, although the nomenclature 'grammar school' which was indiscriminately applied to the schools was defined by the 1840 Grammar Schools Act as a foundation where Latin and Greek were taught. Nicholas Carlisle's two volumes entitled *Concise Description of the Endowed Grammar Schools in England,* published in 1818, revealed these wide differences, and gave numerous examples of misapplied funds, empty schools, hereditary offices and nepotism on a vast scale. Much depended on the energies and endeavour of the master and trustees.[18] For example, at Dorchester, Dorset, when the master took over in October 1814 he found only ten boarders, most of whom left when he was appointed. In four years, he had built up the reputation of the school and it was claimed that by 1818, the work done was similar to that at Winchester. Manchester Grammar School was outstanding in its achievements through a succession of first-rate High Masters.[19]

The lucrative practice of accommodating boarders often resulted in the exclusion of the free pupils. The school at King's Lynn was open to the sons of burgesses, free of expense for classics only. At the time of Carlisle's writing, there were no foundation boys, but the Master took boarders at 32 guineas a year.[20] Since 1840, when the Grammar Schools Act allowed a widening of the curriculum, fees could be charged for subjects other than classics; many pupils with the advantage of 'local preference' by virtue of the founder's will, were unable to take up the education offered. At Oundle, only three boys from the town attended the school. Moreover, since Carlisle's survey, little had been done to correct these anomalies.

The bulk of the middle classes were dependent on the facilities offered by the local endowed school for a number of reasons. Because of the high fees, public schools were beyond their reach; travelling to schools outside the immediate neighbourhood could be difficult and there was often a lack of suitable private venture schools as alternatives. The number of endowed schools had declined during the course of the century and there was a greater demand from the new middle classes, especially Dissenters, for educational facilities for their children.[21] Matthew Arnold articulated the aspirations of 'this great class' shortly before the Schools Inquiry Commission began its work:

... in this land of education it should henceforth get something out of the millions given annually for this purpose to every class except itself. ...

Arnold pointed especially to the endowments given in earlier times to universities and public schools not only for the benefit of the upper classes but for the middle classes who were now virtually excluded.[22] In many instances, the situation was aggravated by the vested rights of inhabitants under the terms of original endowments, which entitled their sons and daughters to be educated free at the endowed school. Changes in the schools were difficult, as they involved the cumbersome machinery of Chancery proceedings (see this chapter, p. 10): the original terms of the endowment made for inertia. Some of the more ambitious headmasters encouraged fee-payers and boarders in direct imitation of the public school and eventually achieved this status, for example, at Tonbridge.[23] By the time of the Schools Inquiry Commission, the need for drastic reshaping of the endowed school system was widely felt.

We must now briefly examine both the attitude of the poor towards education and the aspirations of the middle classes before the Endowed Schools Act came into operation in 1869.

It was widely held, as the Revised Code of 1862 made explicit, that only a minimum of education was necessary for the children of the poor.[24] The concepts of the 'ladder' and the *carrière ouverte aux talents* were of a later age. In many cases, education above the elementary level was considered a luxury, a view often expressed by the middle classes. As Dobbs put it, 'The criticisms which appeared at the commencement of the nineteenth century are governed by the same traditional preconception, that education is normally a means of rising in the social scale and that any widely-organized instruction of the people would incapacitate them for necessary labour and diffuse an atmosphere of social unrest.'[25] The economic argument was a powerful one and would be used to stabilize the social structure after the upheavals following the Industrial Revolution.[26]

By the eighteenth century, education for the poor was provided by charity schools, whose origins were either endowed non-classical foundations or were sustained by subscriptions. The schools aimed at the moral improvement of the poor, based on religious knowledge. Where possible, instruction was free and in addition clothing and apprenticeship doles were given to the pupils.[27] The voluntary schools of Lancaster and Bell at the beginning of the nineteenth century both had as their goal the employment of the child, with elements of education as a charity. The early leaving-age of pupils, estimated by Dobbs as eleven in the first half of the nineteenth century with an average school life of one year in 1835 and two in 1851,[28] was to be expected in a newly-industrialized society with unregulated hours of work.

The poor appeared to accept their position as part of their lot[29] and one has to look to the second half of the century for any articulate demand by the working classes for universal education.[30] The Chartist movement expressed the feelings of the semi-educated; at the Chartist Convention of 1851, Ernest Jones asserted: 'As every man has the right to the means of physical life, so he has to the means of mental activity. It is as unjust to withhold aliment from the mind, as it is to deny food from the body. Education should, therefore, be national, universal, gratuitous and to a certain extent, compulsory.'[31]

By the 1850s the economic crises had passed and the working classes were experiencing the advantages of a trade boom.[32] Agricultural workers drifted into mining but the lot of the factory worker improved: trades union organization had made for better physical and material conditions. However, class feeling as between labour and capital was not antagonistic. Deference was the keynote and inequality was accepted as part of the social order.[33] But the prosperity of the working classes was only a relative matter. In 1867 Dudley Baxter estimated that the skilled, the less skilled and unskilled labouring classes, and agricultural workers, some 6,782,000 people, earned less than £100 a year. Michael Ross, the brewer M.P., making an independent estimate of money wages in the United Kingdom at about the same time, estimated the average income for a working-class family was 31s. per week.[34] Education for their children, involving more than a nominal payment, was out of the question.

Working-class initiative was directed to the field of adult education.[34a] The popularity of newspapers from the end of the eighteenth century and the spread of debating societies in towns indicated an urge for self-improvement. The attempts to canalize this thirst for knowledge to further a stable society by the Society for the Diffusion of Useful Knowledge is well known. As one writer has stated, 'it is evident that the poor were far from indifferent to the missionary efforts of their betters. On the contrary, they recognized a relationship between knowledge and freedom and were able to discriminate between education offered for the purpose of maintaining the existing order, and that designed ultimately to release them from economic restraints'.[35] Birkbeck Schools and the Mechanics' Institutes reflected the quest for knowledge, but by the 1850s enthusiasm had dwindled as the teaching became less systematic and the quality of instruction declined. 'The Institutes had become not only mere training schools for local industries, but poor training schools, at that.'[36] By the time our period begins, the Mechanics' Institutes had passed into the hands of the lower middle-class clerks and were shunned by the working classes. The intellectual ferment caused by Owenite schemes can be seen in the emergence of a number of outstanding self-educated individuals, such as Thomas Cooper and William Lovett. It is important to note that the seeking of knowledge amongst the more intelligent workers was considered as an end in itself, not a means by which they might rise out of their social class.[37]

To sum up: the rise of the middle classes after the Napoleonic Wars provided the dynamic for translating the need for reform into action. The claims of this class to a stake in national education was irresistible and made its voice heard in many spheres. O. R. McGregor has shown[38] that from the time of the Crimean War at least, the reform of public administration was inevitable and raised the question of the location and uses of power. 'The territorial aristocracy still retained political initiative through control over parliament, the civil service and peripheral agencies of government. The established Church and the army, for example, may be defined simply as those sections of the landed interest with spiritual and military functions and pretensions. The political system remained in large measure a property system deriving from landownership. Accordingly its reform presented middle class people with peculiar difficulties. They wished to strip exclusive privileges from landownership without condemning the principle of private property.' The creation of the instrument of the Royal Commission was one answer to this difficulty. Brougham's Select

Committee on the Education of the Lower Orders (1816-18) had discussed the problems at the endowed schools; Oxford and Cambridge had been investigated by Commissions, resulting in legislation in 1854 and 1856. The findings of the Clarendon Commission in the following decade demonstrated the need for a re-examination of the endowed school system. In the same year that the Clarendon Commission's report was issued the Schools Inquiry Commission took up the work of dealing with the remainder of the endowed schools and the provision of education above that of elementary throughout the country, with special reference to future needs.

The Schools Inquiry Commission and the state of secondary education, 1864-68

The agitation for reform of the endowed schools reached its climax when the National Association for the Promotion of Social Science sent a deputation in June 1864 to wait upon the Prime Minister, Lord Palmerston.[39] It asked for a Royal Commission to be set up to enquire into the state of the endowed schools of the United Kingdom 'on behalf of that large portion of Her Majesty's subjects who cannot look for the education of their children either to the great public schools on the one hand or the National Schools on the other'. The deputation included the Association's President, Lord Brougham, Edwin Chadwick, Lord Lyttelton and the Bishop of London. The setting up of the Schools Inquiry Commission [hereinafter referred to as S.I.C.] followed. The Commission, better known as the Taunton Commission, consisting of some twelve Commissioners, was charged with the task of inquiring into the education given at those schools which had not already been dealt with under the Public Schools Commission 'and also to consider and report what means, if any, are required for the improvement of such education, having special regard to all endowments applicable or which can rightly be made applicable thereto'.[39a] The Chairman, Lord Taunton, was a Liberal politician who had held several ministerial offices and was acknowledged to be a sound administrator. Amongst the Commissioners there were some with strong views on educational matters. Thomas Dyke Acland, a close friend of Gladstone and an authority on middle-class education, had also been responsible for the introduction in schools of examinations

which were administered by Oxford and Cambridge Universities.[40] Frederick Temple, then headmaster of Rugby, described by
Acland as 'a man of singularly strong independent power and of
unusual candour',[41] eventually drafted major sections of the
Report. George William, 4th Baron Lyttelton, an influential
member, had served on the Public Schools Commission and was to
be Chairman of the Endowed Schools Commission. W. E. Forster,
an advocate of state education, agreed to join, but urged that the
Commission should not be 'over-churched': opposition to any
practical measures would be most likely 'from the Bainesite
direction'.[42] However, Edward Baines was chosen to represent the
Dissenting interests and rendered valuable service.[43] Stafford
Northcote, who like Lyttelton had been a member of the Public
Schools Commission and took an interest in reformatory education,
was also appointed.[44] The S.I.C. undertook its four years' work with
great thoroughness: the evidence, recommendations and reports on
the schools run to some twenty-one volumes. The Endowed Schools
Commissioners, who were later appointed as a direct result of the
recommendations of the S.I.C., repeatedly publicized the fact that
they based their policies and actions explicitly upon the findings of
that Commission. It is therefore important to look at the work of
the S.I.C. and the conclusions it reached.

The terms of the Commission included the examination of all
types of school catering for education above that of elementary.
This meant that proprietary and private, as well as endowed
schools were to be scrutinized. The former two types depended
entirely on the fees from pupils and, as has been seen, the endowed
schools by this time included a fee-paying element. However, it was
to the endowed school[45] only that poor children as such were
admitted, under the terms of the original endowment, and it is to
these schools that attention will be directed.

The report of the S.I.C. was a landmark in the history of
secondary education in England and Wales. It was the first attempt
made to deal with the problems arising out of the social composition of the endowed schools and to suggest remedies for defects
found as a result of examination of the schools. The radical nature
of the Commissioners' recommendations followed the suggestions
made by some of the Assistant Commissioners, notably Matthew
Arnold, James Bryce and T. H. Green.[46]

From a study of the evidence and report, four major concerns can be identified which had a bearing on the subsequent work of the Endowed Schools Commissioners in relation to the poor. They are:

1. The application of endowments.
2. The definition of the term 'poor' children.
3. The social class of those attending endowed schools.
4. Current views on gratuitous education.

1. *The application of endowments*

For the most part, the Commission reported gross inefficiency in the handling of the endowments and their application. Often, the income from a modest portion of land which was to contribute to the endowment of the school had, by the time of the Commission, increased enormously in value. This was particularly so in the large towns and in London. By the nineteenth century, misapplication of funds had reached serious proportions, due mainly to either apathy, ignorance or greed on the part of the trustees. Remedies were not made easier by disputes having to be taken to the Court of Chancery, which traditionally supervised jurisdiction over all charities and had the power to make new regulations where required. Litigation was a long and costly process[47] and as the costs of the hearings were paid out of the funds of the charity, it often resulted in the crippling of the charity.

Following on Brougham's investigations, a Select Committee in 1835 had recommended the establishment of a permanent board to supervise the cases brought before Chancery. No action to establish such a board was taken; on the contrary, Chancery Courts were given larger powers under the Eardley Wilmot Act of 1840. James Kay-Shuttleworth, who had been the first Secretary of the Committee of the Privy Council on Education, was responsible for interesting influential members of Lord Aberdeen's Government in 1853 in such a body and suggested what its functions might be.[48] The Charitable Trusts Act,[49] which followed in the same year, authorized the appointment of Charity Commissioners, four in number, three of them paid; at least two were to be barristers-at-law of not less than twelve years' standing, one of them to be Chief Commissioner.

The powers given to the Commission, although apparently of wide application, were in fact narrowly circumscribed.[50] Under s.9, for example, from which most of the Commissioners' powers stemmed, they were charged 'to examine and enquire into all or any charities in England and Wales and the nature, objects, administration, management and results thereof, and the value, condition, management and application of the estates, funds, property and income belonging thereto.' But the Commissioners were powerless to act in a judicial capacity and disputed cases went to Chancery. Applications from private persons for authority to institute contentious litigation on behalf of charities, called Relators Suits, drained the funds. Again, although powers were granted for framing schemes on application to the trustees, the Commissioners could not initiate schemes without first being approached by trustees or interested persons. Only where the annual income of a charity was less than £30 per annum could the Commission intervene. A power which was widely exercised by the Commission was the dismissal of trustees if negligent in performing their duties either through old age or immoral conduct. County Courts provided a cheaper method of dealing with a charity where its assets were less than £50 a year in value.

The Charitable Trusts Act of 1860 extended and strengthened the Commission in dealing with charities. Powers so far exercisable by Chancery and County Courts were given to the Commission, giving it henceforward an administrative and judicial aspect. The £30 limit was raised to £50, bringing many more charities within its reach; but as Graham Balfour has shown,[51] all the English charities at this time over £50 per annum income represented 85 per cent of the total value of charities, although numerically they were only 10 per cent. Thus, the important fish escaped the net.

The importance of the Charity Commission lay in the appointment of Assistant Commissioners to examine charities; they could require the attendance of witnesses and both examine them on oath and cause local inquiries to be held in or near districts where the majority of the beneficiaries of the charity resided. The Commission, in its Report for 1860, first mentioned the need to change the strict application of endowments from their original purposes.[52]

The S.I.C., charged with an examination of facilities for secondary education, was interested mainly in endowments which were applied to education. To a great extent, the Commission agreed with the Charity Commission in its findings. It argued that where there was a genuine *cy-près* application of a charity, that is, the doctrine that general charitable intentions by a donor had to be applied as nearly as possible to the way intended,[53] this must inevitably lead to wastefulness as the original terms of the endowment were no longer applicable in a modern setting.[54]

The application of the *cy-près* rule was to be one of the main points of contention between the Endowed Schools Commissioners and the champions of the poor after the passing of the Endowed Schools Act in 1869. The Courts of Equity and the Charity Commission were not able to establish schemes involving a substantial departure from the declared intention of the founder. This meant that the 'dead hand' fossilized the uses to which endowments could be put.[55] But it was agreed that any changes made must safeguard the class for which the charity was originally intended, whilst on the other hand account had to be taken of changing social and economic conditions since the charity was founded.

The S.I.C. enumerated several categories which they considered were not being used to their fullest advantage: grammar schools which had been converted to elementary schools, endowments which had been given to elementary schools and which were not now needed, and endowments for clothing and unnecessary boarding facilities. The main condemnation of the Commissioners was reserved for endowments originally attached to schools and which no longer served a useful purpose. The poorest class was to have benefited from them but the funds were now subject to widespread misapplication. The chief headings were: doles in money or kind, such as bread and coals; apprenticeship fees; marriage portions; loan funds; charities for objects which had failed altogether; and charities for general public purposes.[56]

The main source of opposition to change came from the trustees, who often had the most to lose by such a change. Robert Lowe, giving evidence to the Commission as the Parliamentary Member of the Commission, an unpaid post, pointed out that the Charity Commission were obliged to execute schemes with strict regard to the *cy-près* principle. 'If they (the Charity Commission) go beyond this limit the schemes, when they have been settled by the Charity Commissioners, must be passed through Parliament, through all the stages of a bill. The effect of that, therefore, is only that the schemes are relieved from the payment of fees and from being sent before a Committee of the House like a private bill'.[57] He also made clear that unless the scheme had the consent of the trustees, it would certainly fail to pass. The S.I.C. stated that in their view, there was need for relaxing the *cy-près* rule. If it was argued that the poor came out of it having gained more in benefit than other classes of the community, then this could be shown to be a false picture.[58] The difficulties involved in interpreting the founder's intentions were made clear in evidence. An Inspector of Charities under the Charity Commission posed the problem of a draper in the London parish of St. Andrew Undershaft, who directed that the proceeds of his estate were to be divided among poor drapers, aged men and women living in the parish. 'Are we to consider his principal object to be the benefit of poor drapers, or the parishioners of St. Andrew Undershaft, or that he means the benefit to be chiefly for aged persons? You see it may mean all these things, and each suggests a different *cy-près* rule. We have no power of definition, nothing but pure guesswork, which no declaratory Act could possibly prescribe'.[59]

The S.I.C. therefore felt that endowments were not being fully utilized to the best advantage; nor were the poorer classes benefiting to the extent that the founders would have wished. A re-examination of the *cy-près* doctrine in the light of the changing needs of the time was required.

2. The definition of the term 'poor' children

The meaning attached to the term 'poor' in the evidence given before the S.I.C. and subsequent Select Committees on the working of the Endowed Schools Act varied widely according to the social class of the witness or the interest which he was representing.

The ranking of social classes in mid-nineteenth century Britain was still essentially based on that of a pre-industrial society. The S.I.C. quotes the School of Sir John Wynne of Gwydir at Llanrwst reported on by the Charity Commissioners of 1837, where school fees were settled on the following basis:

	Entrance Fee	Quarterly Payment
Every knight's son	2s. 6d.	2s. 0d.
Ditto or squire's son	2s. 0d.	1s. 6d.
Gentleman or minister's son	1s. 0d.	0s. 9d.
Yeoman's son of £20 p.a. and rich tenants	0s. 9d.	0s. 6d.
They of the poorer sort	0s. 6d.	0s. 3d.
Poor indeed	gratis	gratis 60

Usually, the term 'poor' was equated and interchangeable with 'working class'. The Privy Council rules for Schools of Art provided a definition of a working man:

1. Artisans or operatives in receipt of weekly wages, supporting themselves by their own manual labour, or the children of the same sort earning their own livelihood.

2. Persons who, though paid at longer intervals than a week or for piece-work, support themselves by their own manual labour.

3. Persons not supporting themselves by manual labour but being of the same means and social level as those who do so (e.g. small shopkeepers having petty stocks and employing none but members of their own family and small tradesmen not employing apprentices), village carpenters and the like, policemen, coastguards, etc.

4. Persons supporting themselves by manual labour, but such as it would be unreasonable to expect to pay the fee of middle-class students, as some descriptions of clerks, shopmen, etc.

H. J. Roby, Secretary of the S.I.C. and later an Endowed School Commissioner, stated in evidence before the 1873 Select Committee on the Endowed Schools Act that the term 'poor' was a very variable one, used in foundations such as Eton as well as in connection with elementary instruction.[61] Later, Roby gave a more restricted definition: those attending a public elementary school for a considerable period of time, and orphans under adversity.[62]

In the first half of the nineteenth century, the so-called working classes could be divided fairly simply into skilled and unskilled workers: the former, 'this aristocracy of labour', as Dr. Kitson Clark called it, 'should be grouped with the middle-class, many of whose prejudices about keeping down the rates and maintaining social order they probably shared.'[63] It was the unskilled or semi-skilled workers who were unable to organize themselves into craft unions who became the 'poor' dealt with by the S.I.C. Outside the towns, the wage-earning agricultural labourer presented a picture of a comparatively depressed section of the poor throughout the century. Classified under the heading of the poor were those boys from 'sunken' middle-class families, orphans of professional families and often sons of retired Army officers and the clergy.

The growth of class-consciousness, with its new terminology, did not become obvious until after the death of Palmerston and gained momentum with the second Reform Act of 1867.[64] In the Report of the S.I.C. the employment of such terminology was loose; the subtler distinctions of social class were absent and the quest for sociological definition was not pursued. The instructions given to the Assistant Commissioners in 1864 before their inspections of endowed schools took place provided a picture of what was considered to be the class immediately above that of the working class: 'It is not possible to draw the boundary precisely in a country in which no class of society is separated from that which is above and that which is below. But you will understand that you are required to give your chief attention to the schools attended by the children of such of the gentry, clergy, professional and commercial men as are of limited means, and of farmers and tradesmen.'

3. *Social class of children attending endowed schools*

In well-established endowed schools, catering for an urban population, the picture which emerges in the larger school is one of a socially stratified society, each department catering for a fairly homogeneous social group. More commonly, classical and commercial (sometimes called modern or English) schools existed side by side, the former providing candidates for the University or the Army, the latter for entry into the business world. A three-tier division was not uncommon – upper, middle and lower – as in the instance of Liverpool College: the upper, for merchants, brokers and bankers, the middle for better-class shokeepers and 'wealthy' clerks, the lower for small shopkeepers and educated artisans.[65] Many middle-class parents, not having the means with which to send their sons to public schools, felt that the endowed schools should at least attempt to emulate the former.[66] The Headmaster of College School, Taunton, had this in mind. 'I do not desire only to instruct the middle-class. I desire to improve and elevate them, and I think I can do that most by bringing them in contact with the class above them, so that I should shrink from a system which eliminated the upper-class; I think that by contact with the gentleman's son the tradesman's son learns that refinement and

polish which through life he will find of great service to him: and I
should be sorry to deny him the opportunity of acquiring it.'[67]

Many factors contributed to the educational separation of social
classes. A feeling of social distance between different economic
groups was translated into terms of physical separation within the
schools.[68] It was not confined only to the middle classes, for
working-class parents expressed the wish that their sons should not
mix with other boys above their own social station. This was due
partly to custom, to the difference in manners, expense of superior
dress and the cheap education provided by the National and
British Schools. On the other hand, there was much resentment by
the middle classes where social equality existed in endowed
schools. R. R. W. Lingen, Secretary to the Committee of the Privy
Council on Education since 1849, replying to the question why
farmers sent their boys to different schools from those of labourers
remarked, 'It is partly a feeling of social pride; but there is also a
better reason for it, namely, that farmers' sons will have to
maintain command afterwards over those persons and there is a
sort of quarter-deck feeling, that the one is the officer and the other
the common seaman.'[69]

The entrance requirements of the Universities of Oxford and
Cambridge, since the reform of their degrees, were becoming more
rigorous. Further, the 1805 Eldon Judgement and the Grammar
Schools Act of 1840 both strengthened the hands of grammar
school headmasters. The first, by reiterating the necessity for
schools to teach Latin and Greek in order to avoid a breach of
trust, offered an education which appealed more to the middle
classes. The second, by allowing extra subjects to enter the
curriculum for which fees were chargeable, presented a convenient
opportunity for those schools wishing to exclude poor scholars.[70]
Parental pressure was directed towards establishing a curriculum
which distinguished the school from those below.[71] Despite the
lip-service paid by the S.I.C. to the growing need for scientific
education, the Commissioners made Greek the hall-mark of a first
grade school, Latin that of a second grade.[72]

Nevertheless, the evidence before the Commission showed many
instances of a desire to establish a 'ladder' of education, carrying
the poor boy from the lowest rungs to the university, a concept to be
taken up by T. H. Huxley in the next decade. Kay-Shuttleworth
pleaded for 'equality of privileges in a republic of letters for all

ranks of people' and suggested a graduated series of steps taking a boy from the National School, through the preparatory school of a grammar school, to the grammar school itself.[73] No details were given by the S.I.C. to show how such a scheme could be effected. Indeed, the Commissioners had in mind not a system of transfer from a lower to a higher school but rather a series of grades of schools, each catering for a different social grouping and differentiated by the length of stay of the pupil and the ability to pay the stipulated fees. It was suggested that there should be three grades of school. The first grade, with a leaving age of 18 to 19, would be for intending university entrants; the second grade up to 17 years of age, for those going into professions and trade; and the third grade for boys up to 14, would cater for the sons of small tradesmen and shopkeepers and superior artisans.

These gradings provided the basis for the policy of the Endowed Schools Commissioners. The main need was for third grade schools, for the lower-middle-class strata of sons of small shopkeepers, established clerks and retired army officers who did not attend the National and British Schools.[74] For such pupils it was suggested that preparatory schools for entry to the third grade at 12 to 13 should be established. This would differentiate the pupils from the sons of labourers. 'The class who have above all others seemed to need such Preparatory Schools are indeed the class who insist most strongly on the exclusion of labourers' children, but they are also a class who scorn to receive alms and will either pay for what they require or will put up as best they can with the want of it.'[75]

How the endowments of the schools could best be utilized in the pursuit of such ends exercised the minds of the Commissioners and witnesses. One thing was certain; the extent and application of the endowments was inadequate for the needs of this class. Some mixing was inevitable, especially where the terms of admission of the original benefactor still applied. In such cases the school was divided into departments, and a distinction drawn between fee-payers and free boys; physical boundaries were common – separate playgrounds, partitions within classrooms, the segregation of those with local rights from others, and separate curricula and teachers.

Whilst the majority of witnesses accepted the need for differentiation of treatment, voices were raised to defend the view that in any projected reform, the poor could not be left out of the picture.

References were made to the honourable positions now occupied by sons of humble parents, and the obvious loss to the education system if the brighter and most industrious section of the working class were excluded from the proposed new schools. The very active religious and social conscience of the mid-Victorian era made it impossible to ignore this problem; but it was to remain subsidiary to the main task of the reorganization of the endowed schools.

4. Views on gratuitous education

The foregoing section is incomplete without an examination of the problem of the financing of endowed school education. It was generally agreed[76] that the original founders had stipulated that the poor were to be exempt from all payment, and in many cases the school was free to all.[77] By the time of the S.I.C., as we have seen, the majority of endowed schools accepted fee-paying pupils; additional subjects to the curriculum had to be paid for in order to engage suitable teachers. The S.I.C. argued that the presence of a number of non-paying pupils was a burden on the endowment and the expansion of ambitious schools.

The question turned on the interpretation of the word 'free' which was described in many ways before the Commission and was widely held to mean that entry to the school was open to all but not necessarily gratuitous. Much of the argument tended towards the need for re-endowing the schools for middle-class education, especially as by the time the S.I.C. had reported, the first indication of the future provision of elementary education on a national scale was apparent.[78] If, therefore, the endowed schools were to become largely the property of those above the working classes, the fear of an educated leavening of this class invading and carrying off the prizes of middle-class schools had to be minimized.

To combat the notion that the poor were entitled to free education in endowed schools, many arguments were advanced. Stress was placed on the wastefulness of endowments. The High Master of Manchester Grammar School gave evidence that of 250 free boys at the school, at least 100 were well able to pay the fees, many of these having brothers at Rugby;[79] only 50 to 60 from the poorer classes obtained education there. Gratuitous education therefore worked in favour of the middle classes. Chancery, in framing new schemes for schools, was against the principle of free education. It was pointed out that such provision would encourage improvidence on the part of the parents by abrogating their responsibility for their children's education. Again, were the middle classes expected to subsidize places for the poor as well as pay fees for their own sons? There was also the question of free places attracting the wrong type of boy and thus driving away boarders, who not only gave status to the school, but provided a lucrative source of income.

Many witnesses urged that, whilst the endowed schools should become the prerogative of the middle classes, some provision should be made for those displaced under the proposed reforms. It was agreed that the most able working-class boys should be allowed to enter. The main problem was the method of selecting those who would benefit most by such an education. Patronage was too closely associated with jobbery on the part of the trustees. Competition was the true test: 'it puts the free scholar in the place of honour instead of the place of reproach.'[80] This could be done in three ways:

(a) a leaving examination from the elementary school, carrying with it an exhibition;

(b) an entrance examination into the endowed school, carrying a scholarship;

(c) a leaving exhibition from the endowed school, for further education.

The difference between a 'scholarship' and an 'exhibition' was that the former was to be awarded for use in the school itself, the latter to be taken from the school and to be used at another school or at an institution of higher education. In practice, the terms were often interchangeable. Both types of award were to cover fees and in some cases, books. Witnesses suggested the need for mainten-ance allowances in order to compensate parents for loss of earnings in allowing the boy to stay on at school.[81] Scholarships were not commonly awarded, but examples are found in isolated instances. The S.I.C. praised the use of this system in Doncaster, Yorkshire. A Trustee Scheme of 1862 established Corporation Scholarships at the grammar school; a sum of £250 per annum was set aside for ten free boys' capitation fees of £25 each. The three vacancies per year were advertised in the town's elementary schools and a competitive examination was held. In the first year of the scheme, seven out of ten of the successful scholars entered the classical department and subsequently did well.[82] Little attention seems to have been paid to the social class of entrants for such awards, provided that they were in attendance at elementary schools, but it is likely that the bulk of the prizes were carried off by the upper-working- and lower-middle-class children attending elementary schools.

The age of entry to an endowed school ranged from seven to thirteen years of age. If the exhibition was gained into the school at a late stage, it was of little use to an early leaver. The Latin requirement was seen as a great stumbling-block in scholarship examinations.

Although the S.I.C. did not face up to many of these problems, the reports of the Assistant Commissioners on the individual schools provided valuable data for the Endowed Schools Commissioners who followed up this work.

Commissioners' views and current social thought

Many changes in the social and political structure of Britain had taken place during the time the S.I.C. had been taking evidence (1864-8). The Crimean War, the first war in which England had been involved for over forty years, had ended in disillusionment and resulting political bitterness. The American Civil War revived strong feelings. The 1867 Reform Act, which had a profound effect upon the working man in the political field,[83] widened the franchise with one adult in three now possessing a vote. An educated electorate was a prerequisite of stable government. Demands for a fuller system of education had been made by individuals such as Robert Applegarth, for the purpose of bridging the gap of ignorance and misunderstanding which existed between master and employees.[84] The rising status of the skilled and semi-skilled craftsmen and their growing feeling of group identity found expression in the foundation of the Trades Union Congress in 1868 as a working-class equivalent of the Social Science Association. A resolution carried at its second meeting in 1869 echoed the words of the Birmingham Education League, 'That this Congress believes that nothing short of a system of national, unsectarian and compulsory education will satisfy the requirements of the United Kingdom.'[85]

Certainly, the need for a system of national education was apparent in many different spheres. The low standard of British manufactures at the 1867 International Exhibition in Paris compared with those of other countries graphically illustrated the advance in technical and scientific education made by competitors abroad since the 1851 Exhibition.

That a centrally administered national system of elementary education for the bulk of the working-class population was likely to be accomplished shortly was appreciated by the Commission. One historian of secondary schooling, R. L. Archer, explained the lack of state interference in this sector up to this time as follows: 'Whereas the State was driven by an imperious necessity to intervene in regard to elementary education because without such intervention great masses of people would remain uneducated, some sort of system existed already in regard to higher education and theory was not confronted with an irresistible obstacle of fact'.[86] In fact, the Commission now put forward a plan for a radical reorganization of secondary education which involved Government control. It was suggested that two central authorities should be established; an enlarged version of the Charity Commission, to supervise educational trusts and appoint inspectors, and an examining authority whose job was to appoint Courts of Examiners for secondary schools in each county. Below this were to be the provincial authorities, to consist of either Government Inspectors, Crown nominees and local residents, or chairmen of Boards of Guardians of the county and Crown-nominated, or elected rate-payers, two from each Union, and half as many more Crown-nominated members. In towns of over 100,000, town councils and trustees of endowed schools were to constitute the authority. Supervision was to be exercised by the central authority, with a wide range of tasks given to provincial authorities, such as the fixing of grades of schools in each district, the appointment of headmasters and the determination of the subjects of instruction in schools. Two important provisions were linked with the above. Local rates for secondary education in towns and parishes were recommended for the purpose of building new and enlarging old schools, but not for maintaining them. Rates could also be used for paying the school fees of meritorious scholars elected from the elementary schools. Connected with this last point was the recommendation that free education was to be abolished and the imposition of capitation fees should be made to remove, as the S.I.C. put it, the deadweight of boys not requiring grammar school education.

A few months after the Commission's Report was issued, a Liberal Government was returned to power. Gladstone now led a party with a larger radical element than would have been possible under the autocratic rule of Palmerston, consisting of both middle- and working-class elements.[87] Reforms in education followed, including the abolition of university religious tests; many of the new voters were both Liberal and Nonconformist with long memories of the monopoly of Church education. The recommendation of the S.I.C. with regard to freedom of conscience in religious education, that no religious test was to be imposed on candidates to the schools and that the headmaster need not be in Holy Orders unless the foundation was a specifically Church of England one,[88] fitted in well with the new situation. But on one point both supporters of the Church of England and Dissenters were in agreement: they believed that independence, thrift and self-help on the part of the working classes was to be encouraged and that reliance on the State was both degrading and demoralizing; where help was essential, sufficient should be given to restore a feeling of self-respect but not enough to encourage a relapse into dependence upon others.

The S.I.C. had already pointed out that indiscriminate gratuitous education had unfortunate effects upon the schools and individuals concerned. This was not a new sentiment. Lord Lyttelton, a member of the Commission, and later Chief Endowed School Commissioner, had written in 1855, 'Now pauperism is the casting upon the community of a legal charge by tax, for the supply of that which we are duty bound to provide for ourselves. And free education is moral pauperism, just as free relief is physical pauperism. It is no more just or politic, if it can be avoided, that ratepayers should pay for the schooling of a child, than that they should pay for the dinner of that child.'[89]

In such a milieu,[90] the work of the Charity Organisation Society, founded in 1869, typifies the view then held of the attitude of the poor towards charity. The Society's deep concern with the easing of the application of the Poor Law by the State led to an attempt to co-ordinate voluntary charities.[91] For instance, the Metropolitan Poor Act of 1867 had created a Common Poor Fund for the

Metropolis to which all the Unions contributed. Hospitals and asylums were provided by the Metropolitan Asylums Board and district Poor Law Schools were also constructed under the Act. These became a charge upon the Common Poor Fund and made indoor relief more attractive. It was estimated in 1871 that in England and Wales, 4.6 per cent of the population were classified as paupers at a cost of nearly £8m., or 6s. 11¼d. per head of population.[92] The Society believed that a more scientific approach to poverty could be found; charities, which were being established in large numbers, were to be centralized in one fund. By applying such charities to the aid of the poor in conjunction with the Poor Law authorities, the problem of the poor could be dealt with without the direct necessity of State intervention; for, as the Appendix to the 8th Annual Report of the Society warned with reference to one case, 'if he is taught that as they [debts] arise they will be met by State relief or private charity, he will assuredly make no effort to meet them himself.'[93]

Such a view meshed in well with the findings of the Commission which had reported on the wasteful and degrading uses to which charities were being put. The word 'charity' connoted 'poverty' and the notion that education should be a part of charity in the 1860s was widely discounted on both political and religious grounds. Education in the elementary schools was largely by payment. It was an anomaly that the endowed school should be otherwise.

In sum, the S.I.C. findings reflected faithfully the spirit of the times. The thorough investigation into the social, religious and financial aspects of the endowed schools revealed the need for change and the conclusion to the Report of the Commission was that 'though the changes required are large, they are in truth not larger than have been actually wrought by the uncontrolled drifting of the schools, or the uncertain interference of Parliament and Courts of Chancery.' The legislation which was to follow the Report was confidently expected to confirm the Committee's findings.

NOTES

1. R. L. Archer, *Secondary Education in the Nineteenth Century* (1921), reprinted Cass, p. 83.
2. The Fleming Report: *The Public School and the General Education System*

(1944), p. 8, footnote, does not agree with A. F. Leach in his *History of Winchester College,* Chapter VIII (1899), where he stated that the education of labouring classes did not exist in the fourteenth century. See articles on Leach as an educational historian, W. N. Chaplin, *British Journal of Educational Studies,* Vol. XI, No. 2, May 1963; J. Simon, Vol. XII, No. 1, November 1963; W. N. Chaplin, Vol. XII, No. 2, May 1964.

3. 'Speaking generally, the Foundation Boys are, in the eyes of the Law, the School.' Clarendon Report, P.P. 1864, XX, Vol. I.

4. The period 1660-1730 was the 'golden age' of endowments. One third of all grammar schools in existence in 1842 were founded during these seventy years, or received new endowments. J. E. G. de Montmorency, *State Intervention in English Education* (1902) Appendix II, pp. 243-4.

5. Quoted in I. Pinchbeck and M. Hewitt, *Children in English Society,* (1969) Vol. 1, p. 287.

6. M. Girouard, *Life in the English Country House* (1978), p. 18.

7. L. Stone, *The Crisis of the Aristocracy 1558-1641* (1965), p. 686.

8. The difference between a public school and a grammar school stemmed from the ability of the former to attract boys from a distance.

9. It can be seen from Table 1 in T. W. Bamford's article, 'Public Schools and Social Class 1801-1850', *British Journal of Sociology,* Vol. XII, No. 3, September 1961, that at the beginning of the century the 'lower class' had been eliminated from Harrow, Rugby and Eton.

10. Clarendon, Vol. I, p. 10. The Commission recommended that entrance to the foundations of all schools be made a matter of competitive examination, thus effectively debarring the poor. E. C. Mack, *Public Schools and British Opinion Since 1860* (1941), p. 31.

11. At Eton at the time of the Clarendon Commission there was one Foundationer to twelve Non-Foundationers: Harrow one to thirteen; and at Rugby one to six, Clarendon, Vol. I, p. 8.

12. For examples of this, see Fleming Report, op. cit., p. 16.

13. B. Simon, *Studies in the History of Education 1780-1870* (1960), p. 314.

14. H. C. Barnard, *A History of English Education from 1760* (2nd edn. 1961), p. 128.

15. It has been argued that the headmaster's power to appoint staff, recognized under the Act, was a strong blow on behalf of the forces of internal school reform, and ultimately led to a widening, rather than a narrowing, of the curriculum (Rupert Wilkinson, *The Prefects – British Leadership and the Public School Tradition* (1964), pp. 10-11). But see R. D. Altick, *The English Common Reader* (1957), pp. 179-84 for an account of the state of English teaching in these schools at this time.

16. However, it must be noted that although public schools were reformed in matters of administration, the formidable traditions associated with such schools – bullying, unruliness of the boys, the narrowness of the curriculum and the cost of fees – induced many of the less prosperous middle-class parents to turn to the proprietary schools. Starting in the 1830s, they quickly became a popular substitute for the public school. The three main types were the day schools, modelled on Merchant Taylors and St. Paul's, both of which had been excluded from the Public Schools Act; the boarding schools, such as Cheltenham and Marlborough; and the County Schools, started by Earl Fortescue, modelled on the public school system, as at West Buckland, Devon. For an account of this school, see Earl Fortescue, *Public Schools for the Middle Classes* (1864), pp. 8, 13.

Proprietary schools were often started where the local endowed school had either failed or had become elementary in character. A typical example is that of Leicester, which was one of the first in the provinces. H. Temple Patterson, *Radical Leicester 1780-1850: A History of Leicester* (1954), pp. 241-2.

17. M. E. Sadler, 'The Scholarship System in England to 1880 and some of its Developments' in M. E. Sadler (ed.), *International Institute Examinations Inquiry* (1935), p. 63.

18. Although in the Preface to Vol. I, Carlisle mentions 'the negligence or cupidity of ignorant or unprincipled Trustees who have silently, or by connivance, suffered the furtive alienation of the very lands which they were called upon so solemnly to defend.'

19. J. A. Graham and B. A. Pythian, *The Manchester Grammar School, 1515-1965* (1965), p. 202.

20. Many pamphlets of this period pointed out existing evils. For example: 'The *masters* have rarely been paid in the double proportion of the depreciation of the value of money and of the increase of that of the funds: they have consequently been interested to encourage stipendiary pupils at the expense of the Foundation boys. This lucrative compensation wd. make them averse to enforcing their own rights; and the trustees would not be anxious to put down practices which precluded demands upon the estates they were devouring.' *A Letter to Henry Brougham, Esq., M.P., from a Master of Arts of Queen's College, Oxford, upon the best method of restoring decayed Grammar Schools* (1818).

21. For this, see H. J. Perkins, *Economic History Review*, Vol. XIV, 2nd series, August 1961: after 1830, the expansion of more specialized non-manual work required more formally appropriate kinds of education. There is evidence to suggest that in some places such as Northamptonshire, efforts to provide a suitable education for the middle classes had been made well before the Schools Inquiry Commission came into existence. D. Alsobrook, 'The Reform of the Endowed Schools; the work of the Northamptonshire Educational Society 1854-1874', *History of Education*, Vol. 2, No. 1, 1973, pp. 35-54.

22. Matthew Arnold, *A French Eton or Middle-Class Education and the State*, (1863-4) quoted in G. Sutherland (ed.) *Arnold on Education*, (1973), p. 134.

23. Complaints about the high fees in the school by Tonbridge inhabitants in August 1854 to the Governors. Tonbridge School, PRO Ed 27/1978 Resolution, 11 August 1854.

24. Although Robert Lowe claimed that schools did not have to confine themselves to the basic subjects. 'What we fix,' he said, 'is a *minimum* of education, not a *maximum*.' In practice, school managers ignored this possibility. J. Hurt, *Education in Evolution* (1971), pp. 208 ff.

25. A. E. Dobbs, *Education and Social Movements, 1700-1850* (1919), p. 148. Cf. with Sadler, op. cit., p. 71-2.

'In spite of its growing humanitarianism, the English middle-class (differing from their Scottish contemporaries), were uneasy as to the ultimate effects of giving the strong stimulus of an invigorating education to the minds and ambitions of the mass of working people in town and country. Many were instinctively jealous, on their own account, but still more on behalf of their children, of future rivals springing from below with the formidable equipment which would be given to them by a prolonged education, largely at public expense.'

Robert Owen had in 1835 organized the Association of All Classes of All Nations with the purpose of educating people 'towards a new social order in which the interest of each should be the concern of all, where competition should be supplanted by co-operation, reason should rule over impulse, thus

affording full opportunity for the development of human character.' M. Hansome, *World Workers' Educational Movements: Their Social Significance* (1931), pp. 24-5.
For the period 1780-1832, see E. P. Thompson, *The Making of the English Working Classes* (1963), p. 712ff. See also H. M. Pollard, *Pioneers of Popular Education* (1957), chapter 12, for an account of education at this time.

26. A speaker at the Oxford Political Economy Club posed this question: 'Can the social disadvantage of raising the best minds of every class of the community to the top be regarded as in any way economically a set off to the detriment accruing to the particular industries from which they are withdrawn? Would not the working classes be able to do much more for the economic progress of the community, even than they do at present, if they could keep their best men amongst them instead of being helped by public money to surrender them into the ranks of classes who do not share their feelings, and to whom they are at present in temporary opposition?' C. E. Appleton, *The Endowment of Education, A Paper read before the Oxford Political Club, November 28, 1874,* n.d.
For an account of the condition of the poor during the first half of the nineteenth century, see A. F. Young and E. T. Ashton, *British Social work in 19th Century* (1963 edn.), pp. 8-15.

27. M. G. Jones, *The Charity School Movement* (1938, reprinted Cass, 1964), p. 19.
28. Dobbs, op. cit., p. 151.
29. A. Tropp, *The School Teachers* (1957), p. 8. The influence of Chartism on Whig educational reform should not be overemphasized. The establishment of the Privy Council on Education in 1839 was the result of agitation concerned with the provision of education for the working classes. Asa Briggs (ed.), *Chartist Studies* (1959), pp. 400-1. Note should be taken here of the extent and influence of the working-class press by the middle of the century. R. K. Webb, *The British Working Class Reader 1790-1848* (1955), pp. 158-63.
30. For a brief review of adult education in the early part of the nineteenth century, see J. Lawson and H. Silver, *A Social History of Education in England* (1973), pp. 258-62.
31. Quoted in Simon, op. cit., (1960), p. 275.
32. G. D. H. Cole, *A Short History of the British Working-Class Movement, Vol. II, 1848-1900* (1927), p. 187 ff.
33. It was perhaps a sign of the times that the Amalgamated Society of Engineers, founded in 1851, did not claim that it was its duty to secure the objects of a 'class' 'but rather to exercise the same control over that in which we have a vested interest, as the physician who holds his diploma or the author who is protected by his copyright.' A. Briggs, 'The Language of "Class" in Early 19th-Century England', in A. Briggs and J. Saville (ed.) *Essays in Labour History* (1960).
34. M. T. Hodgen, *Workers' Education in England and United States* (1925), p. 54.
34a. A detailed account of this movement can be found in T. Kelly, *A History of Adult Education in Great Britain* (1962), Chs. 8 to 13.
35. G. D. H. Cole and R. Postgate, *The Common People* (1938), p. 347.
36. Hodgen, op. cit., p. 54. The early fears of the middle classes aroused by the educational influences of the Mechanics' Institutes are well described in H. Silver, *The Concept of Education* (1965) pp. 210-26.
37. 'Only the exceptional man would be able to do this. But that was not to say that the majority had not also improved themselves and thereby enhanced their children's chances of rising in the social hierarchy.' J. F. C. Harrison, *Learning and Living 1790-1960* (1961), p. 216.

38. O. R. McGregor, 'Social Research and Social Policy', *British Journal of Sociology*, Vol. VIII, No. 2, June 1957, pp. 150-1.

39. 'An exclusively middle-class body, the Social Science Association existed to save society from the twin perils of aristocratic government and the doctrines propagated by Owen and St. Simon. From the '30s onwards, middle-class people were continuously digging channels by which working-class demands could be drained away from the foundations of property.' Ibid., p. 154.

39a. S.I.C., Vol. I, p. 1. P.P. 1867-8, XVIII. It is worth mentioning in this connection the work of an older society which carried out investigations into social problems, the Manchester Statistical Society, founded in 1833. Its early members included such figures as James Phillips Kay (better known as Sir James Kay-Shuttleworth), William Langton and Benjamin Heywood. They were eager for reform in all aspects of economic and social life arising from the growth of Manchester, including education. For list of papers read at the Society, see T. S. Ashton, *Economic and Social Investigation in Manchester 1833-1933* (1933), pp. 165-79. Also M. J. Cullen, *The Statistical Movement in Early Victorian Britain* (1975).

40. J. Roach, *Public Examinations in England, 1850-1900* (1971), pp. 85-6. Even a political opponent, Stafford Northcote, urged his appointment on these grounds. Northcote to Lyttelton, 27 August 1864. Lyttelton MSS, Letter 163.

41. T. D. Acland to his son, C. T. D. Acland, 2 Oct, 1865. Acland MSS, 1148M/Box 8/1.

42. W. E. Forster to H. A. Bruce, 25 Oct, 1864. Granville MSS, PRO 30/29/19/25.

43. T. D. Acland, who was given the task of drafting part of the Final Report, wrote to Baines, 'I have benefited greatly by your objections to my former attempt and I must frankly confess that I owe very much to your strong expressions of opinion about endowments and private owner schools.' Acland to Baines, 1 Jan, 1868, Baines MSS.

44. A. Lang, *Life, Letters and Diaries of First Earl of Iddesleigh* (1890) Vol. I, pp. 128-139.

45. An endowed school was defined as 'those which have usually, besides buildings, some income from charitable lands permanently appropriated to the school.'

46. See M. Ritcher, *The Politics of Conscience: T. H. Green and His Age* (1964), pp. 352-7; and P. Gordon and J. White, *Philosophers as Educational Reformers* (1979), Part II, Section 6.

47. Suits by the Attorney-General during the period 1818-37 lasted for between five and ten years. Graham Balfour, *The Educational Systems of Great Britain and Ireland* (1903), p. 144.

48. See *Journal of the National Association for the Promotion of Social Science*, Vol. 1, No. 1, 2 November 1866, p. 8.

49. 16 & 17, Vic. 137.

50. The original Bill had contained provisions for the reappropriation of charitable endowments, where in the judgment of the Board the design of the founder of any charity had failed. Any charity founded more than sixty years having no beneficial results could be applied to other objects in the same district. These provisions were not included in the Act. 14th Annual Report of the Charity Commissioners for 1866, P.P. 1867, XX.

51. Balfour, op. cit., p. 146.

52. 7th Annual Report of the Charity Commissioners for 1860, P.P. 1860, XXIV, p. 6.

53. J. Burke (ed.), *Osborn's Concise Law Dictionary*, 6th edn. (1976), p. 108. See also L. A. Sheridan and V. T. H. Delany, *The Cy-Près Doctrine* (1961), p. 8.

The Charities Act of 1960 (ss. 13 and 14) has widened the scope of *cy-près* applications. The Secretary of State for Education is still solely in charge of purely educational endowments. 'The Charities Act 1960', *Social Science Quarterly,* Winter, 1960.

54. 'It may, we think, be reasonably assumed, that the particular form and mode of distribution are objects of secondary importance with a benevolent donor (enabled by an exceptional law to settle his property in perpetuity for the benefit of posterity) to that of conferring the largest advantage on the subjects of his bounty; and that the specific application of that bounty may well be modified after a sufficient interval of time, and with reference to new surrounding circumstances, without any substantial violation of the founder's principal intentions.' 7th Annual Report of the Charity Commissioners for 1860, P.P. XXIV, pp. 6-7.

55. Thus W. S. Gilbert, in Act I of *Ruddigore,* the action of which was set in the fishing village of Rederring in Cornwall early in the nineteenth century, could still poke fun (1887) at 'the only village in the world that possesses an endowed corps of professional bridesmaids who are bound to be on duty every day from ten to four.'

56. S.I.C., Vol. I, pp. 216-19.

57. S.I.C., Vol. IV, Q. 6547.

58. See, for example, S.I.C., Vol. I, p. 221. Fearon inspected 33 schools in the Metropolitan area, 30 specifically designated 'for poor children, preference to the very poorest.' Of these, 3 did not exist, 1 master had no scholars, 1 had no master pending new scheme, 8-9 were now elementary, none educated girls. Two wealthy foundations were Christ's Hospital and Dulwich.

59. S.I.C., Vol. V, Q. 12982.

60. S.I.C., Vol. V, Appendix.

61. 1873 Select Committee on the Endowed Schools Act, (1869), P.P. 1873, VIII, Q. 182.

62. Ibid., Q. 598.

63. G. Kitson Clark, *The Making of Victorian England* (1962), p. 132. It is undoubtedly the 'labour aristocracy' who wished to take advantage of the facilities available in secondary education during the period 1860 to 1890. Dr. Kitson Clark's statement quoted above over-simplifies the situation. For an exhaustive treatment and penetrating analysis of the structure of the working class in England at this time, see E. J. Hobsbawm, 'The Labour Aristocracy in 19th Century Britain' in J. Saville, (ed.), *Democracy and the Labour Movement* (1954), Chapter VII. Hobsbawm uses the criteria of an average wage of more than 28s. per week (vide Baxter) and membership of the trade union before 1889. By the first criterion, the aristocracy (1840-90) accounted for 11 to 15 per cent of the working class; by the second 10 per cent, pp. 208-9. It has been calculated that 'middle' middle-class income ranged from £200 to £1,000 after the 1850s, the 'lower' middle class £150-£200 (clerks, elementary school teachers, etc.). 'Middle Class Education and Employment in 19th Century', F. Musgrove, *Economic History Review,* 2nd series, Vol. XII, No. 1, August 1959.

For problems arising out of attempts to use the nineteenth century censuses to interpret the class structure in terms of occupational distribution, see D. C. Marsh, *The Changing Social Structure of England and Wales 1871-1951* (1958), Chapter VI, and J.M. Bellamy, 'Occupation statistics in the nineteenth century censuses', and J.A. Banks, 'The social structure of nineteenth century England as seen through the Census' in Richard Lawton (ed.), *The Census and Social Structure* (Cass, 1978).

64. Briggs and Saville, op. cit., p. 69.
65. S.I.C., Vol. IV, Q. 2556.
66. Matthew Arnold wrote of the endowed schools, 'by giving them a national character, it can confer on them a greatness and a noble spirit, which the tone of these classes is not in itself at present adequate to impart. Such schools would soon prove notable competitors with the existing public schools; they would do these a great service by stimulating them, and making them look into their own weak points more closely.' Leonard Huxley (ed.), *Thoughts on Education chosen from the writings of Matthew Arnold* (1912), p. xi.
67. S.I.C., Vol. V, Q. 13199.
68. The unwillingness of one class to mix with the class below it did not exist at the same intensity in all parts of the country: it was stronger in the South than in the North. S.I.C., Vol. I, p. 109.
69. S.I.C., Vol. V, Q. 13069.
70. S.I.C., Vol. V, Q. 16624. J.M.Sanderson, *British Journal of Educational Studies*, Vol. XI, No. 1, November 1962, pp. 38-40, shows the danger of exaggerating the importance of the Eldon decision. A study of Lancashire schools following the case reveals that of 76 of the schools mentioned in Charity Reports, only 8 were following Eldon's intention of free classics and charging for extra subjects. 'For a small village grammar school to invoke the Eldon decree would entail immediate loss of pupils; for a larger school to cease basic subjects or to force them to be taken with others, again entailed parents' resistance and the school had merely cut off its own feed to the upper school. No trustee of good faith wished to manage an empty building, a disgrace to themselves, and thus each worked out a status more or less relevant to its neighbourhood.'
71. This feeling permeated to the National Schools. A Minute of the General Committee of the National Society of 1 November 1865 authorized the establishment of a sub-committee 'on the upper divisions of poorer classes' to see whether the society can assist and if so, how best. in promoting the education of the children of the class of poor just above those who usually attend the National Schools. From 16 January 1867, it was called the 'Middle Class Schools Committee' to be conducted on principles of the Church of England. See E. L. Edmonds, *The School Inspector* (1962), pp. 68-70.
    The Spens Report mentions examples of the movement to graft superior schools on to existing National Schools as early as 1839.
72. S.I.C., Vol. I, pp. 190-1.
73. S.I.C., Vol. V, Q. 17490.
74. S.I.C., Vol. IV, Q. 3583. The City of London School divided middle class into three strata: (a) Professional men – clergy, barristers; (b) Trade; (c) Lower Public Offices – clerks in Bank of England, etc.
75. S.I.C., Vol. I, p. 192.
76. See S.I.C., Vol. I, p. 144.
77. For an account of free scholars in the eighteenth century grammar school, see R. S. Tompson, *Classics or Charity?* (1971), pp. 79-93.
78. Tropp, op. cit., pp. 103-4.
79. S.I.C., Vol. V, Q. 11039. The attitude of economists towards education was divided between the followers of J. S. Mill and Adam Smith. Smith favoured the private school, arguing that the competitive market principle had not been allowed to operate because of the hindrance of endowments. E. G. West, 'The Role of Education in Nineteenth Century Doctrines of Political Economy', *British Journal of Educational Studies*, Vol. XII, No. 2, May 1964.
80. S.I.C., Vol. I, p. 154.

81. But it was not suggested that such sums would adequately represent the market value of earnings. An exhibition might save a father £4-£5 in fees, but the boy would lose £8-£10 in earnings. S.I.C., Vol. I, p. 208.
82. S.I.C., Vol. I, p. 159.
83. The London Working Men's Association was formed in 1866 to organize London trade unions in support of the Bill. See D. Thompson, *England in the Nineteenth Century* (1950), p. 146.
     The American Civil War had its effect on this issue. 'The final victory of the North, followed immediately by Palmerston's death, opened out the way for the enfranchisement of the working classes.' G. M. Trevelyan, *British History in 19th Century and After* (1937), p. 330.
84. 'To understand the working classes in 1860 or in 1856, there is little need to go beyond Applegarth. He believed in the class from which he sprang, and considered it as a class and not as a conglomeration of individuals; but he held that it could only advance by education and superior organization, not by picking up railings in Hyde Park or by accepting a "scientific" theory of tactics and objectives.' Asa Briggs, *Victorian People* (1954), p. 206.
85. B. C. Roberts, *The Trades Union Congress 1868-1921* (1958), p. 60.
86. Archer, op. cit., p. 49.
87. Kitson Clark, op. cit., p. 176.
88. See Lord Lyttelton's reasoning for supporting the Conscience Clause principle in S.I.C., Vol. I, Appendix IA. But the problem remained: 'No party would have dared to turn the Bible out of the schools and no two parties could agree as to the terms upon which it should be admitted.' G. M. Young, *Victorian England* (1953), p. 115.
     Nevertheless, as G. M. Trevelyan remarked, 'The bulk of the working and middle classes and the leaders of the professional and academic world were united in demanding religious equality, educational opportunities and the release of the public services from autocratic control.' op. cit., p. 348.
89. Lord Lyttelton, *Thoughts on National Education* (1853).
90. There is a useful list of references on self-help in Chapter V, 'Getting on in Victorian England'. Harrison, op. cit., pp. 203-11.
91. Charles Loch Mowat, *The Charity Organisation Society, 1869-1913, Its Ideas and Work* (1961), for much of what follows.
     See also reasons for unpopularity of C.O.S. in M. Bruce, *The Coming of the Welfare State* (1960), p. 106; K. de Schweinitz, *England's Road to Social Security* (1943), pp. 140-53.
92. Mowat, op. cit., p. 4, quoting from Local Government Board, 1st Annual Report, 1872.
93. A remarkable feature of the second half of the nineteenth century was the swift increase in voluntary charities. 'The number of such charities in London increased by a quarter in the decade 1850 to 1860, and their income by 35 per cent. Although this rate of increase was not maintained in the following decades it did not fall far short, and by the end of the nineteenth century the trend of donations and subscriptions was still on the upward move. Voluntary societies had become, in the second half of the nineteenth century, the main means by which those in need received private as distinct from State and mutual assistance.' K. Heasman, *Evangelicals in Action. An Appraisal of their Social Work in the Victorian Era* (1962), p. 8.
     Dr. Heasman gives three reasons which would account for this:
     (i)   publicity of the National Association for the Promotion of Social Science (founded 1857) apropos of social distress;
     (ii) deepening sense of guilt at inequality of wealth;
     (iii) desire for publicity and power on the part of the donors.

CHAPTER 2

Reform and Reaction: The Endowed Schools Acts and the Work of the Commission

The years 1869 to 1874 were crucial ones in determining the extent to which the findings of the Schools Inquiry Commission could be put into operation. Much pressure was brought to bear on the Endowed Schools Commissioners in Parliament and by the schools, leading to the modification of important proposals and finally to the demise of the Commission itself. The importance of these pressures in shaping the future development of secondary education in England can be assessed by examining the forces of opposition to the Endowed Schools Act of 1869.

As a party of change, the Liberals once in power enthusiastically set about the task of implementing the findings of the Schools Inquiry Commission.[1] W. E. Forster, now Vice-President of the Committee of the Privy Council on Education, was put in charge of the Endowed Schools Bill, the second reading of which was introduced into the Commons on 15 March, 1869. Forster's interest in education, according to his biographer, was awakened after his marriage to Dr. Arnold's daughter in 1850.[2] As a Bradford man, he was in contact with the leading educational reformers, his friends including Sir James Kay-Shuttleworth, Dr. Hook, Canon Jackson of Leeds, and Canon Robinson of Bolton Abbey, who was later to be named as one of the Endowed School Commissioners. Forster, having served with distinction as a Schools Inquiry Commissioner, appreciated the enormity of the task of reforming the schools and the problems which it would involve.

He accepted the system of gradings of endowed schools as defined by the S.I.C. as a working proposition. In his speech on the second reading of the Bill, Forster made clear that his greatest concern would be with the third grade school. 'Parents in the first

31

grade, being generally persons in affluent circumstances, are able to take care of themselves and I think it is hardly necessary to legislate for them, though we spent a considerable portion of last session in discussing a measure relating to our great Public Schools. The same remark applies to the second grade, but if we are to look after education at all in the country, we must direct our attention to the third grade which I have mentioned.'[3]

The Bill was divided into two parts:[4] the first part dealt with the reorganization of educational endowments, the reconstruction of governing bodies, the lessening of religious disqualification, the reapplication of non-educational charities for educational purposes in certain circumstances, and the establishment of the Endowed Schools Commission. Part 2 of the Bill dealt with the internal organization of the endowed schools. An Educational Council was to be set up, consisting of six representatives of the Universities of Oxford, Cambridge, and London and six Crown nominees. Endowed schools would be liable to be examined in any subject by Inspectors of the Council, the cost to be paid by the school.

Provision was also made for registration of teachers, again under the control of the Council. A register of suitably qualified teachers was to be drawn up under the supervision of the Council; those whose names were not on the register would not be allowed to teach. This part of the Bill had another purpose. 'In effect these clauses were designed, not to set up a professional register similar to the Medical Register, which gave the body of practitioners effective control of their profession, but for the very different purpose of bringing the secondary school teacher under the control of the State and of instituting a certificate which would be parallel to that already prescribed for elementary schoolteachers.'[5]

Headmasters' opposition to the Bill

Opposition to Part 2 of the Bill was immediate and widespread. Although Forster had been at pains to point out that the reform of the endowed schools was not to be regarded as an attack on or an attempt to supplant established private and proprietary schools, the wide powers given to the Commissioners in the second part appeared to contradict Forster's promise. For one thing, the schools were not to be represented on the Council; for another, the power of the Headmaster would be limited to the selection of staff and choice of examinations. That it might be possible to levy rates for municipal schools could lead to further interference in the internal running of a school, and grants might eventually have had to be 'earned' as in the elementary sector.

The most vociferous elements of the headmasters were those who had been aggrieved at being omitted from the provisions of the Public Schools Act of 1868.[6] This attitude was summed up by G. G. Bradley, Headmaster of Marlborough: 'I cannot believe it possible,' he wrote, 'that Parliament would pass an Act which should perpetrate an act of most uneven injustice. It cannot be maintained for a moment that Marlborough, for instance, Cheltenham and Uppingham should be taxed, controlled and examined while Rugby or Eton are left wholly untouched.'[7] Edward Thring of Uppingham poured scorn on the idea of a Council and argued that it was dangerous to treat the endowed schools as an aggregate. 'And what adds very much to the unworkable character of the scheme is the fact that neither Commission has ever raised the question of what is meant by a good school, much less come to any conclusion on that point.'[8]

Championing the Endowed Schools Bill was Dr. Frederick Temple, then Headmaster of Rugby, and one of the moving spirits of the Schools Inquiry Commission. Temple had been responsible for the two key chapters of the Commission's Report – Chapter II, 'Kinds of Education Desirable,' and Chapter VI, 'Recommendations of the Commissioners',[9] and he looked upon the establishment of the Educational Council as of fundamental importance. He was anxious that his fellow headmasters should not regard the seven public schools, which were to be exempted from the workings of the Endowed Schools Act, as a different species from those great schools which would come within the Act. 'There is no reason,' he wrote, 'why the seven schools should not be examined by the Council proposed in the Endowed Schools Bill. If we are really worthy of special distinction, our proper place is not apart from the great body of English education but at the head of it. . . . . . If we are excluded, the Council is damaged by a false impression that it is only inferior work that ought to be examined; and we ourselves are damaged by being shut out from the discharge of a most important duty to the whole country.'[10]

Writing to Harper, Temple stated that he regarded leaving the reform of the seven schools in the first instance to their own trustees a blunder, if the other schools were to be dealt with by a Council. As he saw it, the answer was not to put all first-grade schools on the footing of the seven excepted schools, but to put the seven schools on the same footing as the others.[11] Indeed, it is significant that when the Headmasters' Conference was formed in December 1869 to oppose the demands of the Endowed School Commissioners, that body consisted of headmasters and was not an association of governing bodies, thus showing 'the dominant position of the Endowed School Headmaster and his identification with the institution which he ruled.'[12]

Under the terms of the Bill, the headmaster's authority would be diminished, in a number of ways. An external examining body was to be established; the Council would have the power to choose textbooks for this purpose and charge the school up to £500. The effect on the curriculum, Bradley argued, would be dramatic, with the content of education being taken out of the hands of masters.

It was not only the provisions relating to inspection and examination of schools which led headmasters to oppose the second part of the Bill. Headmasters like Harper had striven to make their schools equal in status to the best public schools. Since accepting the post at Sherborne in 1850, where he found only two boarders and forty day boys, Harper had transformed it, by the time of the Commission, from a mere provincial grammar school to one of the leading English schools.[13] Modelled on public school lines, it possessed its own chapel; when the headmastership of Rugby had fallen vacant, Harper had applied for the post, not for financial betterment 'but it had been represented to him that where so many others were standing, the Headmaster of Sherborne ought, for the sake of his own school, to put in an appearance on the field.'[14] He anticipated the system of the Oxford and Cambridge 'Locals' examinations by inviting university men to examine his boys annually.

Harper pointed out that examination by a Council must be inferior to an outside assessment by university dons.[15] Harper's main concern was with the passing of the control over selection of staff, under the new Bill, from the headmaster to the Council. The composition of the staff was a reflection of the type of school the headmaster wished to make it. Under the new dispensation, the headmaster would be limited in his choice. The class of degree was the best method of certifying a master; a certificated man, as found in the elementary school, might be marked off as inferior, both in intellect and ambition. The choice of staff would be limited and the appointment of distinguished men to headships direct from the universitites, as in the past, would no longer be possible. Forster had already rejected the notion of training colleges for secondary school teachers on the ground that it would give too much power to the Government.[16]

Temple's enthusiastic support for the whole Bill involved him in a long but friendly debate, carried on in the correspondence columns of *The Times,* with his old friend George Granville Bradley of Marlborough. It also throws an interesting sidelight on the differences in temperament and backgrounds of the two educationists. Bradley[17] was at Rugby at the time of Dr. Arnold and after Oxford, returned as assistant master under Dr. Tait. A scholar of great learning, he was autocratic, fear-inspiring, and inclined to sarcasm. He had become Headmaster of Marlborough in 1858 and gathered round him a staff of athletes as well as scholars in the best Arnoldian tradition.[18] Temple, as Head of Rugby, could be accused of viewing the situation from a safe vantage-point, his own school being exempt from the operation of the new Bill. But his support of the Bill was motivated solely by his desire to see the establishment of an efficient system of secondary education; his own early struggles prompted his great interest in this project.[19]

Bradley argued in a cogent fashion that Part 2 of the Bill had no necessary connection with Part 1 and that the schools could be reorganized without need for an examining Council. Temple's reply was unequivocal: 'Certainly they may. But if they are [exempt] within twenty years, half the work will have been undone. No-one could study, as I did for three years, the condition of these schools without coming to an assumed conviction that one cause, if not the main cause, of their present state is that they were never submitted to any periodical public test – their services and their shortcomings never brought to the clear light.'[20]

Temple's hopes for a unified system of secondary education were over-optimistic in the light of events. A further matter of importance was the retention of classical languages in the schools. The two reports of the Public Schools Commission and the Schools Inquiry Commission show a difference in attitude towards what was considered appropriate in the two types of school. The first favoured the retention of Greek and Latin in public schools, as providing good models for language; the latter, whilst acknowledging the need for good Latin teaching, nevertheless recommended Greek only for first grade schools sending scholars to universities, for the most part stressing the need for a modern scientific education.[21]

The loss of status which the large schools would have suffered under Part 2 of the Bill – the setting up of the Teachers' Registration Council, the Educational Council, the loss of headmasters' predominance in shaping the character of the school free from outside pressures, and the doubts prevailing over the future of classics teaching in the endowed schools – led to strong pressures being brought to bear against this part of the Bill.

In the debate on the second reading, the Bill ran into difficulties. John Walter, the proprietor of *The Times*, who had been prominent in Parliament in the movement against the certificated teacher in government schools following the Revised Code,[22] opposed the extension of the system to secondary schools. Forster had already jettisoned many of the provisions that were originally envisaged. After the crucial debate on the second reading, *The Times* commented: 'In reality, the Bill is not a very strong Bill. It falls far short of what the Schools Inquiry Commission recommended. It bears within itself marks of mutilation. Nevertheless, the Bill was too much to be pushed bodily through the House of Commons. Shorn as it had been of all that was necessary to accomplish the characteristic recommendations of the Commission, it still had not enlisted enough support to overbear opposition.'[23]

In the circumstances, the Bill was referred to a Select Committee of the House (1 April 1869), a sure sign that it would be toned down in the process. Bradley observed: 'Any step towards the transference of the direction of our higher education to a London Board – whether desirable or not – is well worth the full and mature consideration which I doubt not it will receive at the hands of the Select Committee and of both Houses of Parliament.'[24] As seemed likely, Part 2 of the Bill was 'reserved for future consideration' in order to ensure that at least part of the Bill became law. The attempt to revive it ended in August 1869.[25]

Although the greater schools had triumphed in this matter, the effect on the bulk of the endowed schools was to bear out Temple's prophetic utterance. Uniform standards between schools in similar grades were impossible without compulsory examination,[26] and the recruitment of staff remained a fortuitous exercise. More serious still was the fragmentation of the system of endowed schools. A minority was able to enjoy an exclusiveness which increased with time and which contradicted Forster's claim in a speech at Leeds in May 1869. 'He believed that the day was gone by when men were born rulers and no arrangement would be more unjust to the gentlemen of England than to give them educational establishments exclusively to themselves. The more efficient the education of great schools was made, the more efficient would be the education in the schools for the poorer classes. It had been his duty to enquire into the education of the working-classes and he found that unless they made the Grammar Schools teachers of what was wanted, they would be no longer schools of the greatest use, schools in which the cleverest boys of the working classes could be brought up.'

The work of the Endowed Schools Commission to 1874

The Endowed Schools Act[27] was to be administered by three full-time Commissioners, who were to be appointed when the Act came into operation. Forster described them as 'merely officers assisting the Government. . . . I believe some persons have thought that the Commissioners have in themselves the power to alter trusts and settle schemes; but the Commissioners alone have no power whatever.'

Some uneasiness was expressed in Parliament over the method by which the Commissioners had been chosen. In the Public Schools Bill, the Commissioners had been named and their nomination debated in the Commons. Here, the Commissioners were to be chosen by the Government. Unlike the Public Schools Commissioners, they were to be paid by and responsible to the Government rather than to Parliament. A. J. Beresford Hope, M.P. for Cambridge University, referred to the Commissioners as 'three anonymous gentlemen, forming an all-powerful triumvirate... appointed by the direct exercise of the Prerogative.'

The Chief Commissioner was Lord Lyttelton, 4th Baron Lyttelton of Frankley (1817-76),[28] a personal friend and brother-in-law of Gladstone. Together they had translated into Greek part of

Milton's *Comus* and into Latin *The Deserted Village*. Lyttelton's qualifications for the post included a one-time Principalship of Queen's College, Birminham, the founding of Saltley Training College, and, as already mentioned, membership of the Public Schools Commission and the Schools Inquiry Commission. He took a keen interest in Church affairs and, as Under-Secretary of State for Colonies under Peel, was responsible with Edward Gibbon Wakefield for founding the province of Canterbury in New Zealand in 1850; the town of Lyttelton, named after him, commemorates this link. Subject to fits of melancholy,[29] Lyttelton took his own life in 1876.

Two other Commissioners were appointed. The first, Canon Hugh George Robinson (1819/20-82), was a friend of Forster, a barrister as well as priest, who had served as Principal of the York and Ripon Diocesan Training College, 1854-64, then as rector of Bolton Abbey, 1864-74, in which capacity he also carried out his duties as a Commissioner.[30] The other Commissioner was Arthur Hobhouse, later 1st Baron Hobhouse of Hodspen (1819-1904), who had been called to the Bar in 1845 and soon acquired a large Chancery practice, becoming a Q.C. in 1862. Illness had forced him to give up his practice and Hobhouse accepted the post of Charity Commissioner from 1866 and was subsequently appointed as an Endowed Schools Commissioner.[31] In politics, he was an avowed Liberal.[32]

The Secretary of the Commission was Henry J. Roby (1830-1915). As a Fellow and Lecturer at Cambridge, he examined for the Classical Tripos and Law, but upon his marriage in 1861 he automatically forfeited his Fellowship; he became second Master at Dulwich, and was thus the only member of the Commission to have had teaching experience in an endowed school. Roby had served as Secretary to the S.I.C.[33] and was the natural choice for the Endowed Schools Commission five years later upon Hobhouse's retirement in 1872.[34] In later life he became a Liberal M.P. and a supporter of Gladstone.

Of the three Commissioners, Lyttelton and Hobhouse had already before their appointment expressed themselves in favour of sweeping reforms in the matter of charitable endowments. In 1869, Lyttelton, commenting on the probability of Hobhouse and himself becoming two of the Commissioners, claimed 'that if they were to be allowed to do what they would certainly feel it their duty to

attempt in very many cases, the "pious founder" would go to the
wall.'[35] At the same time, Hobhouse wrote, 'To talk of the piety or
benevolence of people who give property to public uses, is a misuse
of language springing from confusion of ideas. As a matter of fact, I
believe... that donors to public uses are less under the guidance of
reason and conscience, and more under the sway of baser passions,
than other people.'[36] Hobhouse's strong personality and firm
conviction of the rightness of his attitude towards charities affected
the judgement of the Commissioners in their work during the first
few years.[37]

Lyttelton, conscious of the fact that the new Commissioners
should be able to 'set about their successors' delicate negotiations
with minds unfettered and free from all previous conclusion', at
first declined the post but was eventually persuaded by Gladstone
to accept.[38]

The immediate work of the Commissioners was to frame a
number of model schemes as a basis for future working; this task
occupied the Commission to December 1869. The only exemptions
from the jurisdiction of the Commissioners were those foundations
endowed within the previous fifty years, cathedral schools, and the
schools dealt with by the Public Schools Act. Briefly, its tasks were
to redistribute charitable endowments which were not being fully
utilized and to widen the area which would benefit from them; to
ensure that schools were financially efficient; to establish the
'grade' of school in a given area; to reform governing bodies and
trustees; to destroy the Church basis of qualification for headships,
assistant masters and conditions of entry to schools; and to provide
in the schemes for pupils of ability the opportunity of benefiting
from exhibitions and scholarships tenable at the reformed
schools.[39] The education of girls was omitted from the original
terms of reference, but persistent pressure by a committee concerned with the higher education of women led to its inclusion.[40]

This enormous task was to be completed within three years as it
was anticipated that the schools could be remodelled in a short
space of time. Forster himself was not so optimistic.

When the Bill was in preparation, Lyttelton had discussed with
him various aspects of the Commission's work. In evidence before
the 1873 Select Committee on the Endowed Schools Act, Lyttelton
recounted his conversation with Forster on this matter: 'I said to
him, "Do you suppose that much can be done in 3 or 4 years?" He

said to me, "Certainly not, 10 years would not have been too much." What he said was (and it has come to pass) that in 3 or 4 years Parliament would be able to see how the work had been carried on, and would be able to judge, as it is now attempting to judge, whether the Commission should be retained, and on what terms it should be continued.'[41] The Commission therefore was on trial with the possibility that a premature termination of its existence would leave the field of secondary education in a chaotic state.

The process of preparing and submitting a scheme was a complex and cumbersome one. A draft scheme was prepared after either an examination or a public inquiry by the Commissioners. After printing, the scheme was submitted to governing bodies, headmasters, and other interested parties; a three-month period following publication was reserved for receiving objections, suggestions and alternative schemes. The Commissioners (or any one of them) were to take these into consideration and could then either hold another public inquiry or frame and submit the scheme directly to the Committee of Council on Education for approval. If the governors had submitted a scheme to the Commissioners before the latter had prepared a draft scheme, then both schemes could be considered by the Education Department. If the Department did not approve the Commissioners' scheme, another was then prepared, the governing body being given a further three months to submit a new one. Alternatively, if the governing body felt that the Commissioners' scheme was disadvantageous with regard to compensation for vested interests, or that the scheme modified privileges or educational advantages to which a class of persons was entitled, it could, within one month of the approval of the scheme, petition the Judicial Committee of the Privy Council or bring their grievance to the attention of Parliament. Either House could present an Address within forty days against the whole or part of the scheme; if this was successful, the scheme was to be remitted to the Commissioners for amendment. It could then either be reframed or resubmitted to the Education Department with the necessary amendments. Finally, every scheme had to receive the approval of the Sovereign in Council, when it acquired the force of an Act of Parliament.

These safeguards written into the Act resulted in slow progress and encouraged delaying tactics by those affected by the schemes.

The constitutional position of the Commissioners was somewhat analogous to that of the Poor Law Commissioners. As an administrative body, it was responsible directly to the Government of the day and therefore enjoyed neither the anonymity of the Civil Service nor the privilege of being answerable to Parliament for its actions. A fourth Commissioner was appointed to overcome this difficulty. He was a Member of Parliament, chosen by the Government of the day and unpaid, and it was hoped that, by attending meetings of the Commission, though not taking part in the formulation of policy, he would become fully cognizant of the Commissioners' work and could represent them in the Commons. This was not successful because of the lack of continuity of office and infrequency of attendance at meetings as well as political opposition to a purely administrative body. There was also the fact that Parliament was able to intervene in the process of scheme-making at the end, only when acceptance or rejection were the alternatives.

The task of the Commissioners bristled with problems. The preamble to the Act stated that its intention was to 'render any educational endowment most conducive to the advancement of boys and girls with special reference to the Schools Inquiry Commission... and of carrying into effect the main designs of the founders thereof, thus putting a liberal education within the reach of children of all classes.' In order that this could be accomplished, unusually wide powers, many of them discretionary, were given under the Act. Despite the 1840 Grammar Schools Act subjects taught and entry into schools were still fairly narrowly prescribed by the Courts.[42] Under s.9 of the Endowed Schools Act the Commissioners could ignore previous schemes relating to the foundations and were given powers to consolidate, re-endow and move schools, as well as change what were traditionally considered to be 'grammar school' subjects. By this section, the Commissioners 'should have power in such manner as may render any educational endowment most conducive to the advancement of education, to alter and add to any existing, and to make new trusts, directions and provisions which affect such endowments, and the education promoted thereby, including the consolidation of two or more such endowments, or the division of one endowment into two or more endowments.'[43] Thus the Commission was given powers formerly entrusted to the Courts.

Linked with this was s. 99, which stipulated that endowments attached to schools for the payment of apprenticeship fees, clothing, etc., were to be classed as educational endowments. Apart from these, a list of non-educational charities, almost identical with those suggested by the S.I.C., was set out in s. 30. If donated for charitable purposes before 1800, and if the consent of the governing body was forthcoming, the endowments could be applied to educational schemes by the Commissioners.

To compensate for the loss of educational privileges the famous 'due regard' provision, s. 11, was inserted, which was to cause so much dispute at a later date. It stated that where a scheme 'abolished or modified any privileges or educational advantages to which a particular class of persons are entitled, whether as inhabitants of a particular area or not, the Commissioners were to have due regard to the educational interests of such class of persons' without defining the term 'class of persons'. This was to be taken in conjunction with s. 13 which provided for the saving interest of boys in attendance at the time of the Act on the foundation of an endowed school as well as exhibitioners and teachers entitled to pensions at the time of the passing of the Act; for the governing bodies, provision was made for any rights of patronage exercised by individual members.

The Commissioners encountered much opposition in the course of their work from individuals and institutions likely to be affected by the wide-ranging powers given to them by the Act. Chief amongst the objectors was the Church of England: unless the governing bodies could produce evidence that they were originally 'Church foundations' and thus under s. 19 exempt from the workings of the Act, schools were likely to become secularized.

Alternative schemes

The Church of England basis of many of the schools was, as we have seen, assumed by virtue of the original endowments. The close connection between the Church and education was strengthened by the almost universal rule that the headmaster was in Holy Orders. By the time of the Endowed Schools Act, the majority of schools had lost their exclusively denominational character except in the case of Cathedral schools and similar institutions. In many cases, entrants were expected to belong to the Church of England

and received instruction in the catechism, but no great importance was attached to such provisions.

Only in the case of the Woodard Foundations had any effort been made to link middle-class education with religion. Nathaniel Woodard in his pamphlet, *Plea to the Middle Classes* (1848), had pointed out that the 'trades class' were comparatively illiterate, and that the nation faced the danger of lapsing into barbarism. Woodard's philosophy has been summed up by his biographer as follows: 'Positively, he asserted that this state of things constituted a dramatic challenge to the Church. It was her business to rouse herself and to do for the middle classes what she had done for the poor, by means of National Schools, forty years earlier. Negatively, however, in addition to using language which suggested that the Church, in interesting herself in the middle-class schools, should use them mainly for the purpose of propagating doctrine, he maintained throughout his life that it would be disastrous for the State to assume even a moderate degree of control over the educational system of the country.'[44]

Woodard anticipated that the coming of State participation in secondary education would lead to unbridled denominationalism. He wished to restore the position of the established Church in education by setting up a system of Church secondary schools.[45] The country was to be divided into five areas, with one body to supervise the work of each area; the Lancing Society, for example, consisted of a Provost and 24 fellows, half of whom were resident clerics, the other half, non-resident laymen. The five Provosts and 120 fellows could make by-laws for all the schools. The Bishop for each diocese was to be the Visitor; appeals could be made to the Upper House of Convocation.[46] Underlying Woodard's desire to start such schools was the growing popularity of Methodism whilst that of the Church declined; he openly set out to win back Dissenters to the Church.[47]

Woodard's scheme attracted widespread interest from those sections of the middle classes who could not afford a public school education yet who were dissatisfied with that provided by the endowed schools. The structure of the new schools made clear Woodard's educational philosophy. He appreciated that professional and trading classes would never mix in a single school, so a series of graded schools needed to be set up, called respectively 'upper', 'middle' and 'lower'. Boarding accommodation was an essential part of the scheme. Lancing, equivalent to a first grade school, Hurstpierpoint a second grade, and St. Saviour's, Shoreham 'for poorer members' of the middle classes, later in 1870 removed to Ardingly, were established. The so-called third grade school disappeared as the boarding school aspect, combined with the high fees, raised it above the level of an equivalent third grade endowed school. Its place was taken by day schools.

The Taunton Commission had examined the schools (Lord Taunton himself had been a patron of the schools) and found them efficient. Lyttelton too had been a friend of Woodard but had disagreed with Woodard's policy in a long and bitter exchange of correspondence.[48] Woodard's ideas were directly opposed to the spirit of the Schools Inquiry Commission. In 1869, Woodard issued his *Letter to the Marquis of Salisbury*[49] which showed him as neither an educational reformer nor the promoter of a national system of secondary education. His interest, which lay in the essentially denominational character of a school, flew in the face of much contemporary opinion.

Private means were insufficient to expand the Woodard Schools and attempts were made when the Commission began its work to obtain funds from dormant endowments to establish schools on the Woodard plan. In Yorkshire, a Middle Class Schools Association was formed under the auspices of the Rev. Robert Howard of Rawdon, Leeds. His aim, as he wrote in a letter to the Commissioners, was to found a 'lower grade boarding school in the West Riding'.[50] A pamphlet written by Howard at this time makes clear his aims.[51] The Church should take a lead in questions of education. He was against the establishment of isolated schools belonging to a single grade which 'would necessitate the establishment of other schools, one by one, each with its own repetition of a governing body, but wholly isolated and separated, the one from another.'

The Association was to consist of a society of clergy and lay members of the Church of England. Howard would open schools of each grade as funds permitted; the head of each school was to have a seat on the Board of Trustees. The aim of the Association would be to help the poorest of the middle classes by establishing a third grade boarding school at Sherburn in the West Riding for 300 to 500 boys. At the time of the Schools Inquiry Commission, Sherburn were catering for four boarders, all orphans, who were clothed and given elementary education and taught the Church catechism. For this the Master received £60 per annum. The intention of the Association was to stop the election of further orphans and to devote a proportion of the annual income to repair or rebuild elementary schools (if required) and place them under inspection. Endowments attached to the Sherburn school were to be supplemented by those of three neighbouring schools, Drax,[52] Snaith and Tadcaster. The Association would deal drastically with these foundations.[53] Drax educated twelve boys who were later apprenticed at a cost of £300 per annum, with another £400 spent in providing gratuitous education, part of which went to maintain three infant schools which were part of the foundation. The endowment was to be withdrawn from the infant schools and used for a lower-middle-class grammar school at Drax, the rest to be allocated to a boys' school at Sherburn. Snaith had a free grammar school, the premises of which were situated in the churchyard and were in a dilapidated condition,[54] and Tadcaster possessed a free school which, according to the S.I.C., 'demoralizes the town' and 'receives children whose parents will not pay to send them to the National School.' These two endowments were to be wholly transferred to Sherburn. Howard's proposals were that all gratuitous education was to be abolished and 'such fees only charged as are fitted to the means of the parents of the class which is contemplated in order to provide schools at Sherburn and Drax.' Provision was to be made for exhibitions for deserving boys and girls during their stay at school and for entrance into a trade or employment, although no details were given. This scheme was closely modelled on Woodard's own, except that the complete range of schools was not provided, merely one foundation.

The Commissioners turned down Howard's scheme, stating that whilst 'it is their duty to consider the interests and requirements of the middle-classes', they were limited by the provisions of the Act itself. For example, ss. 15-18 laid upon the Commissioners the obligation to introduce undenominational instruction in the schemes, except in the case of foundations connected with Cathedrals or Collegiate Churches or if the founder had specifically stated otherwise, in which event denominational instruction could be given up to fifty years after his death. No such clauses were to be discovered in the original foundations of the schools mentioned. The other point on which the scheme failed was that 'they [the

Commissioners] must secure the fullest liberty of conscience for the scholars and must also provide that no-one shall be disqualified from being a member of the governing body by reason of his "religious opinions" or his attendance or non-attendance at any particular form of religious worship.'

This naive attempt to aggregate endowments for purely sectarian ends was bound to fail because of the nature of the Endowed Schools Act. However, the scheme was not without merit. Woodard and his followers aimed at providing sufficient secondary education for all who could afford to pay, according to their means. The division of the country into areas governed by 'Societies' came near to the Provincial Boards envisaged by the Schools Inquiry Commission and by W. E. Forster, as means of obtaining uniformity of standards within an area. The Woodard plan failed because of its conservative nature in educational thinking and the narrowness of its terms of admittance to the schools, although Church co-operation on a county basis with the Endowed Schools Commissioners followed.[54a]

Local opposition

The Commissioners' policy of downgrading schools to meet the real needs of an area, coupled with a broadly-based concept of education, favouring scientific rather than classical aspects of the curriculum, was unpopular with schools and parents. A number of old foundations had been reformed in the years prior to the establishment of the Commission and were now offering a curriculum similar in content and level to the public schools. The Commissioners' policy was an attempt to rationalize the use of resources in any given area.[55] The preservation of vested interests of boards of governors and trustees was jealously fought for: and the openings provided by the Commissioners for the admission of able poor boys to the schools on favourable terms were resisted.

Most of these pressures were at work during the life of the Commission (1869-74) and can be seen in a study of a number of schools of this period.

Teaching of Greek

The Commissioners, on taking office, were confronted with the problem of the place of classics in the endowed schools. It has been seen earlier[56] that the Public Schools Commissioners recommended the retention of Greek and Latin to the exclusion of modern subjects. A line of gifted teachers – Arnold, Kennedy, Vaughan, Bradley and Temple – had firmly established these languages as the hall-mark of a public school.

The S.I.C. had concluded that Latin should be taught in endowed schools but that Greek should be confined to the first grade schools and then only to those boys proceeding to the universitities. Many private schools had sprung up to supply the language teaching which was often lacking in the schools. It seems clear that for many parents who intended their sons to receive a university education, the demand for the teaching of classics was a real one,[57] and that without such teaching the gap between school and university would be too great.

The views of the Commissioners alienated a large section of such parents. Forster had mentioned the threat of the 'German clerk' in Bradford and stressed the need for modern scientific education in the schools in order to retain Britain's industrial and commercial superiority over her European competitors. Thus, the Modern side of the school should be stressed, with efficient instruction given in European languages and one or two branches of science; to many, this looked like a thinly-veiled 'commercial' or 'English' school for potential clerks. The Commissioners came out strongly against the teaching of Greek and advocated that there should be only one school in an area teaching Greek at which those pupils who required instruction could attend.

One of the first schools dealt with by the Commissioners, Bradford Grammar School, illustrates the opposition to the abolition of Greek. The Commissioner in charge of the case, Canon Robinson, who as a local knew the problems of the area well, in his instructions to D. R. Fearon, the Assistant Commissioner at Bradford, suggested that besides providing a first grade school out of the endowments, a good second or third grade school should be established, offering a useful practical education to the sons of tradesmen and well-to-do artisans. Robinson anticipated opposition from the headmaster and trustees on the issue of classics.[58] 'If these – as seems possible – try to make a stand for the conditions of the original foundation they must be strongly resisted. The school as a classical school is doomed.'[59] This was because of the proximity of Leeds Grammar School which already provided for these subjects. Fearon agreed with Robinson on this: the danger was that if Greek were allowed, an élite, representing the ambitions of the school, would be formed: 'The Headmaster will come at last to have a small picked lot of Grecians to be worked up for the University.'

A Memorial to the Commissioners from the governors of the Grammar School (9 November 1870) made clear the keen interest in education in Bradford. The population at the beginning of the century had been 13,264; by 1870, within a radius of four miles, it was 254,230. The Memorialists claimed that 'a large and affluent middle-class has sprung up within the last generation, the members of which are anxious to give their sons educational advantages that were denied to their own youth, and who feel that thus only can they enable those who are to succeed them in the management of important commercial or industrial establishments, to take their proper position among English gentlemen.'

Some three months[60] earlier the governing body had asked the Commissioners to include Greek in a 'liberal' education, after unanimously agreeing that it should be taught. Its value for those going on to university was stressed. Medical and scientific terms were chiefly derived from the Greek. The gulf between first grade and public schools could be bridged in this way. 'What the State wants from schools are men who have a common basis of instruction up to a certain point and can meet on common literary grounds afterwards whatever their special line of technical or professional study may be.'

The Commissioners resisted this point of view. It was contrary to the spirit of the preamble of the Act. The needs of the locality and a broader curriculum were paramount. Certainly in the case of Bradford, an industrial town with allied scientific establishments, a classical school in such surroundings would have been out of place.[61] The attitude of the Commissioners at this early date is brought out clearly in reply to a deputation of Governors:

> The Commissioners fear that in relation to this question, there is a fundamental difference of opinion between themselves and many of those with whom they anxiously wish to co-operate. There seems to be a widely prevailing notion that a good school ought to teach everything: that, at least, the limits of a school

course may be very wide. Hence no difficulty is felt in urging that not only Greek and Latin but 2 or 3 Modern Languages, Mathematics, Science and a variety of subordinate subjects should be included in the school curriculum. Of the fallacy and mischief of this notion in itself and as conspicuously illustrated in the history of education, the Commissioners are deeply persuaded. For the sake of thoroughness and reality in education, they desire to limit in each case the course of study and give to each school its own definite line of work.

They are satisfied that the teaching of Greek in addition to Latin will be apt entirely to dominate the school course, to force all other subjects into a subordinate place and to fix in a classical mould the type and character of a school.[62]

The system would tend to be a self-perpetuating one, with the headmaster selected on classical attainments, who would devote an inordinate amount of time to Greek and Latin.

The Commissioners opposed the suggestion of confining modern and scientific instruction to the junior school. 'The effect of this will be to put the Modern and Scientific Instruction in an inferior and subordinate position and to reproduce the old plan of a classical and commercial school in juxtaposition, a state of things which has seldom been found to work satisfactorily.' The junior department in this instance catered for boys 8-15 and the senior department 13-19, with entrance by examination to both departments.

In response to constant pressure from those wishing to see a classical school established, the Commissioners gave consent for a local inquiry to be held to see 'whether there is such a proved demand for instruction in Greek as to justify the claim urged by the Governors in its favour. Whatever be the result of the proposed enquiry, the Commissioners sincerely hope that it may lead to the establishment of a school in Bradford which shall give a liberal and practical education to as large a class as possible without attempting to achieve aims that are incompatible with one another, and without sacrificing the interests of the less opulent many to the wealthy few.'

The inquiry, held 10 January 1871, brought forward some thirty to forty gentlemen[63] to testify in support of the governors. Faced with unanimous opposition, the Commissioners were obliged to amend their scheme. Cl.41 now read: 'Within the limits fixed by this Scheme, the *Governors* shall prescribe the general subjects of instruction, the relative prominence and value to be assigned to each group of subjects.' The headmaster was to have control over both departments, junior and senior. Entrance requirements into the junior school were: reading simple narrative, writing texthand, easy sums in first and second rules of arithmetic; for the senior department, in addition, English history and Latin grammar were required, with ability to translate and parse simple Latin sentences. The curricula of the two departments naturally differed. Roby, on giving instructions for the Inquiry (7 January 1871), allowed that Fearon should sanction Greek being taught in the upper department.

This outcome was undoubtedly a defeat for the Commissioners in their efforts to liberalize education and prevent endowed schools becoming pale imitations of the public schools. The introduction of Greek kept fees at a high level, in the case of Bradford Upper School £10-£20 per annum with a £2 entrance fee. The consequence of the Bradford scheme was to encourage other schools to adopt the Greek cry. Lyttelton and his colleagues appreciated that the source of trouble could be traced to the universities, where Greek predominated.[64] To break the circle, the Commissioners addressed an open letter to Oxford, Cambridge and London to ascertain what support the Commissioners could expect from the universities with reference to entrance requirements and quoting the Bradford scheme. This attempt was unsuccessful, all three institutions refusing to sanction Lyttelton's proposals.[65]

The Commissioners' policy in dealing with the Greek question was more idealistic than practical. Whilst the language was held as the hall-mark of a good education, middle-class parents could be expected to urge its retention, and in many cases, its introduction into, the school curriculum. For a first grade school, it also served as a social selector for entry into the school and it marked it off from the schools below.

The Commission at work

Of the 3,000 endowed schools, more than 2,200 were classified as being elementary in character; these came within the purview of the new Commission. Because of the urgent need to deal with the larger foundations, the elementary schools were not given new schemes. By the 1873 Endowed Schools Amendment Act, the bulk of these schools were transferred to the jurisdiction of the Education Department in cases where the gross average annual income of the endowments did not exceed £100.

Four of the biggest endowments – Bedford, Birmingham, Dulwich and Christ's Hospital – were allowed by the Act (s. 32) a year in which to submit their own schemes to the Commissioners, i.e. until August 1870; until such time, the Commissioners' powers to make schemes were suspended. At the time of the passing of the Act, Bedford presented in an enlarged form the problems attendant upon many of the larger schools in their relationship with the Commissioners. In November 1869, there were 1,700 scholars out of a population of 16,400. This was largely due to the great number of 'squatters' who came to the town for the free education which the foundation, Harpur's Trust, offered. Many of these were of the poorer middle-class families which the Commissioners envisaged as the class entitled to receive greater benefits under the dispensation of the Act – army officers, clergy, civil servants, and their widows. The schools – consisting of the Grammar School, a Commercial School and three elementary schools – offered a free education to all inhabitants of Bedford and were unselective. A letter from a former head of the Medical Department in Madras (October 1869) to the Commissioners bears this out. Giving his reasons why, after settling in Bedford especially for the benefits of education, he withdrew his four sons from the school, he stated: 'The boy who cleans my sons' shoes was in the same class with them. I do not mention this unkindly, but it is not very probable that Latin or French would be of much use to him afterwards.'[66]

At the same time, a master at the Modern School complained that 'the endowment, being intended both for educational and eleemosynary purposes, the rival interests have clashed to the detriment of the cause of education.' This was to a great extent true: the foundation dated back to the reign of Henry VIII when Sir William Harpur, then Lord Mayor of London, had made over to the foundation thirteen acres of land in London, the rents and profits of which were to be devoted for ever to the instruction of Bedford children, 'in grammar and good manners.' The surplus was to be used for maintaining almshouses, for providing Bedford girls with marriage portions and general charity work among the poor of five parishes. The eleemosynary portion of the charity, due to the great rise in land values in London, had increased in wealth and the trustees, elected on the qualification of paying 'Scot and Lot', dominated the educational side;[67] from the charity was maintained a Hospital School which boarded, clothed and educated 26 poor children at the cost of £40 per child a year. The Grammar School, which had flourished under the headship of the Rev. F. Fanshawe, had a body of non-local trustees, nominated by the Warden and Fellows of New College, Oxford. With two separate boards of trustees, friction between the two aspects of the endowment was inevitable.

Lyttelton remarked on the file (16 April 1870): 'We have no more important case, I think, as when I reported on it to the former Commission,[68] that it is probably the most glaring instance of abuse in some important particulars, that can be found.' It was on this school that the crucial debate took place between three of the Commissioners on the policy to be followed. Both Roby and Hobhouse felt that as the school possessed such a large endowment, the poorer sections of the middle class should be helped. They set out their views for Lyttelton's comments. Roby wrote: 'Bedford is regarded as a place where widows and others in poor circumstances can reside and obtain for their children a better education for a smaller sum than is obtainable for that amount elsewhere. It seems to me by no means clear that this is not a good way of using *one* of the large endowments which comes under the Commission.' For this purpose, Roby would diminish or do away entirely with the appropriation of endowments to elementary schools, except by exhibitions. 'But I would not attempt to make the fee paid by the parents generally at all adequate to the cost of education. It at present affords a means of helping poverty... and Bedford affords an opportunity of showing that, where it is possible to befriend poverty without injuring education, the Commissioners are willing to do so. For it is a distinct benefit to the community that persons belonging to an educated class hit by an accident or the loss of a husband, are [sic] unable to give their children an education like their own, should be able, though at some inconvenience to themselves, to get this education for their children. Why should not Bedford be allowed to continue as a place especially adopted for sojourners?'[69] Hobhouse concurred with this view in a footnote: 'There is a good deal to be said for this view of the case and deserves to be considered.'

Lyttelton's memorandum in reply displayed his determination to enforce a universal principle regarding the payment of fees. In his view, it would be wrong to exempt Bedford from the necessity of charging reasonable fees to those in poor circumstances on that ground alone, irrespective of merit and industry. The general principles of the Commissioners had been determined and should be followed in all cases; nowhere should the general charge be much below its real value.

> We submit to its being so in the case of poor schools, simply because we cannot help it. We cannot get the modicum of schooling that we think indispensable for labourers – and that on political grounds, not personal ones relating to the parents – without paying for it very much more than it is possible for the parents to pay. But that is by no means proved as to the class above them and the experiment has to be made. . . . The very ground on which we proceed is the assumption that these funds are now, as a general rule, wasted in giving gratuitous education. But I do not know that it follows that the effect on the general education of the country will allow the soundness of the general principles on which we go and will leave the result to be ascertained by experience.[70]

Lyttelton, who stated that 'the town is a small one, and seemed to us absolutely gorged with this endowment,' was responsible for the new scheme in 1873 which embodied the Commissioners' policy. The secondary schools were now given 8/11ths of the revenue and the elementary schools 2/11ths.[71]

Protection Societies

'Protection Societies', under various names, were set up to watch over local interests. At Exeter, where a scheme was to be put forward in 1871, two rival committees were established: the City Committee was 'to consider the application of the Endowed Schools Act to the foundations of the City and to make suggestions to the Commissioners.'[72] A resolution to the Commissioners (28 April 1871) asking for the Exeter endowments to be confined to the town was sent. The County Committee, consisting of a number of influential persons, urged the wider extension of benefits from the endowments. Both bodies were essentially middle-class in composition, having as their object the establishment of a first grade school in the district. Similar committees proliferated in many parts of the country. The Yorkshire Education Society appointed a committee to draw out a scheme of re-organization and included among its members the Archbishop of York, the Bishop of Ripon, and the Duke of Devonshire. In the case of the Leicestershire County Committee, the secretary was Master of Kibworth Grammar School whose school was shortly to be visited by the Commission.[73]

The Birmingham Grammar School Reform Association is an example of a well-organized pressure group which affected the course of a school's scheme. As the school's historian commented, 'A private body with modest and reasonable aims put forward certain proposals for a less radical alteration on the administrative side and also for important reforms in the educational function of the school. To that body, far more than to the Town Council, the School owes changes that were beyond question beneficial.'[74] It consisted of many prominent Liberals, Nonconformists, manufacturers and influential Old Boys. It was founded the same year that the Schools Inquiry Commission began taking evidence and was therefore one of the earliest committees of its kind, and later gave evidence before the Commission.[75] Some of its most active members, such as George Dixon, M.P., and the Rev. R. W. Dale, were active Radicals and prime movers of the National Education League, which had as its main aim the universal free and unsectarian education of every child in the country. This was with reference to elementary education, but the relationship between secondary and elementary stages was brought into focus by the demands for the reform of the Birmingham Grammar School. The Association was concerned both with the raising of existing standards at the school, linking it with the elementary schools, and at the same time with avoiding rivalry between the school board and grammar school. A Report of the Association[76] showed that it believed the endowments should remain in the grammar school foundation: 'One great difficulty that will present itself in the future will be the appropriation of funds. A popularly elected School Board would consider, in all probability, whether the income should not be applied in reduction of the elementary education rates, and leave the higher grade of education to maintain itself entirely by capitation fees. The Endowment will, undoubtedly, do the most good, and stimulate education most widely, if chiefly applied to promote the highest form of intellectual training and at the same time render it accessible to every boy whose industry and mental power give promise of future eminence.'

When the Assistant Commissioner, Mr. Hammond, was given instructions on visiting Birmingham (26 November 1870), the Association was one of the three bodies 'which to some extent may be held to represent the public opinion of the town, so far as it takes interest in the question', the other two being the Town Council and the governing body of the grammar school.[77] Its desire to employ endowments for secondary education was not intended to preclude the poor from enjoying the benefits of them. In a five-hour meeting with Hammond, it urged that the elementary schools of the foundation should become third grade schools. There would be a range of fees from £1.10s. to £5 but with as much as 50 per cent of admissions to the school free, by competition, 30 per cent to the second grade and 20 per cent to the first.

A test case: Emanuel Hospital

In the first years of the Commission, those mainly affected by the proposed changes were not organized in any systematic defence. It was to be expected that the main opposition would spring from attempts at the reform of the London foundations. The case of Emanuel Hospital, Westminster, brings out, in a graphic manner, the support for the poor from unexpected quarters – the Church of England, the Conservative Party and the Court and Aldermen of the City of London.

The Hospital was founded by the will of Lady Ann Dacre in 1594, in which the executors were to build a convenient house with accommodation for 20 poor folk and 20 other children 'bestowing thereon £300'. Letters patent of 1600 vested the property in the Lord Mayor and Aldermen of London, the Governors of the Hospital and the poor of Emanuel Hospital. From 1736 both boys and girls were admitted, from the parishes of St. Margaret's, Westminster, Chelsea, Hayes and later, the City of London and Brandesburton in Yorkshire, where was situated the principal property of the Hospital. Admission was by election, with some limitation for Protestant children.

By the second half of 1864, Emanuel School was classified as non-classical third grade.[78] There were no day pupils but the school boarded thirty sons of poor tradespeople or persons holding public offices, entitling them to free board and education and three meals a day. An entrance qualification was that boys on admission must be able to read words of two syllables. Religious instruction consisted of a Church service in the morning and evening prayers. At the time of Roby's inspection in 1871[79] 30 boys and 30 girls were boarded and educated at the Hospital, 46 from London and Westminster. The affairs of the Hospital appeared to be managed by a committee of aldermen. As to the type of child receiving benefit from the Hospital, Roby wrote: 'The children belong to a class above the ordinary primary schools. The parents are Policemen, Master Artificers, Messengers [House of Lords] and the Brandesburton children are children of farm bailiffs, governesses, etc.'[80] Six boys and twelve girls were orphans. Roby found that the majority of girl leavers took service with families and the boys became clerks and apprentices to trades.

As the Hospital possessed an educational endowment of more than £1,000 per annum, it was entitled to draw up and submit a new scheme to the Endowed School Commission for consideration; the Lord Mayor and Aldermen of the City of London took advantage of this and a scheme was submitted on the 28 January 1870. In it, they named themselves, as a body, to be governors and visitors, with power to close the school, sell the site and erect a new building in the Home Counties. The eleemosynary side of the charity provided, under the scheme, for the abolition of in-pensioners, and out-pensioners' provisions were to be restricted to certain parishes, the recipients to be over 56 years with goods not exceeding £30 in value.

The school was to be divided into upper and lower and the children classified as either 'children in the Hospital' or 'out-scholars'; the former would receive free board and education, the latter were to be admitted on payment. The upper school would provide instruction in Latin, Greek, Bookkeeping, etc., with fees of £5-£10 per annum. Admission, except for certain preferences for City of London, Westminster, Brandesburton, Hayes and Chelsea, was open to all comers, and pupils of the school would stay until eighteen years of age. The lower school, giving an elementary education, was to limit its pupils to the above parishes and the parish where the school was to be situated. Fees would be between £1-£4, with a leaving age of fifteen. Both schools were to admit, under the scheme, at eight years of age. For the Hospital, there were to be not less than seventy poor children and an equal number of boys and girls elected. To qualify for entry a child had to be an orphan or from a family that had been resident at least twelve months previously in a prescribed parish. The Hospital children were to be placed initially in the Lower School, where they would remain until fifteen, but were eligible thereafter for promotion to the Upper School.

The Commissioners questioned the authority of the Lord Mayor and Aldermen to frame such a scheme. Section 7 of the Endowed Schools Act could be interpreted to show that, nominally, Emanuel Hospital possessed two governing bodies. A governing body was there defined as 'any body corporate, persons or person who have the right of holding, on any power of government of, or management over, any endowment or any endowed school.' This charity showed the Corporation of the City of London as possessing the power of government and Emanuel Hospital as holding the endowments. The solution was not to make over power to the City of London: a reply from the Commissioners stated that they were unwilling 'to commit the whole government of important educational endowments to a single corporation, however eminent and dignified' (11 February 1870). They believed that a more representative governing body should be formed. D. C. Richmond, an Assistant Commissioner, commented that nothing had been mentioned in the scheme regarding the selection of foundation scholars. Pecuniary benefits contemplated under the scheme 'should be given not as matters of privilege or patronage but as rewards of merit'; an efficient entrance examination with remission of fees for merit and some exhibitions for further education was necessary. It was finally stated that a school with a great age range and different standards of instruction and catering for pupils with different future careers was bound to fail.

The Commissioners' outline scheme (20 June 1870) showed a much more drastic treatment of the existing foundation. Emanuel Hospital was to be absorbed into a group of schools with which it was connected – the Grey Coat, Green Coat and Blue Coat Schools, Palmer's Hospital and Emery Hill's Hospital.[81] The consolidated foundation would be made into a great day school for boys and a duplicate of this was to be established in the suburbs with boarding facilities. The day schools, divided into upper and lower, were to be called the United Westminster Schools of third grade status with an age range of seven to fourteen years. The school could charge £3-£5 and the boarding school £20-£35. Latin was to be taught in the upper but not the lower school. Foundation scholars would account for a sixth of the total number in each school, with remission, total or partial, of boarding fees. There were to be exhibitions for further education as well. Of these benefits, a third was to be reserved for boys of the public elementary schools in the parishes of St. Margaret and St. John and another third to boys at public elementary schools who had lost one parent.[82] The governing body, of twenty members, would consist of three *ex officio,* seven nominated and ten co-opted governors, with minority representation to the Aldermen and the City of London.[83]

Reaction from the latter body was soon forthcoming. The proposed loss of identity of the foundation was deplored; the introduction of competitive examinations, it was claimed, would eliminate the poor. 'The school has been for the poor and the Court of Aldermen desire that it should so remain, according to the desire of the Founder' (31 May 1870). It was not necessary to use the endowments of Emanuel Hospital, as the Elementary Education Bill, then before Parliament, 'will provide for primary education of the people without the Commissioners touching for that purpose the funds of Emanuel Hospital' (8 July 1870). It was pointed out that girls' education was not envisaged in the Commissioners' scheme and strict 'due regard' had not been paid to the loss of privileges then enjoyed by certain parishes. The religious aspects of the Commissioners' scheme, which included the freeing of the foundation from its denominational origins, was not overlooked. The Master of Emanuel, the Rev. J. Maskell, welcomed the abolition of eleemosynary education from the foundation but was 'not quite so satisfied with the destruction of the religious character of the instruction for the sake of disconnecting it with the Church of England.'[84]

Because of the fundamental objection to the Commission's scheme, the governors refused to take advantage of the opportunity to submit their objections. They told the Commissioners, 'The Governors, in coming to this conclusion, have borne in mind that in their previous correspondence with the Commissioners, they have fully stated their views and their intentions, if it be possible to preserve this endowment for the poor, whilst the Commissioners on the other hand have avowed their intention of carrying universally into effect the maxim that there should be no gratuitous education except as the reward of merit. The two bodies would appear therefore to be so much at issue upon a cardinal principle as to leave no room for any common ground of agreement between them, and to render it probable that the final determination will have to be by another tribunal.'

In giving their 'Observations on Objections of Governors', for the Committee of Council on Education, the Commissioners rejected the cry of 'robbing the poor': 'The Commissioners do not think it necessary in this case to dwell much on the well-known topics that of late years great assistance has been given, and that now full provision is made by law, for the education of the poorest classes; whereas nothing has been done for those just above them; and that it is a very old principle of dealing with endowments to apply them to purposes not provided for by the ordinary course of law. For in this case they conceive that by their scheme they offer to the very class which is now using the Endowments, benefits which will reach a larger number in a more healthy way than is at present the case.'

The Lord Mayor convened a public meeting on 21 April 1871, to consider the position of Emanuel Hospital, Greycoat and other foundations which were threatened. As a result, a School Trusts Defence Committee was established a week later, with its head-quarters at the Mansion House. Its aim was to prevent the removal of the endowments from the locality and it sought support from many quarters. Endowed schools throughout England were can-vassed for support and the Committee attempted to link up especially with those schools which at that time were being subject to the scrutiny of the Commissioners. Circulars were sent to all municipalities, requesting them to address the Commissioners on the Emanuel scheme and adding, 'if they [the Commissioners] succeed against us, resistance anywhere else will be hopeless.' The councils were also asked to support Emanuel Hospital when the case was brought up before Parliament, a course which was hinted at in the Corporation's reply earlier to the Commissioners.[85] 'The most effective way in which you can help us will be by communica-tion with your members and with any members of the House of

Peers to whom you have access, as we are really fighting a common battle.'[86]

Political support for the Committee was not difficult to find. The Liberals were in a state of disunity after the 1870 Elementary Education Act came into operation. The passing of the Criminal Law Amendment Act in the following year had alienated many of the working class.[87] The defence of charitable endowments, which now appeared to be in the process of being swept away, presented the Conservative opposition with a chance of championing the cause of the poor. Both W. H. Smith and the Marquis of Salisbury spoke at the initial meeting, the former to give his support to the Huxleyian concept of providing a ladder whereby a child in the lowest elementary school could ascend into a grammar school, the latter to suggest the establishment of a Defence Committee.[88]

The Church of England supporters had cause to encourage the work of the Committee against the Commissioners. The disestablishment of the Irish Church had been recently accomplished; the compromise Cowper-Temple Clause in the 1870 Education Act had resulted in the banning of denominational teaching in elementary schools; and the University Tests Act was passing through its final phases, which would allow Dissenters to enter the universities, end the compulsory attendance at college chapels and throw open to all denominations fellowships and posts in colleges.

On 25 April 1871, the Marquis of Salisbury gave notice of a motion he would introduce in the Lords 'to draw attention to the proposals of the Endowed Schools Commission in reference to the Emanuel Charity'. Salisbury, equally a keen Churchman and a fervent Conservative, was busy behind the scenes.[89] In the House of Lords, an 'Address to Her Majesty to withhold her Assent from the scheme' was presented, which was carried by 64 to 56, thus destroying the scheme. As one paper put it: 'The Marquis of Salisbury and the Opposition peers saw an opportunity of wounding the Government through the Endowed School Commissioners and the "Whip" was so peremptorily sounded through the Conservative ranks that the Opposition benches were as crowded as if an Irish Church Bill had been upon the paper.'[90]

Having been defeated, the Commissioners now had to draw up a new scheme. They informed the governors that 'The principal attractions will be in the Clauses relating to Exhibitions, in which greater securities will be taken for confining them to the poorer classes'. The governing body would be simplified, exhibitions would be extended to boys already at the school and not confined to boys entering the school. Three-fifths of the charity was to be spent on education, not two-thirds as formerly, a concession to the eleemosynary part of the charity. A policy statement by the three Commissioners (19 July 1871) made clear their wish to find a speedy solution to the deadlock: 'Our course shall be guided mainly by reference to two events. First, the vote of the House of Lords and secondly, the change of circumstances effected by the creation and operation of the London School Board. With regard to the London School Board, we are very anxious to invite its criticism on our plans, and that, if possible, before publication.'[91] The statement showed a realization of the necessity to co-operate with existing institutions. As a sign of this, the Commissioners altered the basis of the award of exhibitions. Formerly, one-third of them were for boys at an elementary school or resident in St. Margaret's and St. John's, a further third to orphans and the rest to be left open: under the new scheme, the exhibitions were now devoted entirely to public elementary school boys and extended to include all the School Board district of Westminster.

The Governors, now more confident, objected to the revised scheme and submitted one of their own (5 December 1871) which contained much more generous provision for the eleemosynary side of the charity at the expense of the educational, with 100 poor boys and girls to be lodged, clothed and fed. The school was to be an elementary type with 300 scholars admitted at a small fee. This deliberately went against the Commissioners' plans, guided by ss. 9 and 10 of the Endowed Schools Act, to consolidate four of the five foundations, and if possible the fifth. An amended scheme of the Commissioners (25 April 1872), submitted to the Committee of Council on Education, was sanctioned on 1 May by that body. An appeal by the governors to the Privy Council (November 1872) failed; Parliamentary action was the only course now open to the governors.

Other charities, disturbed by the Commissioners' work, looked to Emanuel Hospital as the test case which would decide the course of future events.[92] A Motion for the rejection of the second scheme of the Commissioners was brought before the House of Commons by R. W. Crawford, M.P. for the City of London. The implications of the outcome of this debate were summed up by one observer: 'It is impossible to exaggerate the importance which will attach to the vote to be taken next Tuesday. If it gives a triumph to the Commissioners, every educational foundation in the kingdom will be endangered. Lord Lyttelton himself declared that the fate of Christ's Hospital, and of every Hospital School in England, depends upon the decision of Parliament on the Emanuel Hospital scheme.'[93]

This was a suitable juncture for Church opposition to make itself heard. At a meeting of the Lower House of the Convocation of the Province of Canterbury (May 1873), standing orders were suspended whilst a special motion was introduced. The Commissioners had dealt ruthlessly with those foundations unable to produce documentary evidence of an original ecclesiastical charity. Of the 317 schemes published up to May 1873, only 27 had been accepted as falling within the provisions of s. 19.[94] Also, the new schemes abolished the Bishop as Visitor and tended to diminish the number of vicars appointed as *ex officio* trustees. Prebendary Fagan, who introduced the Motion, accused the Commissioners of not keeping faith with the pious founder and of directing charities intended for the poor to the middle classes. The following statement was agreed with only one dissentient:

> That the religious educational endowments of the Church of England have been, and are, exposed to great peril under the operation of the Endowed School Commission. That therefore His Grace the President and their Lordships the Bishops, be requested to direct the careful attention of Churchmen in their respective dioceses to the schemes of the Commissioners; and that in as much as the Act expires at the close of the present year, their Lordships be earnestly entreated that in any future legislation on the subject, care be taken to secure for the Church of England the undisturbed possession of those endowments which have been left by the piety of founders and benefactors for the Christian education of her children.

The Debate on Emanuel Hospital took place on 13 May 1873.[95] Crawford's presentation of the case on behalf of the school stressed mainly the position of the governing body under the new scheme rather than condemning the Commissioners' policy. This line of attack was easily met by Gladstone who, in a rallying speech, referred to the City of London as the only unreformed municipal corporation, with aldermen appointing each member of the Court in turn. Under the existing system, it was very difficult to compare claims of competitions for the charity. Forster intervened shortly before the division was taken, to ask 'whether, having passed the Elementary Education Act, the House would be content to allow these endowments to be devoted to the promotion of elementary education which was otherwise provided for, or whether the endowments should not be applied to the encouragement of higher education.'[96] The subsequent vote resulted in a victory for the Commissioners, the Motion being rejected by 286 to 238, a majority of 44. The scheme was then approved by Order in Council (26 June 1873) and the charities consolidated. The new governing body consisted of twelve City aldermen and twelve burgesses of the City of Westminster. The lower of the two schools, by 1875, housed 261 boys, paying fees of 10s. a quarter. History, geography, French and mechanical drawing were taught[97] to scholars 'selected from those occupying advanced positions in the elementary schools of the district.'[98]

During May 1873, with the prospect of another scheme, that of Birmingham, being debated in the Commons, a Committee of the Church Defence Association was established in London, with Salisbury as the moving spirit and later, as an active member.[99] A deputation of Birmingham governors attended one of its earlier meetings in order to discover if there were grounds for the school being treated as a Church foundation.[100] The governing body, consisting entirely of Church members, was to obtain the help of Sir John Pakington, a former Minister interested in educational issues, to move an Address in the House of Commons, praying Her Majesty to withhold consent from the Birmingham scheme. One of the main complaints of the governors was the provision under cl. 50 for 'religious education' in the various schools of the foundation without specifying its nature. Pakington, in his Address, stated: 'They consider that in the present state of public feeling the effect of this clause will be to make the Body an arena of religious discord, and the nature of the religious instruction, whatever it might be, should be fixed in the scheme itself.'

The night Pakington was to introduce his Motion, Gladstone crushed the opponents of the Emanuel scheme; as the Birmingham scheme was likely to meet a similar fate, the Motion was dropped but re-introduced on 19 May into the more convivial atmosphere of

the Lords: the passing of an Address in either House was fatal to
the scheme's success. With Salisbury leading the Opposition attack
and Lyttelton feebly defending the scheme, the Commissioners
were defeated (106-60). This was a great victory for the Church but
a setback for educational reform. One paper, commenting on the
debate in the Lords, remarked: 'The rejection of the Commissioners' scheme would be a smaller matter if it stood alone, but it is
part of a policy. A rash Prelate was so mindful of the reticence
which was displayed on the Conservative side as to blurt out the
truth. The Bishop of Bath and Wells said that the projects of the
Commissioners all took away something which the Church had
deemed to be her own, and that they ought to be resisted for her
sake. Hence, he would begin with the Birmingham scheme, and
deal with others as they presented themselves.'[101]

The end of the Endowed Schools Commission

The fall of Gladstone's Ministry shortly afterwards, in February
1874, was bound to have its effects on the Commission. As W.
Latham, an Assistant Commissioner, wrote to Roby in a letter (13
March 1874), 'I suppose we shall have the Conservatives in now,
and what will they do with the Commission? I fear it will arouse
our foes to double resistance, and our own friends in the House
may be intimidated by the prospect of meeting their constituents.'[102] It was clear that the new Government would review the
work of the Commission and the hostility of Salisbury and the
Church authorities would make themselves felt.

In the first session of Disraeli's Government, two Bills were
introduced into the Commons, the Regulation of Public Worship,
concerned with Church practices, and the Endowed Schools
(Amendment) Bill, which aimed at abolishing the Endowed
Schools Commission and transferring its functions and powers to
the Charity Commission.[103] Because of their controversial nature, it
was unlikely that both Bills could have negotiated the hazards of
the Commons in the same session. The first Bill was talked out by
A. J. Beresford-Hope, Salisbury's brother-in-law, (a strong opponent of the Commission)[103a] and the Endowed Schools Acts
(Amendment) Bill was proceeded with, Lord Sandon, the new
Vice-President, being in charge. The Times leader of 23 July 1874
found four major faults with the Bill: Cl. 7 did not make provision

for the 'conscience clause'; nonconformists were not to be trustees and masters were to be in Holy Orders; the Endowed School Commissioners were to be unfairly treated; and Dissenting boys were to lose their scholarship rights.[104]

Support for the Bill came from those schools whose Church character was likely to be changed by the Commissioners. One pro-Government newspaper expressed its views thus: 'As for the complaint that the Bill will prevent the sons of Non-Conformists from gaining Exhibitions etc., in the Endowed Schools, it appears to us that Non-Conformists would at once show greater respect for their own dignity and for the rights of others, if they set about founding Endowed Schools of their own and providing scholarships for the youths of their own denominations – as Churchmen have already done – instead of attempting to appropriate for such purposes what does not happen to belong to them.'[105]

The Bill was introduced into the Commons on 14 July 1874. Those children likely to be affected by such a Bill amounted to half the population, according to one paper.[106] However, the more contentious religious clauses, which alone made it of great value to Churchmen, were eventually dropped. In the hectic final stages of the Bill, much to the dismay of Government supporters, the security of the conscience clause to nonconformists and their scholarship rights remained intact.[107] Sandon introduced an amendment allowing nonconformists to remain on governing bodies; he also conceded that if an instrument of a foundation did not specify the religious or secular membership of a governing body, the matter was to be settled by the Commission's successor.

Disraeli's reasons for giving way on these vital clauses are not altogether clear.[108] What did remain in the Bill when it finally became an Act in July 1874 was the dismantling of the Endowed Schools Commission and the transference of its duties to the Charity Commission. Whatever the relief felt by many at the schools' reprieve from Church domination,[109] there was little protest at the demise of the old Commission. This was summed up by a Liberal newspaper and echoed widely-held sentiments: 'There has been one good thing saved out of the wreck. The transfer of the business of re-organizing our endowed schools to the Charity Commissioners will be a change for the better; it could hardly be for the worse.'

The decline in the fortunes of the Endowed Schools Commission had been a gradual but inevitable process; the change of government in 1874 was only the final blow and not the root cause. Opposition to the Commissioners had come from religious, educational and other interest groups who were affected by reforms carried out by the Commission.[110] Much of the animosity was directed against the Commissioners themselves. The Report of the Select Committee of 1873 had remarked, 'The published opinions of some of the Commissioners on the subject of endowments have caused alarm and have, in some cases, seriously impeded the harmonious action which might otherwise have been secured between them and the Governing Bodies of the Charities with which they have had to deal.'[111]

Politically, the Commission was the creation of a Liberal Government and much of its policy was interpreted in this light. When the Endowed Schools Department of the Charity Commission was formed, only Canon Robinson of the original Commissioners, who opposed the sweeping treatment of endowments favoured by Lyttelton and Roby, was retained.[112]

As a new venture in central control, the Commission attracted the suspicions of members of both parties, who feared that secondary schools would become a State responsibility in the same way as elementary schools had done.[113]

Administratively, the Endowed Schools Commission was handicapped by its lack of contact with the Education Department, whose experience and advice would have saved the Commissioners from making fundamental errors of judgment. Lyttelton, on giving up the Chief Commissionership, sketched out the relations between the two bodies up to 1874 in a speech replying to Sandon: 'Never once, from the day that they [the Commissioners] took office to the time when I had a private note from the noble Duke (of Richmond)[114] informing me that the Commission was to be abolished, was there any direct communication from the heads of the Education Department, to the heads of the Commission. Sometimes, when from want of information they could not help themselves, they sent their Secretary to see ours, or instructed him to write a note; but that is all. I doubt whether at this moment the noble Duke knows by sight either of my colleagues. And yet we are not only their colleagues in office, but our office is actually part of theirs.'[115]

An Amending Act of 1873[116] had earlier attempted to meet the criticisms made in the Report. By it, the government of the day was able to exercise greater influence over the form of the final scheme. The Education Department was to be brought more into the picture. So far it had been able only to approve or disapprove a scheme; now, a scheme could be remitted to the Commission for amendment. Elementary schools with endowments of less than £100 per annum were excepted from the Commission's jurisdiction and greater protection was afforded to denominational schools. These changes did little to meet the main criticisms of the Commission, and the last two years of its life (1873-4) saw the slowing down of the machinery of reform.[117]

Such piecemeal reforms were not adequate for the situation. The Commissioners had tackled the larger institutions in a somewhat quixotic fashion armed with quasi-judicial powers and without public support: their attacks foundered in the face of powerful vested interests. This opposition has been seen in the case of Emanuel School, where those affected by the scheme took on the role of champions of the poor, although opposition was here motivated by fear of the poor.[118] The Endowed Schools Department of the Charity Commission from 1875 onwards attracted less criticism on the score of personalities, whilst continuing to pursue policies similar to those of the old Commission.

NOTES

1. Gladstone, writing to Lord Lyttelton in 1861 declared, 'It is our habit in this country to treat private interests with an extravagant tenderness. The truth is that all laxity and extravagance in dealing with what in a large sense is certainly public property, approximates more or less to dishonesty, or at the least lowers the moral tone of the persons concerned.' J. Morley, *Life of Gladstone,* (1905), Vol. 1, p. 946.

    Morley expresses the view that the class immediately concerned with reforming the schools showed little interest, and singles out a few men 'of superior energy and social weight' as leaders of this movement: Jowett and Temple, both active in Civil Service reform, Dean Lidell and Goldwin Smith, who had been Joint Secretary to the Commission dealing with Oxford Reforms 1850-2. Ibid., pp. 39, 50, 512.
2. T. W. Reid, *Life of Rt. Hon. W. E. Forster* (1888), p. 29.
3. *Hansard,* Ser. 3, CXCIV, 1868-9, House of Commons, col. 1359, 15 March 1869.
4. 'That it be an Instruction to the Select Committee on the Endowed Schools Bill that they have power to divide the said Bill into two Bills, and to report such two Bills, on either of them separately, to the House.' Report of the Select Committee on Endowed Schools Bill, 11 May 1869. P.P. 1868-9, VIII.

5. G. Baron, 'The Teachers' Registration Movement', *British Journal of Educational Studies*, Vol. 2, No. 2, May 1954.

6. Schools dealt with under the Public Schools Act were exempt from the workings of the Endowed Schools Act, although falling within the category of 'endowed schools' – Harrow, Winchester, Eton, Westminster, Charterhouse, Rugby, St. Paul's, Merchant Taylors' and Shrewsbury. In the case of the latter, its inclusion in the investigations of the Public Schools Commission resulted subsequently in a substantial increase in pupils. J. B. Oldham, *A History of Shrewsbury School* (1952), p. 127.

7. *The Times*, 7 April 1869. H. D. Harper, Headmaster of Sherborne, expressed similar sentiments in a letter to a Member of Parliament: 'If the words "Endowed School" in Section 53 are to be explained by the definition in Section 5 and *every* endowed School is to be subject to the Educational Council, whether Eton, Winchester, Rugby etc., *or* Repton, Uppingham, Sherborne etc., I have nothing to say. I do not believe in the operation of such a council; I defy any council to find out by mere examination, or to examine Schools efficiently, except by able examiners on the spot. But if the State takes Education into its own hands, and treats all Schools alike, *even* if it goes so far presently as to start a "revised code" and pay by the results, of the number of boys who can say the Latin Primer &c, &c, *I* bow submissively: *only* let the State be fair and submit all Teachers to the same ordeal.' L. V. Lester, *Memoir of Hugo Daniel Harper,* D. D. (1896) p. 73.

   Harper's school was the first to be dealt with by the Endowed Schools Commission and his apprehensions proved to be unfounded. The scheme left Harper in supreme control and finally freed him from the necessity of personally financing the School. 'For the first time since I have been acquainted with it,' he wrote in 1871, 'the School promises to be able to pay its way.' A. B. Gourlay, *A History of Sherborne School* (1931), pp. 119-20.

8. G. R. Parkin, *Life of Edward Thring* (1898), p. 173. For an account of Thring's views, see P. Stansky, 'Lyttelton and Thring: a Study in Nineteenth Century Education', *Victorian Studies*, Vol. 5, No. 3, 1962, pp. 220-2.

9. E. G. Sandford (ed.), *Life of William Temple*, (1906), Vol. 1, p. 135.

10. *The Times*, 2 April 1869. Temple's enthusiasm for and attitude towards education were the result of his own struggles, when a boy, to obtain scholarships in order to take him to the University. An account of these struggles appears in the *Exeter and Plymouth Gazette* for 18 May 1871. He praised the Doncaster Scheme (see Chapter I, p. 19 above) in the Lords and held it to be a model for future schemes (*Hansard* CCV 1871, col. 1574, 24 April 1871), and in his own diocese of Exeter, Temple visualized a system whereby Elementary School children might rise, by merit, through each grade of school by means of Exhibitions. Report of the Endowed School Commissioners to the Committee of Council on Education, Appendix 6, P.P. 1872, XXIV.

11. *The Times*, 7 April 1869.

12. G. Baron, 'The Secondary Schoolmaster 1895-1914', Ph.D. London, 1952, p. 90. For the early years of the Conference, see A. Percival, *The Origins of the Headmasters' Conference* (1969), pp. 42-3.

13. *The Times*, 15 April 1869.

14. Lester, op. cit., p. 38.

15. Arthur Faber of Malvern asked whether schools already externally examined should not be exempt. *The Times*, 22 April 1869.

16. *Hansard,* Ser. 3, CXCIV, 1868-9, House of Commons, col. 1378.

17. F. D. How, *Six Great Schoolmasters* (1904), p. 258.

18. D. Newsome, *Godliness and Good Learning: Four Studies on a Victorian Ideal* (1961), p. 217.
19. Temple, whilst appreciating the anxiety of the clergy with regard to religious education in the reformed schools stated, 'For my own part, I do not feel, nor have I ever felt, any hostility to secular education even taken by itself.' *'Middle Class Education': A speech delivered to the Devon County School, West Buckland, 23 September 1873.*
20. *The Times*, 15 April 1869.
21. M. L. Clarke, *Classical Education in Britain 1500-1900* (1959), p. 95.
    At Rugby Temple, a pioneer in expanding the curriculum, introduced French, and from 1864 Science was compulsory for all forms below the Fifth. G. G. Coulton, *A Victorian Schoolmaster – Henry Hart of Sedbergh* (1923), pp. 24-5.
22. Tropp, op. cit., pp. 98-9.
23. *The Times*, 2 April 1869.
24. *The Times*, 15 April 1869.
25. See Special Report from the Select Committee on the Endowed Schools (No. 2) Bill, 8 June 1869. P.P. 1868-9, VIII.
26. Some twenty years later, W. H. Smith, replying to A. H. D. Acland's motion in the Commons (27 April 1888), insisted on the preservation of the independence of Secondary Education and suggested that examination of Secondary Schools should be rather superintended and directed by the State 'than originated by it'. For further details, see H. Longley to Lord Cranbrook, 16 March 1891. Cranbrook MSS, T 501/34.
27. 32 & 33 Vic., c. 56.
28. *Compact Dictionary of National Biography* (1975), Vol. I, p. 1264. For details of the friendship existing between the two men, see Philip Magnus, *Gladstone* (1954), pp. 43-4 and 125.
29. See letter from Lyttelton to Henry Solly, 4 July 1873, Solly MSS. Vol. 18, f. 37.
30. F. Boase, *Modern English Biography* (1897, reprinted Cass), Vol. 3.
31. T. D. Acland, an old acquaintance of Gladstone, protesting about a proposed scheme for Exeter in 1871, mentioned 'the long elaborate arguments from the pen of Hobhouse who has the fluent pen of an equity draughtsman and Charity Commissioner.' T. D. Acland to Gladstone, 8 April 1871, Gladstone MSS. BM Add. MSS. 44092 f. 104.
32. *Compact Dictionary of National Biography,* (1975), Vol. II, p. 2697.
33. For an assessment of Roby's abilities at this time, see F. Temple to W. E. Gladstone, 9 Aug. 1864. Granville MSS, 30/29/19/4.
34. W. E. Forster to Gladstone, 21 Feb. 1872. Gladstone MSS, BM Add. MSS. 44157 f. 50.
35. *Journal of the Social Science Association,* 8 July 1869, p. 600. See also Hobhouse to Granville, 1 March 1869, Granville MSS, PRO 30/29/19/25.
36. Ibid., p. 595.
37. H. J. Roby, in L. T. Hobhouse and J. L. Hammond, *Lord Hobhouse, A Memoir.* (1905), p. 50.
38. Lyttelton to Gladstone, 15 June 1869. Gladstone MS. BM Add. MSS. 44240 f. 98. Gladstone to Lyttelton, 16 June 1869. Glynne-Gladstone MSS.
39. Some aspects of this work had already been accomplished by the Suspensory Act of 1868 which followed on the disclosures of the S.I.C. and suspended the acquisition of new vested interests under trusts for endowed schools.
40. See J. Kamm, *Hope Deferred. Girls' Education in English History* (1965), chapter XIV, and D. Beale, *Schools Inquiry Commission on the Education of Girls* (1869).

41. 1873 Select Committee on the Endowed Schools Act (1869), P.P. 1873, VIII, Q.1246.
42. Ss. 1-3 provided that wherever a question came before a Court of Equity 'concerning the system of education thereafter to be established in any Grammar School, or the right of admission into the same' the Court was to make such an Order as seemed expedient for altering the subjects taught or the right of admission, due regard being had to the founders' intentions.
43. In fact only one school, Hemsworth Grammar School, Yorkshire, moved from a mining village to Barnsley, was transferred to a different locality, and only after an eight-year battle, in 1887. See Hemsworth Grammar School, PRO Ed. 27/5641, 5642, 5643 and 5645 for a fascinating and detailed account of this. Writing a few years later, an Assistant Commissioner stated: 'the enormous difficulty which was encountered from local opposition in closing the Hemsworth Grammar School, and applying the endowment to Barnsley Grammar School will, I should think, discourage any public body from attempting such a task again, however advisable it may be' – Bryce Report, Vol. VI, pp. 233-4. P.P. 1895, XLVIII. See also Vol. V, p. 76, P.P. 1895, XLVII.
44. K. E. Kirk, *The Story of the Woodard Schools* (1937), pp. 31-2.
45. Woodard was probably trying to emulate the very successful Quaker schools, such as Ackworth, Yorkshire, which had been founded in the previous century. See W. A. C. Stewart, *Quakers and Education* (1953), pp. 60 ff. After 1871, Dissenters were admitted to the universities. The Friends' Public School Company was established.
46. J. W. Adamson, *English Education 1789-1902* (1930), p. 278.
47. F. C. Pritchard, *Methodist Secondary Education* (1949), p. 191.
48. Sir J. Otter, *Life of Nathaniel Woodard* (1925), pp. 181-247. Lyttelton was particularly hurt by Woodard's remark that State and Government were 'wholly anti-religious', p. 212.
49. Nevertheless the pamphlet ran to a second edition as late as 1883.
50. PRO Ed. 53/263.
51. *A Plea for the Establishment of Additional Public Schools in Yorkshire for the Upper and Middle Classes* (1870).
52. S.I.C., Vol. 9, p. 118.
53. Ibid., pp. 77-81.
54. Ibid., pp. 270-1.
54a. B. Heeney, *Mission to the Middle Classes. The Woodard Schools, 1848-1891* (1969), pp. 179-80.
55. F. E. Balls, 'The Endowed Schools Act 1869 and the Development of the English Grammar Schools in the Nineteenth Century', *Durham Research Review*, No. 19, September 1967, p. 214.
56. Chapter I, p.2.
57. But cf. Clarke, op. cit., p. 8, on apathy in language teaching in schools of this period. It is interesting to note that Cambridge had to wait until 1869 for a Chair in Latin to be established.
    The universities played an important part, however, in maintaining the importance of the classics for an educated class. A Professor of Humanity compared the value of mathematics with classics in 1861 as follows: 'Mathematics, exclusively pursued, carry their votary to a region of their own, in the empyrean of pure unassailable truth and far apart from the corners of this nether world: the study of classics, on the other hand, connects the pupil at every step with the sympathies of his fellow-creatures – with the passions, the interests, the duties, the occupations, the history, and the prospects of humanity.' James Pillans, *On the Relative Importance*

of Mathematics and Classics in the Higher Instruction (1861), p. 278.

58. The motives for a town urging the establishment of a first grade school were often as much economic as educational, for example, Report of Assistant Commissioner on Bideford Grammar School, PRO Ed. 27/631: 'The advocates of a Grammar or Classical School look to the education of some small number of the children of the inhabitants but chiefly to the indirect advantage the Town would derive from a large school which would bring money into the place and encourage families to settle in the neighbourhood.'

59. PRO Ed. 27/5721, memorandum undated.

60. PRO Ed. 27/5721, memorandum, 1 August 1870.

61. G. H. Bantock, *Education in an Industrial Society* (1963), pp. 66-9, shows how classical education 'had an appeal precisely on the grounds of its uselessness' as distinct from the vocationally-orientated subjects of a second or third grade endowed school curriculum.

62. PRO Ed. 27/5722.

63. PRO Ed. 27/5723. 22 witnesses were heard, consisting of 4 clergymen, 2 gentlemen of independent means, 3 physicians, 4 merchants, 1 manufacturer, 2 solicitors, 1 surgeon, 1 Dissenting Minister, 1 surveyor, 1 chemist, 1 master printer and 1 warehouseman in receipt of weekly wages.

64. At nearby Batley, in August 1871, for instance, the trustees of the grammar school requested that Greek and Latin should form the main basis of instruction. The Commissioners rejected this suggestion, stating that the curriculum of a school in a manufacturing town should be centred in English, science and modern languages. D. N. R. Lester, *The History of Batley Grammar School 1612-1962* (1962), p. 121.

65. For Oxford University's response to Lyttelton's proposals, see W. R. Ward, *Victorian Oxford* (Cass, 1965), p. 288.

66. PRO Ed. 27/8A.

67. Ibid., 'Formerly this led to the appointment of Butchers, Bakers, two Hair-dressers, and a Horse Doctor'. Letter to Commissioners, 8 November 1869.

68. For accounts of Bedford School before 1869, see S.I.C., Vol. VIII, p. 685 ff.

69. PRO Ed. 27/8A.

70. Joshua Fitch, as an Assistant Commissioner, agreed with Lyttelton's views on the uses of educational endowments on several occasions. At Exeter, where Fitch was sent to hold an Inquiry (17 April 1871), a strongly worded report condemned the continuance of the endowed elementary schools of the town. If the ratepayers were contrived to be relieved, 'the school would not be so well looked after and efficient as if people of the locality had to pay for it.' PRO Ed. 27/695.

Cf. Fitch writing in 1869 *à propos* of fees, stated: 'whilst I am keenly sensible of the evil of a preponderating influence on the part of ill-instructed parents, and have seen several sad instances of its lowering and vulgarizing effects on the schools, I may venture to remind the working-classes that there is a perfectly legitimate deference due from a teacher to the wishes of the parents and that this might be put in peril or sacrificed altogether if the whole duty of finding the money and of directing its expenditure were relegated to the taxpayers.' A. L. Lilley, *Sir Joshua Fitch* (1906), p. 57.

See also his views on this in *Endowments: An Address given at the University of Pennsylvania,* 5 July 1888; 1886 Select Committee on the Endowed Schools Acts, Evidence, B.P.P. 1886, IX, Q. 1397.

71. J. Godber, *The Harpur Trust 1552-1973* (1973), pp. 52-3.

72. PRO Ed. 27/695.

73. 1873 Select Committee on the Endowed Schools Act (1869), P.P. 1873, VIII, Q. 4708.

74. T. W. Hutton, *King Edward Schools Birmingham, 1552-1952* (1952), p. 46.
75. S.I.C., Vol. V, p. 956 ff.
76. PRO Ed. 27/4891.
77. Ibid., Report of the Free Grammar School Association, 1870.
78. S.I.C., Vol. X, p. 83.
79. A letter about Roby's visit appeared in *The Times*, 28 April 1872, from the Chairman of the Committee of Governors, claiming that Roby had been in the school for only half-an-hour and that no inquiry was made.
80. PRO Ed. 27/3363.
81. A very fully documented account of the Commissioners' work, including correspondence, in connection with the scheme for Greycoat School up to 1873 is to be found in E. S. Day, *An Old Westminster Endowment. Being a History of the Greycoat Hospital as recorded in the Minute Books* (1902), pp. 159-226.
82. Both governing body and Commissioners were agreed as to the reallocation of the endowment: two-thirds educational; one-third eleemosynary.
83. The reconstitution of the governing body involving loss of office for influential individuals was a cause of much bitterness by existing governors. A. Hobhouse to Lord Cairns, 21 June 1871, Cairns MSS, PRO 30/51/17.
84. PRO Ed. 27/3363. Letter to Commissioners, 27 August 1870. The governing body had previously (8 July 1870) attempted to claim exemption from the workings of the Act under s. 19.
85. *Bedford Mercury*, 6 May 1871. Report of Council Meeting which passed a Resolution sympathizing with the Corporation of London in its fight with the Commissioners. The Lord Mayor had earlier shown interest in the Bedford case.
86. *Trewmans Exeter Flying Post*, 17 May 1871.
87. G. M. Trevelyan, *British History in Nineteenth Century* (1947), p. 369, gives this as one of the reasons for the Liberal defeat in 1874.
88. *London Mirror*, 22 April 1871.
89. Salisbury's activities included, after taking his seat in the Lords in May 1868, the defence of the payment of doles in endowed schools, opposition to the Disestablishment of the Church of Ireland and the abolition of religious tests in universities. A. L. Kennedy, *Salisbury, Portrait of a Statesman* (1953), pp. 76-8.
90. *Weekly Scotsman*, 3 July 1871.
91. PRO Ed. 27/3363. An ally of the Commissioners was the London School Board. Lord Lawrence, Chairman of the Board, regarded the scheme as providing a stimulus to working men of London for their children's advancement. *Hansard*, Ser. 3, CCV, 1871, House of Lords, col. 1561.
    The Commissioners asked the School Board to nominate governors and were anxious to avoid third grade schools injuring the Board's elementary schools. H. Hobhouse to T. H. Huxley, 15 April 1871. Huxley MSS, Vol. 18, f. 194.
92. A typical comment of the time appeared in *The Globe*, 5 May 1873: 'By persisting in a vexatious and impudent policy, destroying existing authorities, in many cases without any apparent reason, the Commissioners have won for themselves the hearty antipathy of many other bodies besides the Corporation of the City of London; and in fact they have stirred up such a number of enemies (most of them being individuals or corporations of considerable influence) that it only requires a moderate amount of skill in the continuation of the antagonistic elements not merely to defeat the machinations of the Commissioners with respect to Emanuel Hospital, but to secure the speedy termination of their functions altogether.'

93. *The Standard,* 6 May 1873.
94. Ibid., 9 May 1873.
95. *Hansard,* Ser. 3, CCXV, 1873, House of Commons, cols. 1875-1955.
96. *The Times,* 13 May 1873.
97. PRO Ed. 27/3375.
98. *Daily Telegraph,* 16 November 1875.
99. Salisbury had carefully watched the activities of the Endowed Schools Commission, being helped in this work by his colleague, Gathorne Hardy. It was about this time that Hardy told Salisbury, 'I should not be sorry to see an end of the whole Commission for if they have any latitude they are sure to use it adversely to the Church.' Hardy to Salisbury, 24 July 1873, Salisbury MSS.
100. *Birmingham Daily Post,* 27 May 1873.
101. *Daily Telegraph,* 20 May 1873. In the voting on the motion, six Bishops – Bangor, Bath, Chichester, Gloucester, Bristol and London – moved for the rejection of the Commissioners' scheme.
102. PRO Ed. 27/9.
103. Salisbury insisted on the introduction of the Endowed Schools Amendment Bill as a *quid pro quo* for agreeing to the presentation of the Regulation of Public Worship Bill. Disraeli to Queen Victoria, 25 July 1874. G. E. Buckle, *Life of Disraeli* (1926), Vol. V, p. 333.
103a Beresford-Hope to Salisbury, 25 July, 1874, Salisbury MSS.
104. The original Bill, as first conceived, would have negated the main intention of the principal Act, to sweep away the denominational barriers of the schools. See, for example, Clause 6 of the first draft. Endowed Schools Acts (Amendment) Bill, Vic. 37 & 38, as ordered by House of Commons, 2 July 1874, P.P. 1874, II.
105. *Exeter and Plymouth Gazette,* 23 July 1874.
106. *Western Times,* 29 July 1874.
107. A cabinet meeting of 25 July, according to Cranbrook, 'was not agreeable as we had to abandon much work and especially the contested clauses in the Endowed Schools Bill.' Cranbrook MSS. Diary, HA 43 T 501/296, 25 July 1874.
108. Perhaps the most likely explanation is that given by S. Maccoby, *English Radicalism 1853-85* (1938), p. 199. 'When on July 24 Disraeli rose to tell the Commons that the disputed Clauses would be virtually dropped, he was probably doing more than robbing Opposition Radicalism and the Liberation Society of a formidable chance of agitation. He was probably putting Lord Salisbury, his most difficult colleague, in his place for the second time that month and giving the legislative initiative for 1875 to the less ecclesiastical and much safer Mr. Cross.' Sandon had written to Disraeli earlier warning him that 'there is one part of our Endowed Schools Bill which I am confident will do us politically infinite damage in the country, and only gain the admiration of the smaller and most bigoted clergy.' Sandon to Disraeli, 10 July 1876. Hughenden MSS, Box 142, B/XXI/S/38.
109. But this proved illusory. Henry Longley, writing to Lord Wharncliffe privately to persuade the latter to withdraw his opposition to a scheme which was opposed by leading Churchmen, including the Archbishop of York, referred to the 1874 compromise of Beaconsfield which had suppressed religious differences for the last thirteen years:

> ... my only object in troubling you with this somewhat presumptuous letter is to say that which, in the interests of the Church, cannot be proclaimed on the house-tops – nor stated in the Memorandum I have mentioned. The compromise to which I have referred was to the effect that

where schools are not Church schools within the definition of the E.S.A. (and Hemsworth has been decided judicially to be not within that definition) provision shall be made with schemes that religious instruction shall be given in the principles of the Christian faith.

This – which is effectively a large concession, admitting the use of words which may mean anything – has worked admirably for the Church. The Church has been prudently content to accept this substantial gain in silence and to abstain from interfering with this arrangement. Church teaching is almost the invariable rule under this clause.

Hemsworth Grammar School, PRO Ed. 27/5642, 5 May 1887.

110. Roby summed up these groups under the following headings: 'Trustees who objected to any interference, schoolmasters who disliked the sphere proposed for them or their schools in future. Church and Non-Conformist Committees who claimed to have the Act interpreted in ways specially favourable to their educational principles or desires, solicitors who feared their interests might suffer under a new Governing Body or by the simplification of the rules for administering the trusts.' (L. T. Hobhouse and J. L. Hammond, *Lord Hobhouse. A Memoir* (1905), p. 49). Hobhouse remarked later that 'the business we were set to do was to get butter out of dogs' mouths.' Hobhouse to T. D. Acland, 17 August 1874, Acland MSS, 1148M, Box 21 (iv), 7.

111. This sentiment was echoed by Disraeli in his speech announcing his decision to disband the Commission: 'If you find that the Commissioners who have certain duties to perform and trustees who are in a certain position do not work together, you may respect them both, but a responsible Minister must see that the work of the country is done.' *Hansard,* Ser. 3, CCXXI, House of Commons, cols. 481-2, 21 July 1874.

112. For a succinct analysis of the political implications of the Endowed Schools Commission, see Spencer Walpole, *The History of Twenty Five Years* (1904), Vol. II, pp. 292-9.

113. 1886 Select Committee on Endowed Schools Act, Q. 907, op. cit. The new Commissioners – Robinson, Henry Longley and Lord Clinton – were chosen by Disraeli, Cairns and Hardy. Diary, 28 July 1874. Cranbrook MSS, T 501/296. Plans to replace the Commissioners were being formulated as early as March – see letter Salisbury to Duke of Richmond, 25 March 1874, Goodwood MSS 866. Roby complained to Stafford Northcote that he had been singled out as the scapegoat for Lyttelton and Hobhouse, 'because as Secretary he had signed all the Commissioners' letters.' Northcote suggested posts at the Colonial Office and as a Schools Inspector, both of which Roby refused. Northcote to Richmond, 21 June 1874. Iddesleigh MSS 50063B, f. 273, and Northcote to Richmond, 26 June 1874, Goodwood MSS, 886, Z 108-9.

Robert Lowe, as a Liberal, had reservations on the question of centralization in education, see J. F. Hogan, *Life of Robert Lowe, Viscount Sherbrooke* (1893), p. 314 ff. for a reasoned assessment of Lowe's attitude; and Lowe's pamphlet, *Middle Class Education: Endowment or Free Trade?* (1868). Also, A. Briggs, *Victorian People* (1954), in the chapter 'Robert Lowe and the Fear of Democracy', p. 259: 'A single system of schools unified under rigid public control meant dangerously strong government. Lowe's Benthamism did not lead him, like Chadwick, towards an efficient autocratic state: rather it made him afraid of too great a concentration of power at the centre.'

114. I.e. 6th Duke of Richmond, Lord President of the Council, 1874-80, congratulating Salisbury on his appointment in the new Disraeli Government. Lyttelton had written, 'I would rather you had been at the Council office: for the only question is who shall kill us. I would rather it was by a man who is

supposed sometimes to read a book than by a man who never does such as I take the excellent Duke to be.' Lyttelton to Salisbury, Salisbury MSS, 24 February 1874. See also B. Askwith, *The Lytteltons* (1975), p. 185.

115. Lord Lyttelton, *A Speech delivered in the House of Lords, 3 August 1874, on the Endowed Schools Amendment Bill* (1874).

116. Endowed Schools Act (1869) Amendment Act 1873, 36 & 37, Vic. 87: For comment on the effectiveness of the Act, see 1894 Select Committee on Charity Commission, P.P. 1894, XI, Q. 827-30.

117. See the Report of the Endowed Schools Commissioners to the Committee of Council on Education, P.P. 1875, XXVIII, p. 5.

> It is to be borne in mind that in 1873 the work of the office was considerably interfered with by the demands on our time arising out of the inquiry by a Committee of the House of Commons, and uncertainty what might be the issue of the inquiry sensibly affected the action of persons locally interested in endowments, as well as of ourselves.
>
> In 1874 in anticipation of fresh legislation in the first place, and afterwards the nature of that legislation, had the effect of further retarding our proceedings, and of almost restricting our action to cases where there was a probability of substantial agreement between ourselves and all parties concerned.

118. See letter from Hobhouse to a friend on the Emanuel Scheme in Hobhouse and Hammond, op. cit., p. 50.

CHAPTER 3

The Admission of the Poor to Endowed Schools: An Analysis

In examining the system by which the Commissioners secured awards of scholarships and exhibitions to the 'meritorious' poor, a number of interdependent factors can be observed which determined the type and extent of the awards. The prevailing public attitudes to the question of 'free' education, in any form, influenced the actions of the Commissioners. In the schools themselves, these attitudes were reflected in the relationships which existed between the elementary and the grammar schools (especially of the respective headmasters), and the middle schools and the grammar schools. A further factor was the attitude of the headmasters towards foundationers. A study of these different elements throws an interesting light on the extent to which educational opportunities were available for the poor in the reformed endowed schools.

Attitude towards 'Free' Education

(a) *Pamphleteers' views*

Judging by the flood of publications on the subject in the last thirty years of the nineteenth century, it was widely held that gratuitous education, although awarded on merit by means of competition, was *ipso facto* an unnecessary luxury in the scheme of reorganized secondary education. Disappointment felt by such writers at the lack of sufficient grammar school provision for the middle classes turned to bitterness as the Commissioners' work progressed in a slow and piecemeal fashion. After ten years' work, the Commissioners had submitted 118 schemes for approval, representing less than a third of the schools falling under their jurisdiction.[1] One writer, commenting in 1883 on the work of the Commission, found evidence of a singular lack of success: 'In many places, these desirable establishments have never existed; and in others have fallen through for a time, as for example the Taunton Grammar School which has been repeatedly closed. In the case of Trowbridge not only was the school closed, but owing to its collapse, the endowment of £1,200 lapsed to the almshouses of that town.'[2]

An argument much used concerned the school board rate, which was based on the rental of a house, paid for by those who, for the most part, received no direct benefit from such payment; the poorer middle classes were faced with no suitable local schooling for their children, apart from private and proprietary schools. Where endowed schools did flourish, the granting of exhibitions to pupils at elementary schools was interpreted as the giving of a double prize at the expense of their own sons. Further, it seemed ironic that the poor could receive free education at grammar schools whilst being liable to fees if they had remained in the elementary schools.[3] Some of these attitudes were expressed in an essay on secondary education at this time:

It is also largely due to the scholarship system that an eleemosynary attitude is adopted towards education by all classes in England. Our imaginations are engrossed by the 'deserving poor'; we cannot see beyond them, or outside them; we forget that they are a small minority even of the poor, and that the sound training of the fairly well-to-do is at least as important to the State as the relief of amiable destitution. It is to this mental attitude that is due the fact that the public money is recklessly wasted on helping people that do not want help, and in giving that help in a form most expensive to the State, and least calculated to bring about the ends for which alone the State is justified is spending money on education.[4]

The opponents of the provision for helping the able poor which was contained in the proposed schemes of the Commissioners emphasized the danger of over-educating them. At a meeting convened to discuss a scheme for the reorganization of Macclesfield Grammar School, the Mayor, declaring himself to be against gratuitous education or making education cheap, quoted the following story to illustrate his point:

He once complimented a learned physician of Edinburgh on the

number of institutions of all kinds that were to be seen there.
The physician replied that what he [the Mayor] admired so
much was not to the great advantage of the community, adding,
'We have made everything so cheap, and easy to be obtained
that the poor people do not appreciate it, nor do they provide
against coming trouble'. He argued the question very fully, and
came to the conclusion that in the City of Edinburgh more had
been done for the people in the way of education and
emolument than was really good for them.[5]

Another factor militating against attracting the intellectual élite
from the elementary schools was the raising of standards in the
board schools after 1870 and the successful experiments in
advanced teaching by higher grade schools which overlapped the
work of some of the grammar schools.[6] The Charity Commissioners
drew attention to the fact that the higher grade schools were
competing with third grade schools and were able to do so at lower
fees, enjoying the advantage of being aided by rates and Parliamentary grants. That the third grade school was likely to suffer was
evident in the calculations of the Commissioners for the average
fees charged at the two types of school: about 2s. per week at the
third grade and at the higher elementary 9d. per week in 1882. As
one critic wryly remarked, 'One of two things only can relieve the
pressure felt by the middle class; either the curriculum of the
secondary schools must be raised, or that the Board and Voluntary
schools be reduced to a more elementary standard.'[7]

Physical and moral reasons were advanced against the Commissioners' schemes to help the poor. A notable lawyer of his day,
Courtenay Kenny, in a work devoted to the past and present
history of charitable endowments wrote:

The Endowed Schools Commissioners adopted a plan of applying the endowments of primary schools in sending to secondary
schools those boys whom competitive examination showed
worthy of the favour. The plan was endorsed by Mr. J. S. Mill as
'the most enlightened that ever yet proceeded from any public
authority in the United Kingdom'. But it seems open to serious
objections, both physical and moral. The physique of boys is
little adapted to the strain of competitive examination; and
experience seems already to suggest that these prizes are sapping
the health of lads who would otherwise have been the élite of the

working classes and that at best they will tend only to produce the hot house minds of French schools, with a defective physical, and therefore an unhealthy moral, development. There is also an ethical objection to any change of social station effected at so early an age, before family ties have become loosened by maturity. Sir Astley Cooper reported to the House of Commons Committee on Medical Education: 'It has happened to me repeatedly to have an opportunity of introducing into the profession the sons of persons who were in a lower sphere of life. They have generally become bad sons and very bad subjects; they despise their parents; they will not mix with their family; and the system destroys the best feelings of the heart.'[8]

The medical argument against raising the poor through education was reinforced some four years later by a Report of Dr. J. Crichton-Browne which achieved widespread publicity and was published as a Parliamentary Paper.[9] Browne, a Superintendent of the West Riding Lunatic Asylum, received permission to visit a number of schools in the Lambeth and Walworth districts of London in order to investigate the effects of the Education Code on children. Browne claimed, on the basis of these visits, that numerous cases of headaches and illnesses were caused by over-pressure, the result of work done in the schools in order to bring the children up to the required standard; insanity in later life was also attributed to this fact. The concern caused by the new Code of 1882 led to many questions being asked in the Commons (June-July 1884); at a meeting convened at Exeter Hall in March 1884, Lord Shaftesbury had expatiated on the 'tyranny and oppression' of the Code in the elementary schools.[10]

Where the customary rights of the poor were endangered by a proposed scheme of the Commissioners, any resistance which was offered usually failed to affect the outcome. However, one outstanding champion of the rural areas was Jesse Collings (1831-1920), a self-made business man and friend of Joseph Chamberlain, who devoted his life to educational issues. He had been both Secretary and President of the Birmingham Education League and was Lord Mayor of Birmingham in 1878.[11] As a radical M.P. for Ipswich, he became interested in Joseph Arch's National Agricultural Labourers' Union.[12] He believed that 'the ladder of education' was a concept which affected the different grades of education. He

told a Select Committee on Endowed Schools in 1887: 'If
education, meaning by that art, literature and science, is not going
to go to everybody, in the mine and the workshop, and the field
and the factory, everywhere, then education is not anything like
what I had hoped it would be.'[13] Collings was a traditionalist,
wishing to leave the endowed schools available freely to children of
all classes.[14]

His most spectacular success in defence of rural endowments
was at Scarning, Norfolk, in 1882, where the Free School Protection Committee defied the Commissioners' scheme by establishing
a school of their own for fifteen months.[15] In the same year, in
Sussex, Collings also supported the Horsham Free School Defence
Association, a committee of working men who fought the plans of
the Commissioners and the Mercers' Company, who intended to
create a fee-paying day and boarding school in the town.[16] On a
larger scale, Collings supported the inhabitants of West Lavington,
Wiltshire, who resisted the attempts of the Commissioners and the
Mercers' Company to take the major portion of endowments for
building a middle-class school.[17]

But such organized resistance was rare. The entry of public
elementary school boys into the endowed schools was retarded by
the opposition of the middle classes, who regarded the schools as
their own: education was to be organized on class lines as
hitherto.[18]

(b) *Commissioners' Views*

The reform of the schools was as a general principle based on the
imposition of fees. The cost of education was raised to a level which
most ambitious parents of the poor could not afford: but from the
beginning, the Endowed Schools Commissioners felt bound to
make provision from the endowments for those who originally
benefited from them.

The policy of the Commissioners was set out clearly in one of
their Reports:

> In dealing with Educational Endowments in general, we have
> felt strongly the importance of employing them so as to *assist
> deserving scholars* in passing from schools of an inferior grade,
> and more especially from Public Elementary Schools, to places

of advanced instruction, and in some cases to Universities. The *Method* by which this object is provided may be briefly stated. Provisions are as a rule introduced into the Schemes for the establishment of Scholarships tenable in schools, and of Exhibitions tenable according to the grade of the School, at a University or other place of higher education, or professional, scientific or technical training. It is usual to direct that scholarships entitling to exemption from payment of tuition fees may be awarded to the extent of 10 or 20% of the number of Scholars in attendance, and in ordinary cases, not less than half of such scholarships are reserved in the first instance for deserving scholars from Public Elementary Schools.

When the endowment is considerable there is generally a direction in the scheme that separate sums of not less than a specified amount shall be applied for the purposes of maintaining Scholarships and Exhibitions, and in many cases the Scholarships are required to be of such value as to provide not only for the cost of tuition but also for some part of the other expenses incident to attendance at the school.

In Schemes for Elementary Schools to which adequate endowments are attached, it is usual to provide that some part of the Endowment shall be applied in the form of Exhibitions tenable at schools of higher grade, or in such other way as may secure for deserving scholars educational advantages which would not otherwise be within their reach.[19]

One of the main problems of the Commissioners was the interpretation of the phrase 'deserving scholars' in the context of individual schemes. At Ware Grammar School, Herts., the scholarships awarded to boys in public elementary schools under cl. 51 of the scheme, were to be 'awarded and held under such regulations and conditions as the Governors might think fit.' The governors proposed subsequently to make a regulation requiring a list of candidates to be submitted, and then enquired into the circumstances of parents in order to judge the boys' eligibility to compete. The Chairman considered that such a resolution was illegal and submitted for the Commissioners' consideration an alternative resolution, namely that the scheme did not contemplate the scholarships being restricted to poor boys from a public elementary school. In their reply, the Commissioners upheld this view, stating that attendance at such a school was the only condition of admission to competition.[20]

In many schemes, however, the terms were more explicit. At Balshaw's School, Leyland, Lancashire, the poor were specifically mentioned in the scheme: the relevant clause (60) ran:

> A yearly sum of not less than £75 shall be applied in maintaining scholarships. These shall be awarded to poor children who are or who have for not less than three years been scholars in some Public Elementary Schools in the Parish.

The Commissioners' attention was drawn to this school because of local complaints that the scholarships were not being awarded in accordance with the terms of the scheme and that awards were being carried off by others than the 'poor'.[21] The governors stated that they had enquired into the position in life of the parents of the boys and were satisfied that 'without such assistance the boys would not have been able to attend the school'.[22] A comment by a Commissioner on the file summed up the problem: 'I do not see how the Commissioners acting in a quasi-judicial capacity can give a definition of poverty any more than the Supreme Court can give a definition of burglary, although in individual cases they can upon sufficient evidence respectively decide whether a person is poor or a burglar.' The Commissioners concurred with the governors' action, leaving to them the application of the awards and the interpretation as to eligibility.

The Commissioners[23] were obliged to modify their view that the awards should be restricted to those boys who without help would not have been able to attend the school, when five candidates presented themselves for the award who, on the basis of their parents' occupations, which included a stationer and a publican, did not appear to be eligible. Sir George Young, replying to the complaint, wrote, 'It must of course be kept in view that parents may be able to "send" children to school in the first instance who would not, from poverty, be able to keep them in attendance throughout their school course, especially if visited with any of the ordinary misfortunes of life.'[24]

In addition to attending a public elementary school, another condition usually attached to entering for the competition was that the candidate had been in attendance there for some two, but usually three years.[25] (The notion of including the three-year rule in the provisions of schemes originated with a lawsuit *In the Matter of Storrie's University Gift,* where the matter was discussed in detail.[26]) It was assumed that this meant a total of three years spent in such a school until a case came to the notice of the Commissioners concerning exhibitioners to Ulverston Grammar School, Lancashire. There, a boy was ruled as not qualified to be a candidate for an exhibition, as there had been a break of eight months during his last three years at the public elementary school, during which time he attended a higher grade school in Barrow in the capacity of a Monitor. The Commissioners supported the governors' decision that the boy was inadmissible to the competition, although in fact he was the only candidate. Thenceforth, the Commissioners wrote into their schemes that the three years' attendance at the public elementary school had to be immediately preceding entry for the scholarship or exhibition.[27]

Where scholarships and exhibitions were awarded, the Commissioners did not, for a variety of reasons, specify the purposes for which they were to be employed, apart from stating that they were to be of an educational nature. The schemes frequently mentioned that they were to be tenable 'at places higher than elementary'.[28] Evidence taken by the 1886 Select Committee on the Endowed Schools Acts by previous and present Commissioners showed a lack of agreement on how the exhibitions should be awarded. One Commissioner, Sir George Young, whilst maintaining the 'elementary school' test as the basic one, believed that, on that matter of eligibility, 'it includes all such as require the particular help for the particular education intended by the founder', a phrase which, ambiguous as it was, pointed to a higher class than those generally understood by the term poor.[29] H. J. Roby stated that the less wealthy members of the liberal professions who, as a class, could be termed poor were to benefit by the scholarships. This sentiment harmonized with that of Henry Longley, then Chief Commissioner, who quoted Lord Hatherley in a debate in the Lords, 'those who desire and those who deserve a better education – a superior education to that which the circumstances of their parents can afford'.[30] At the same time the Commissioners would continue to encourage the selected poor who wished to take advantage of higher education. J. G. Fitch, taking as the 'poor', wage-earning classes, the artisans and labourers, believed that their best interests as a class were to be served, not 'by claiming for them the exclusive

enjoyment of the very few endowments which, by the original
terms of the trust, might seem to belong to them as a class, but by
obtaining for them free access to all the best schools.'[31] Matters
were made complicated by the absence of principles in fixing the
proportion of endowments allotted to scholarships as distinct from
school expenses. Sir George Young rightly pointed out that the
word 'poor' was not mentioned in the Acts, the 1869 Act referring
to the 'same class of persons' as that of the persons who were
benefited at the beginning of the Act and that of 1873, 'persons in a
particular class of life'.[32]

It is known that the Board Minutes of the Charity Commissioners, which contained all the important policy decisions and
which are now lost, did not have in its index any Minute listing
places at which exhibitions could be held.[33] Each case was
considered on its merit, whenever the Commissioners were called
upon to make a decision. A typical provision in a scheme would be
such as that of Petworth, Sussex, where cl. 19 provided that
'Exhibitions under the scheme shall be tenable at any place of
Education Higher than Elementary or of Technical or Professional
training approved by the Governors'. Scattered references in the
school files show that the institutions at which exhibitions were
tenable, apart from the endowed schools, were fairly narrowly
circumscribed. At Heath, Derbyshire, the vicar and churchwardens
and overseers of the poor, as local trustees of the Earl and Countess
of Devonshire Charities, enquired 'whether being articled as a
Pupil Teacher in a Public Elementary School is apprenticeship for
cl. 22 of this scheme': the Commissioners refused to sanction the
award (13 March 1896). Similarly, in the case of Wynn's Foundation at Penn, Staffordshire, the payment to a boy or girl under the
scheme of 1891 was to be made only so long as he or she remained
a scholar in the public elementary school. The Board resolved in
the negative the question whether a pupil teacher on the staff of
such a school was a scholar (6 November 1891).

Exhibitions were not always attached to grammar schools, and
the scheme for Boothtown-in-Halifax, Yorkshire, in 1882 provided
for exhibitions at Heath Grammar School, Halifax, 'or some other
place of education higher than primary'. The trustees, on enquiring
if the exhibitions might be held at the higher board school in
Halifax, were informed that the latter was 'not a place of education
higher than primary within the meaning of this provision of the

scheme' (24 November 1893). However, an organized Science and Art section of a school was considered suitable by the Commissioners.[34]

An important feature of the exhibitions was that they were not awarded for the purpose of apprenticeship, formerly one of the principal heads of application of endowments. However, Science and Art Department classes at technical colleges were held to be suitable places within the meaning of the term 'higher education' (Poplar, All Saints – George Green's School 12 July 1887).

'Professional training' was frequently included as an object for exhibitions and which was to be conducted at some place approved by the governors. At Petworth, Sussex, an appeal was addressed to the Commissioners against the decision of the governors to the effect that an exhibition could not be properly held by a boy in his father's chemist's shop, receiving instruction from him and also from the headmaster of the parochial schools in order to take the qualifying examination of the Pharmaceutical Society. But the rules of the Society under the 1868 Pharmacy Act required, as a condition of registration, 'employment as a student of pharmacy for three years or otherwise for that period to be practically engaged in the translation and dispensing of prescriptions.' Accordingly the Commissioners agreed with the decision of the governors to refuse the boy entrance to the competition on the grounds that the training constituted an apprenticeship.

The policy of the Commissioners throughout the period was to restrict the scope of exhibitions and scholarships to within fairly narrow academic limits. Novel applications and experimental schemes were discouraged: parents of poor boys who wished their children to be supported in vocationally-orientated education before the time of the Technical Instruction Acts received little help from the Commissioners. The latters' attitude was unrealistic, as the average poor boy would not go on to a university.[35]

Relationships between the Schools

The pattern of English education during the last thirty years of the nineteenth century was a complex one. Within the elementary system were the endowed elementary, the locally rate-aided elementary and voluntary schools, higher grade schools and upper departments attached to elementary schools; at the secondary stage, there were private, proprietary, public and the three 'grades' of endowed schools. There also existed in many places the grammar and the 'middle', 'English' or 'commercial' school, the latter of uncertain grade, the dichotomy being the result of civic pride in founding a 'town' school as distinct from the existing grammar school.

The tenuous link between the two systems was through the 'scholarship' awards although it is true to say that, for the most part, mobility took place within the respective systems rather than between them. Conditions differed from area to area, but it is possible to discern a recurrent pattern of relationships between the schools which had some bearing on the place of those 'poor' who were drafted into the secondary system, especially the grammar school and its immediate rival, the middle school; and the grammar school and the elementary school. In addition, the views of secondary headmasters on the admission of foundationers were important, especially where they reflected public opinion on the subject.

(a) *Views of Headmasters on the Admission of Foundationers*

Where the school was an old foundation, it was likely that the headmaster would continue filling up vacancies on the foundation in the same manner as he had done previous to the Endowed Schools Acts, wherever this was possible, even where the original intention of the donor specified the admission of 'poor boys'.[36]

Two dominant themes which exercised the minds of headmasters of the endowed schools were the exclusion of the 'free' scholars (either as of right or by competition) in order to raise the reputation of the school in the eyes of parents of potential pupils, and the financial loss suffered by the foundation and the headmasters as a consequence of being obliged to admit this class of scholar.[37] Many endowed schools closed throughout the country after the Commissioners had begun their work, due to lack of funds.[38] In the case of Ipswich Grammar School, twenty day boys were admitted, without payment, after being nominated by the Town Council, and were known as Queen's Scholars. At the time of the Commissioners' enquiries into the school (1879), the Headmaster, the Rev. H. A. Holden, showed that the school was sustained mainly by boarders and his own private means. Holden recommended that drastic action should be taken over the free boys. 'At present, there are twenty boys, mostly of indifferent merit, whose parents do not really require the kind of education supplied, and who are therefore a burden on the school and tend to depress the standard of culture.' This statement is borne out by an examination of the numbers in the school in 1878: of the 75 boys in attendance, only 49 paid tuition fees. Next, Holden suggested that at least half, if not all, of the scholarships were to be awarded to boys who had been one year or more at the school; and that all free pupils one year older than the average of their class, if unfit for promotion, were to lose their scholarships. It was only in this way that Ipswich could maintain its place alongside the other schools which were flourishing in the neighbourhood – Haileybury College, Framlingham, Dedham, Felsted and Norwich.[39]

The proposed scheme of the Commissioners at Queen Mary's Grammar School, Walsall, containing a provision for the selection of meritorious scholars from the lower schools, met with opposition from the Headmaster, the Rev. Joshua Vaughan, who complained that 'capitation fees are not due upon Exhibitioners but only upon paying pupils. Such a distinction could only act injuriously upon the school. Moreover, it would be manifestly unjust in my own case, since £45 has been taken from the salary and put upon the fees.'[40] A similar objection registered at Norwich Grammar School in 1880 by the new headmaster, O. W. Tancock, in a letter to the Commissioners, referred to the scheme then in operation: 'These clauses assign no foundation money at all to encourage boys at the school; leave the Governors at liberty to give scarcely any scholarships, if they so please; put the form of scholarships as "exemptions" from fees, a form the most difficult to work, especially where all masterships are badly paid, and need the tuition fees to pay them; and where salaries are paid partly by capitation grants.'[41] One way out of the difficulty which was explored at Lymm, Cheshire, was that such pupils would be admitted to the Grammar School and exempted from paying tuition fees, but would still pay the capitation fee of between £2 and £5 per boy.[42]

A somewhat different problem arose at Christ's Hospital Girls' School, London, whose educational status was raised by the scheme of 1891. One-third of the places were free, subject to competition, and girls' endowed schools were canvassed in order to fill the places. A number of headmistresses came to the school, complaining that the procedure was poaching on their preserves.[43]

Although it was usual, where a scheme of the Commissioners provided for free scholars, to allow a sum equivalent to the amount of fees of paying scholars from the endowment for staff salaries, no such money was made available at Wigan. In 1879, the Grammar School had embarked on an ambitious programme of schoolbuilding; the trustees, in order to gain the use of town and apprenticeship charities, had in return promised to educate thirty-five children from the public elementary schools without charge. This class of pupil, because of the nature of the Wigan endowment, proved to be a heavy drain on the school's finances, the free boys representing almost a third of the school in 1894 (74 paying and 32 gratuitous scholars). The schoolhouse had been let as a private residence, the boarding school had been let off for art classes and another room for a dancing class as a result of this arrangement. As the Assistant Commissioner reporting on Lancashire schools, F. E. Kitchener, remarked: 'No self-respecting headmaster could long continue such a state of things'.[44]

By 1897, there were only sixty-five paying scholars and the headmaster resolved to reorganize the school on a novel basis: there was to be an upper school, giving a complete education from kindergarten to university, and a commercial grammar school, teaching commercial and technical subjects and mainly for elementary boys. The novel aspect arose from the proposal to have two physically separate buildings, each with its own playground, but with one headmaster and the same staff for both schools. All the free scholars were to be deposited in the lower (third grade) school. 'There would be no change in staff necessary at first, because one or other of the present staff can deal with every subject needed in the Third Grade School.' At an interview with a Commissioner, the headmaster explained what would be gained by such a change. 'The Upper School would be relieved of the large number of Public Elementary scholars which was believed to interfere with the popularity of the school with parents of a higher social grade, whilst the lower school at the cheaper rate would attract boys whose parents were lower in the social scale and who yet wish their boys to continue beyond the ordinary leaving age at Public Elementary School.'[45] These proposals, although viewed sympathetically by the Commissioners, were finally rejected by them: as Sir

George Young wrote on the file, 'In view of our experience of the failure of "Upper and Lower Department" adjustments I had rather not make a scheme to try the experiment at Wigan. But I expect that either the Lower Department will fail or that it will *become the school*, the other department not being likely to be saved by the separate playgrounds.'

A system by which the award of exhibitions did not lead to the influx of large numbers of clever but 'poor' boys was employed at Emanuel School, Wandsworth, an off-shoot of the former United Westminster Schools. Two classes of exhibitions into the school were awarded: the first, for any poor boys educated for three years at any public elementary school within the parishes of St. Margaret's, St. John's, Westminster and St. Luke's, Chelsea: the second was 'preferentially for poor boys who by reason of orphanage or other adversity shall, in the opinion of the Governors, be proper objects of bounty'. Under cl. 66 of the scheme of 1873, two-thirds of the exhibitions were to be given to class one and one-third to class two. Between 1890 and 1895, the proportions had been reversed, two-fifths being awarded to class one, three-fifths to class two: all but one of these were boarding exhibitions, giving total exemption from fees. By 1895, the first class of awards was confined to boys attending the day school of the foundation. On his visit to the school (5-6 February 1895) R. E. Mitcheson, an Assistant Commissioner, noted how far the conditions for the award of the exhibitions had departed from the original spirit of the scheme.

> The Adversity Exhibitions (Class 2) are awarded not on competitive examination but on selection by the Governors, who receive applications three times a year, regard being had in selection (i) to locality, the parishes of Saints Margaret's, John's, and Luke's being preferred, on the ground that parishioners have under the scheme a prior right to the schools of the Foundation, and (ii) to the circumstances of the child's home as regards income, size of family etc. It is noteworthy that although Clause 65 requires all Exhibitions to be given as the reward of merit, the two classes are referred to respectively as 'Merit' and 'Adversity' Exhibitions, the latter being admittedly not given as the reward of merit.

No details are given in the report on the methods of selecting the

'Adversity' scholars or the schools which they had previously attended. It is known from the Return of Scholars at the school that of the 275 boys, only 9 were the sons of artisans: 62 were of professional parents, 91 of tradesmen, 34 clerks, 21 commercial travellers, 14 farmers and 40 dead or not known. Mitcheson notes that, 'They [the candidates] are drawn from all parts of the United Kingdom, and are generally, though poor, of better social status than the "Merit" Exhibitioners.'[46] Such a system was preferred by headmasters who were thus free to choose those scholars who might add a leavening of social distinction to the school, rather than one based on ability alone.[47]

This tendency is observable in many other schools at this period. It is seen in a similar but more detailed form in the scholarships awarded by Sheffield Grammar School at approximately the same date. The Foundation Scholarships, fifteen in number, were divided into 'Close' scholarships, that is, limited to those who had been not less than three years at a public elementary school in Sheffield, entitling the holder to full exemption from tuition fees; and 'Open' scholarships which were awarded without restriction to boys either already at the school or not, with exemption from half-fees. Awards made in the years 1889 to 1893 in the respective classes were:

WINNERS OF SCHOLARSHIPS

Parents' Occupations

	Open	*Close*
1889	Headmaster of Sheffield Grammar School	Engineer
		Engine Tender
	Steel Merchant	Workhouse Manager
1890	Merchant	Cabinet Maker
	Pearl-flinter	Compositor
1891	Colonel, R. A.	Joiner
	Accountant	Silver Cutter
	Clerk	Grocer
		Blacksmith
1892	Surveyor of Taxes	Commercial Traveller
	Steel Merchant	Cut-glass Manager
	Colonel, R. A. (2)	Clerk
	Accountant (2)	
1893	Steel Merchant	Cooper
	Tool Merchant	Joiner
	Accountant	Silver Piecer
		Head Nailer

Source: Sheffield Grammar School, PRO Ed. 27 6146.

The distinction between the two types of awards becomes clear from this table. Open scholarships were carried off by professional and larger-scale business merchants: the 'Close' scholarships by the superior artisan or small-scale business owners. The only occupation common to both classes of award is that of a clerk.[48] This would seem to refute, to some extent, the criticism put forward by witnesses before the Select Committees on the working of the Endowed Schools Acts that a superior class was at that time in attendance at the public elementary schools in order to carry off the free scholarships at the expense of the *bona fide* 'poor'.

The attitude of the headmasters of endowed schools towards the free scholars was determined partly by financial considerations, by their ambitions for the school and their memories of the 'free' endowed schools.[49] It is now necessary to see the effects of these attitudes on the relationship between the grammar school and the elementary school.

(b) *Relations between Elementary and 'Grammar' Schools*

That there was a connection between the two types of school, because of the boys who were drawn by the awards from the elementary to the grammar school, is obvious. However, the link between the schools was a shadowy one, as the Commissioners did not make clear the standard procedure to be adopted in choosing the exhibitioners: how, for example, to define and distinguish, for practical purposes, between 'merit' and 'ability'.

Lyttelton's ideas on the subject were unambiguous: 'I think that competitive examination, on paper chiefly, a strictly intellectual competitive examination, ought not to take place before eleven years old at the earliest.'[50] Canon Robinson, giving evidence before the same Committee, did not admit to the same view. He stated the Commissioners' aim to be 'not necessarily the principle of competitive examination, but of selection by merit, subject to such particular conditions as the peculiar circumstances of the case may make expedient.'[51] Robinson went on to demonstrate how selection by merit could be made:

> Supposing, for instance, that a number of scholars in a public elementary school had passed the Government Inspector's examination, and that the authorities of the school were authorised to select a certain number of those scholars on the

report of the inspector, seconded by the report of the master of
the school; that would be a fair selection by merit. You could
hardly say that it was a competitive examination, except so far
as the scholars passing in the different standards may be said to
compete with one another: and the report of the master would
have reference, not to the work of the child at a particular
moment, but to his general work, his industry, and his attention,
during the time he had been in the school.[52]

D. C. Richmond, Secretary of the Charity Commission, on the
other hand, pointed out that many of the schemes stated that the
governors of the endowed school into which the boys would pass
should test the merit of the boys; this could be done by setting an
entrance examination at the higher school.

The lack of uniformity in the Commissioners' schemes for the
awarding of exhibitions from the elementary schools led, as will be
seen below, to misunderstanding and sometimes friction between
the schools. Briefly, however, five types of testing the candidates'
ability with regard to 'merit' can be distinguished: in the elementary school, examination by an H.M.I., reports of the headmaster, a
selection examination based on academic subjects: in the endowed
secondary school, an entrance examination into the school or an
examination set by the school to be taken in the elementary school.
There were many variations on this procedure in practice; where
strong opposition was encountered to the application of endowed
elementary funds for secondary education, other criteria were put
forward by the Commissioners as the basis of award. For example,
at Chertsey, Surrey, in the new scheme proposed for Sir William
Perkins School, the trustees expressed the fear that the scholarships
would go to the 'clever scholars'. R. Durnford, the Assistant
Commissioner, met this objection in the following way: 'I said that
one class of scholarship might be given as a reward for diligence
and good conduct, to be tested by the number of attendances made
in excess of that required by the Code as a condition for annual
grant.'[53] In order to encourage younger boys from public elementary schools to compete for exhibitions, the governors of Alleyne's
Grammar School, Stone, Staffordshire, devised separate examinations for pupils under and those over twelve years of age.[54]

Where the scheme provided for the award of scholarships, there
were many difficulties, apart from financial ones, preventing it from

being carried out, not the least of which was the animosity which existed between the elementary and secondary schools. At Tideswell Grammar School, Derbyshire, which had received a scheme in 1876 and was visited by A. F. Leach ten years later, the clauses relating to the award of scholarships were inoperative: this was partly due to the fact that the fund had been used to provide compensation for the previous headmaster. It was not surprising, therefore, that the governors had allowed the present headmaster to conduct the school in effect as a private adventure school, in the way most likely to provide a profit.[55] There were sixty-five boarders and ten day boys, apparently of middle-class parents; the curriculum was mainly classical, Latin and Greek being taught although the latter was not mentioned in the original scheme. Leach pointed out that the scheme was intended to serve the immediate neighbourhood rather than to attract boys from a distance and that science and modern languages would be of more practical value to the boys, as the school did not prepare for the universities. The governors replied that science and modern languages were not the marks of a superior education and that 'the presence of boarders was a far greater benefit to the inhabitants of Tideswell and the farmers round it owing to the money thereby spent in the town than free scholarships or scientific education would be.' Nor were they impressed by Leach's claim that a 'modern' course in the school would make for more productive wage-earners.

These conditions naturally affected the award of scholarships in Tideswell. At the time of Leach's visit, there were three public elementary schools: one National School of 124 scholars and two independent schools of 125 and 62, a total of 311 pupils. Up to 1886 when scholarships ceased to be awarded, five were to boys from the National and three from the independent schools. The principal reason for the lapsing of the scholarships stemmed largely from the hostility existing between the schools. Leach recorded this feeling in his report:

> I went over to the national school and had a conversation with the Headmaster, and could plainly perceive that he was animated by somewhat bitter feelings against the grammar school and the Headmaster. He alleged that the boys were very badly taught in Arithmetic and other elementary subjects at the grammar school and that boys sent there frequently returned to

him because they learned nothing. Though, however, the hostility of elementary schoolmasters and the other reasons assigned by Mr. Fox [the grammar school headmaster] may have had their effect in preventing competition for scholarships, I cannot think that there has been a sufficient trial of the system under him. It seems unlikely that out of an average attendance of 150 boys in the three public elementary schools in the parish there should not be found three in each year or 2 per cent per annum in need of secondary education and able to take it when offered gratis, even with the present course of instruction in the school.

It would seem, however, that the blame did not lie wholly with either side. When Leach persuaded the governors to offer three more scholarships for competition (20 January 1887) only two candidates presented themselves and were selected, although reluctantly, by the headmaster of the grammar school, after an examination conducted by him. According to Fox, the two boys scored 26 per cent and 16 per cent respectively on their arithmetic papers. Each side accused the other of low standards, the grammar school in order not to be burdened with too many elementary school pupils, the elementary schools to assert their independence against the grammar school.

Antagonism often resulted from ambiguities of wording in the scheme as to whether candidates for election were to be selected by the elementary or the grammar school. At West Kirby, Cheshire, five scholarships were to be awarded under the scheme at Calday Grange Grammar School for a period of three years. The Commissioners were asked to arbitrate in a dispute between the Board of Governors of the Grammar School and the Elementary School Committee. The Chairman of the Grammar School Board wrote to the Commissioners (19 December 1887):

> Owing to a misunderstanding which has taken place with regard to an appointment of a Bennett's scholar, I shall be very much obliged if you will inform me whether the election rests with the Governors of Calday Grammar School or whether the Managers of the Elementary Schools have the election of scholars from the individual schools for the presentation to the Governors as Bennett scholars; and if the election rests with the Managers of the Elementary schools (provided the boys can pass the Head-

master's examination and the provisions of Sections 40 and 49 have been complied with), have the Governors the right to prescribe such regulations and conditions under Section 53 as they think fit for the conduct and announcement to the Governors of such election by the Managers?[56]

On the same day, the rector of West Kirby, as Chairman of the Elementary School Committee, wrote to the Commissioners:

I have lately communicated with the Chairman of the Governors a letter announcing the appointment, by the Elementary School Committee of a boy duly chosen and as fulfilling the Conditions laid down in Clause 40 of the scheme.

The appointment has been refused on the grounds that certain other conditions were prescribed by the Governors, which the Committee of the Elementary School have declined to acknowledge.

The Governors in attempting to impose on the Committee regulations with which the scheme gives them no authority to interfere have treated the Elementary Schools as subordinate branches of the Grammar Schools, whereas they are independent institutions, enjoying certain privileges connected with the Grammar School.

The Commissioners ascertained that the 'certain conditions' around which the controversy centred had been imposed by the Grammar School governors almost a year previously (29 January 1887). These required that in future fourteen days' notice must be given of an examination of candidates for the Bennett scholarships; the notice boards of places of worship in the parish were to be used for this purpose. The main reason given for the passing of this resolution was that, according to the governors, there had been much dissatisfaction in the town arising from the system of electing the Bennett scholars, and that many parents had not been aware that elections were about to take place. The resolution stipulated, therefore, 'that the Managers of the Elementary Schools must satisfy the Governors that the provisions of the scheme and of this notice have been complied with.'

Under protest, the Elementary School Committee carried out the instruction concerning the advertising of the forthcoming election only to find, according to the Chairman, 'a further form of instructions requiring me, in sending the boy, to send with him a statement that the former instruction had been duly complied with. I felt unable to continue this line of courtesy, being obliged to look on this second order as a deliberate challenge of the position I had taken earlier.' The Grammar School Board had written previously to the Elementary Committee that 'The selection of boys will be left with you after such an examination as you may prescribe', which thus laid the responsibility for election fairly and squarely on the Elementary Committee. By the end of January 1888, there was a complete deadlock: the Elementary School Committee refused to give the undertaking required by the Grammar School governors, and the latter refused to receive the boy elected by them without it. It was left to the Commissioners to clarify the situation. In a letter to the governors (10 February 1888) the Commissioners found the former body at fault in inviting the managers to 'select' and 'present' a boy to the governors. It was provided in the scheme that the governors of the Grammar School were responsible for the election of Bennett scholars and could not abrogate their responsibility by delegating the task to the Elementary School Committee.

This case affords an interesting insight into the relationships existing between two such bodies. Distrust and petty jealousy on the part of the governors and managers worked to the disadvantage of the scholars who were to benefit by transferring from one school to another and who were used as pawns by the rival bodies.

Entrance examinations into the grammar schools were of various standards, according with the outlook of the headmasters. Where it was felt desirable to exclude elementary boys and where the terms of the scheme did not stipulate that any preference should be given to them, the examination was a difficult one.[57] Headmasters often personally set the examinations. Papers in subjects which included Latin, history, geography and arithmetic were often of considerable difficulty and were moderated by bodies such as the Oxford and Cambridge Schools Examination Board.[58] Applicants for entrance scholarships to Mansfield Grammar School in 1889 were expected to be of a standard equivalent to that of the Oxford and Cambridge Local Examinations and were to compete against holders of the scholarships already in the school, some of them sixteen and seventeen years of age.[59] At Ipswich Grammar School, Queen's Scholarships to the annual value of £15 each were to be awarded to boys whose parents would not otherwise be able to afford a grammar school education. Out of a list of sixteen Queen's Scholarships for the years 1887-1892, four had been scholars in a public elementary school, only one of whom had been elected direct from such a school.

The headmaster wished to alter the entrance examination to the grammar school by abolishing the provision (cl. 55 of the scheme) concerning the translation and parsing of simple Latin sentences, in order to draw boys from the elementary schools, but was unable to effect such a change.[60] Where the grammar school had a middle school, as at Ipswich, the Elementary or Foundation scholars entered the middle school. The Commissioners favoured the policy of the Schools Inquiry Commission, that where competition was confined to the elementary schools, the exhibitions should be tenable at a third grade school, with a system of internal awards operating to enable boys to rise if talented, to a first grade school.[61]

Where open examinations were held, however, this did not favour the elementary boy. Dr. E. Abbott, the liberal-minded Headmaster of the City of London School (1865-89) confirmed from his own experience that such examinations served little purpose unless they were confined to the elementary scholars. In a debate on the subject at a meeting of the National Association for the Promotion of Social Science, Abbott stated that in his school, there were several entrance scholarships for which boys from elementary schools might compete, and he had always desired, as far as was consistent with the impartiality of an examiner, to see his own boys beaten by pupils from elementary schools, but this had never been the case. If the scholarships were confined to elementary schools, the pupils would be able to hold their own.[62]

Girls were at an even greater disadvantage in obtaining scholarships to endowed schools. The S.I.C. had noted that there were only twelve girls' endowed schools in 1864. By the time of the Bryce Commission (1895) this had risen to eighty, but this was still inadequate. At Rothbury, Northumberland, as late as 1901 scholarships open to both boys and girls were not taken up by the latter as no school buildings existed for the higher education of girls.[63] A. F. Leach reported that at Audley Grammar School, Staffordshire, girls received 'very unequal treatment compared with boys'. No scholarships were awarded to them during the nine years after a new scheme had been drawn up in 1877 and the School Board had subsequently withdrawn public elementary school scholarships to the school, but only for girls.[64] In urban areas the creation of the few girls' schools often presented problems of travel and expense.[65]

Much of the resentment of the elementary schools directed against the grammar schools stemmed from the wish not to lose their best pupils. At the United Westminster Schools, London, many exhibitions were not awarded because of irregular proceedings on the part of the headmaster.

> When Exhibitions were taken to Emanuel School direct from the Public Elementary Schools, the Headmasters of those schools often withheld their best boys from the competition, and it was difficult even to get a sufficient number of candidates to fill the vacant places. In other cases it was thought that the Public Elementary Master was using the Exhibitions as a piece of private patronage. The Governors therefore abandoned the system, which was in accordance with the more natural interpretation of the scheme, and instead resolved to make arrangements 'such as should seem to them best adapted to secure certain objects.'[66]

The grant-earning capacity, especially of older pupils, was an added incentive to retain boys in the elementary schools. At Queen Elizabeth's School, Barnet, the scheme provided that scholarships should be offered annually to boys attending the public elementary schools within the Poor Law Union of Barnet. The age range for entering the competition was fixed at seven years to nine years, but the Finchley School Board urged that the upper limit should be raised to twelve, claiming that in the meantime the boys would receive as good a grounding in a primary as a secondary school. The governors, in October 1889, considered this proposal but felt that it was undesirable in the interests of the boys themselves that the age limit should be extended so far. Finally, they agreed that the conditions should be altered so that a boy who was successful in the examination should not join the school until he was nearly eleven years of age.[67]

At Bingley, Yorkshire, the dispute over the age of transfer to the grammar school took a rather different form. Under a scheme of 1873, two exhibitions yearly to the value of £6 each were awarded to boys educated in public elementary schools, tenable at the grammar school for three years. Bingley School was noted for its pioneering work in this sphere and awarded the exhibitions regularly. Up to 1889, the governors had accepted boys for competition at any age under seventeen years. In July of that year, the governors of the Grammar School made an order that no candidate whose age exceeded twelve on 12 September previously would be accepted. In a statement to the Commission, signed by fourteen of the fifteen heads of the Bingley elementary schools (17 January 1889),[68] the limitation in age imposed by the governors was welcomed, for it was shown that most of the children had already left by thirteen and were therefore practically debarred from competing. It can be seen that the elementary schools, in their quest for status, were not anxious for their better pupils to transfer to the grammar schools.

The loss of potential pupil-teachers further strengthened the elementary schools' desire to retain promising pupils wherever possible. One example will suffice for many. Under cl. 97 of the 1872 scheme for Bath Row School, one of the elementary schools of the King Edward VI Foundation, Birmingham, no girl was allowed to remain at the school beyond the end of the school term or half year in which she attained the age of fifteen. Miss S. J. Corbett, who had been the headmistress of the school for thirty-three years, protested to the Commissioners that if the clause became operative, the future efficiency of the Branch schools would be impaired. The supply of teachers and monitors for the schools was provided by the elementary schools: pupils of special promise were retained, becoming assistant teachers or paid monitors and remaining until eighteen or nineteen years of age at the schools.[69] Self-recruitment operated to such an extent that all seven teachers and paid monitors in the school were former pupils: two successive heads at the Gem Street Branch of the Foundation were former pupils and eight of the second mistresses in the Branch schools.[70]

It is arguable that the improved nature of the elementary schools since Forster's Act lessened the incentive for some boys who would otherwise have competed for exhibitions. In 1870, the leaving age was twelve years; by Sandon's Act of 1876 it was raised to fourteen, the same as for the third grade school. Curriculum choice was becoming wider; for example, the annual code of 1875 introduced Latin as a grant-earning subject. Often, too, the facilities available in the elementary schools were superior to those in the endowed schools. At Northwich, Cheshire, parents were unwilling to let their sons compete for six scholarships at the town's grammar school for, as the governors noted, 'there is hardly an Elementary School in the district so badly furnished.'[71] An education comparable in quality with that given in a reformed endowed school was often available with the advent of the higher-grade schools, following the example of the Leeds School Board in 1872. The curriculum offered within elementary schools often compared favourably with the endowed schools in the same town, as at Birmingham:

ELEMENTARY	LOWER MIDDLE
14 years or thereabouts	
Reading	Reading and spelling
Writing	Writing
Arithmetic	Arithmetic
English Composition	English Grammar
English literature	English literature
* Latin	Rudiments of Latin
* French, German	French
* Mathematics	Elementary mathematics
* Mechanics, Botany	Elementary natural
* Animal Physiology	science
* Physical Geography	
Outline of English History	English History
Outline of English Geography	English Geography
* Domestic Economy	–
–	Drawing
–	Vocal Music

* Special subjects, any two of which may be recognised in IV, V, and VI Standard Examinations.

Source: King Edward VI School, Birmingham, PRO Ed. 27 4901. Extracted from the Report of the School Committee upon the development of the schools of the foundation (22 December 1880), Birmingham.

But unlike the endowed schools, the elementary sector had no tradition of extended education. This is borne out by the statistics for the period: in 1886, the number of boys and girls between the ages of thirteen and fourteen at elementary schools was 147,000 but only 40,000 remained in the schools after fourteen years. An added incentive for remaining in the elementary school was that the brighter pupil, who passed the required standards readily, was able to leave school earlier and become a wage-earner.[72]

Perhaps another factor contributing to early leaving in the elementary school was the state of upper schools attached to the former. To encourage boys to continue their education at the school, or where a suitable higher grade school was not within reasonable travelling distance, the Commissioners had directed that upper departments should be created out of the endowment, with exhibitions attached to them. In their Annual Report for 1881, the Commissioners remarked that though the elementary schools under their jurisdiction were on the whole efficiently conducted, the creation of upper departments was not as widespread as might have been expected 'and which as managers of the Elementary School they [the Managers] have direct pecuniary interest in ignoring'.[73] The funds used for such a department meant that a lesser sum was available for the elementary school.

The low educational standards of those children leaving the elementary schools at an early age possessing the necessary ability for more advanced education led to this outburst by John Morley:

> Certainly no child below the Sixth Standard could do any real good in a secondary school. It is clear then that the present system and standards of primary instruction exclude all but a very small minority from so much as the bare chance of partaking of those vast means of educational endowment which be open to the sons of the middle and upper classes. It will not do to say that the children of the poor have neither capacity nor industry nor time enough to come up to Standard VI. Nobody in his senses will believe that there is any disqualification about English poverty so fatal as this.[74]

A form of 'streaming' was adopted in many elementary schools when the time approached for the competition for exhibitions: a group of those who seemed likely to do well in the examinations were chosen by the headmaster for this purpose. Rivalry between the elementary schools of a town sometimes resulted, as success would attract more pupils. At Wigan, for example, the Assistant Commissioner noted that the twenty-five scholarships, competed for by the elementary schools of the town, were greatly in demand. 'There is keen competition among the various schools, and the Grammar School gets the pick of their scholars. At each school, a special class of candidates is formed; this in some cases prevents boys from joining the Grammar School who otherwise might do so.'[75]

Much was heard, from those interested in the endowed schools, on the subject of the exhibitions falling into the hands of those who least needed help and for whom the original Act never contemplated participation in the competition. Certainly, the better-educated parents of children at the elementary schools would have been quick to avail themselves of the benefits resulting from a scheme for the endowed school in their locality. A report in a Birmingham newspaper throws an interesting light on this matter:

> On the 24th June 1868, there were 548 boys in the New Street Grammar School, and of these the parents of 21 only belonged to the working classes. We are officially assured that the proportion is now [1875] about the same as at that time. It may be asked why the working classes do not more largely avail themselves of the school, as the arrangements for admission place no difficulties in their way. The answer is obvious. The middle and upper classes have a better acquaintance with the school and a greater affinity for education. When vacancies occur, they are more prepared to avail themselves thereof, and like the lame man in the parable, the working-classes always find someone stepping in before them.[76]

The following year, a master at the Grammar School wrote to a newspaper:

> In your report of the deputation from the Liberal Association, Mr. Crosskey is represented as dwelling on the zeal of the working man to obtain the higher education for his children and he seems to have mentioned especially Greek and History as objects of this zeal. I have been a Master in the Classical Department for upwards of twelve years, and am in the habit of registering the occupations of the parents of my pupils. I regret, for the sake of Mr. Crosskey, and the working man, that I cannot recall to memory that I have ever registered manual labour in any form as an occupation.[77]

More detailed information was given by the Rev. Charles Evans, a former headmaster of the school, in commenting on the Fortescue Returns (see p. 114, following) in 1885. Evans had made his own enquiries into the working of exhibitions from elementary to higher grade schools.

> I am confirmed in the opinion that such exhibitions are for the

most part carried off not by the children of the very poor, but by the children of the middle and lower middle classes. A few weeks ago, observing that four pupils from a single Board School had won Exhibitions to King Edward VI Grammar Schools in Birmingham, I made enquiries as to the parentage and circumstances of the successful candidates and found that No. 1 was the son of the School Board Attendance Officer. No. 2 of a small shopkeeper, rather poor. No. 3 of a Master Mason, employing five men. No. 4 of a man in easy circumstances. You may accept this as a typical case.[78]

Since the 1878 scheme for the school, however, more poor boys had entered the Classical Department: three such boys had passed to Oxford or Cambridge and two boys to the Mason Science College since that time.[79] It must be remembered, though, that Birmingham was a rather special case among endowed foundations with its graduated system of schools.

The tendency of the middle-class parents to send their children to the elementary schools in order to obtain scholarships was more widespread by the 1880s.[80] There were many incentives for the parents to do so. The Roan Foundation at Greenwich, one of which was a third grade school for boys, gave prior right of entry to those who had attended a public elementary school for three years, having passed the fourth standard, at a fee of £3, which was slightly more than half-fees. The fact that these places were eagerly sought after confirms the presence of a middle-class element in the elementary schools.[81]

(c) *Relations between the Middle School and Grammar School*

'The ladder of education' which was mooted by the Schools Inquiry Commission, and the implementation of which was to be entrusted to the Endowed Schools Commissioners, was a concept which was difficult to realize in practice. Many pages of Evidence from the Select Committees of the last quarter of the century bear witness to the simple yet effective means by which the 'ladder' could become a reality. Lyttelton declared before one of them:

Just as we open the way from the second grade schools through exhibitions, and scholarships, and so on, to the higher schools above them, so we open the advantages of second grade schools to the third grade schools below them, and in the same way the third grade schools to the public elementary schools of the district, which we believe to be far the best way of benefitting the labouring classes in those districts.[82]

In their section on systems of education in other countries, the Taunton Commissioners had praised the Scotch system with its well-established links from the elementary school to the university, dating back to the Scottish Renaissance of the sixteenth century. In England, the vacuum caused by the lack of regional co-ordinating authorities to oversee such a system lessened the chances for making such an experiment. The only hope for success seemed to lie with those large foundations which, within themselves, displayed a diversity of types of school but which were organically linked by a common governing body and a single endowment as in the cases of Bedford and Birmingham.

This optimism was reflected by an Assistant Commissioner in his Report on the Birmingham schools (1871): 'The wealth and local character of the Charity, the number of the population and the diversity of classes composing it, the established reputation of the existing schools, all combine to make the experiment an easy and safe one. The advantage of gradation is that it finishes an unbroken chain of schools connecting the lowest with the highest in the country.'[83] A marginal note by Roby showed a different line of thinking: it ran: 'No chain but parallels. The right symbol is not 3rd – 2nd – 1st Grade but $\overbrace{\qquad}^{\text{1st}}_{\displaystyle } \begin{array}{l} \text{2nd} \\ \text{3rd} \end{array}$.' Roby's interpretation rather than Lyttelton's was to prove to be the more common case. Some thirteen years later Sir George Young, then Chief Commissioner, was asked before a Select Committee:

> If a boy were going up this educational ladder, of which we hear so much, from an elementary school, would you expect him to take in all these steps, into the third grade; then the second grade, then the first and then the University?

He replied,

> No, certainly not. The three grades of school are not steps in the 'ladder of education'. The intention of a third-grade school is to suit boys who are to finish their education in that school. The intention of the second-grade school is, to a very large extent,

the same. The intention of the first-grade school is, for the most part, to train boys for the university ... The 'ladder of education' does not require more than three steps – the elementary school, the secondary school, and the university.[84]

For those who accomplished the first two steps in the 'ladder' a further difficulty confronted them. It will be argued here that the presence of the 'Middle' Schools (alternatively called the English or Commercial Schools) in many instances cut off the exhibitioners from grammar school education.

The so-called middle school can be traced back to before the second half of the nineteenth century. It was the creation of many different sets of circumstances but outstanding amongst these was the rivalry with the grammar school. At Norwich, the middle school split off from the grammar school in 1862, from which it remained separate for nearly fifty years. The town council supported the Nonconformist element in the city, emphasizing that the non-sectarian character of the grammar school endowments had been changed because of the Church of England control of the governing body. A middle school was thus established to cater for sons of tradesmen, with a curriculum similar to that of the grammar school.[85] As in many other instances, the middle school became in time the 'town' school as against the grammar school.[86] An attempt to introduce a Church of England bias into the flourishing new institution met with strenuous opposition from the Corporation.

At Bedford a similar situation existed, where the local trustees, as they were called, 'were set on running the Commercial School, which they regarded as their own, against the Grammar School, which they regarded as New College'.[87] The majority of the trustees were tradesmen of the town and resented the aloof manner of the Headmaster, the Rev. F. Fanshawe, in their dealings with him. When the Commissioners were engaged in making a scheme for Bedford, their proposal to provide a comprehensive system of schools in the town, ranging from the grammar school and the commercial school to the preparatory and elementary schools,[88] was not opposed by Fanshawe except for certain reservations directed against the commercial school. Fanshawe's concern was with the proposal to rename the commercial school the 'modern' school. A Memorial from Fanshawe and the staff of the grammar school requested the Commissioners to withhold this title 'as this would be a misnomer and would mislead Parents in comparison with the Grammar School, in which also modern subjects will be taught'. It also insisted on 'the paramount necessity of preserving fairly the present general limits or spheres of the schools of the Charity'. The grammar school should be made first grade, the commercial school second.[89]

When it became known that the final scheme retained the title of 'Modern' for the commercial school, Fanshawe, a fervent anti-Liberal in politics,[90] claimed that the intervention of the local M.Ps, James Howard and Samuel Whitbread, both Liberals, as arbitrators between the schools and the Commissioners, had been engineered in order to raise the commercial to a first grade school: further, that this was being done because of pressure by the local political party. Fanshawe wrote: 'It is not a case of wholesome rivalry between similar schools. For many years the Trustees have desired to crush the Grammar School. One main cause of the eagerness with which they have suddenly at last come round to support the Commissioners is that they see what they believe to be a severe blow dealt to the Grammar School.'[91] The disparity between the fees of the schools – at the commercial school £1 10s. to £4 per annum, at the grammar school £4 to £12 per annum, also put the former at an advantage. Twelve years later, this rivalry still existed, as was noted by a writer to the Commissioners:

> In many places where, as at Bedford, for instance, there ought to be exhibited a model of a perfect system of graded schools, all harmoniously dovetailing into one another, and by an economical division of labour, each subserving the common good, the elementary school overlaps the Modern School, the Modern School ambitiously wastes its energies in attempting work which might be better done at the Grammar School, and a mischievous see-saw and rivalry are growing-up between schools on the same foundation, and the public interests suffer from the competition, just as the travelling public would suffer if competing railway companies ran only first class trains.[92]

The existence of rivalry between the two types of school cut off effective communication, resulting in each competing for its own boys, and, though often working under a common governing body, they were to all purposes separate entities. At Walsall, too, where the school was divided into commercial and grammar, both sets of pupils met for instruction in the same room but used different, though adjoining, playgrounds. 'The boys from the Commercial seldom pass into the Grammar School and are decidedly inferior in social status,' reported an Assistant Commissioner.[93] It was hoped to remedy this state of affairs by eliminating the middle school, creating in its place a third grade school affiliated to the grammar school. There would be one headmaster for the two institutions and boys would be able to rise to the upper school by internally-awarded scholarships. At Ashby-de-la-Zouch, Leicestershire, the middle school was described in 1889 by an Assistant Commissioner as 'an anomaly and a misfortune.' It ranked as a higher grade elementary school for the middle classes. Scholarships from elementary schools in the town were restricted to this school.[94]

'Middle schools', by one name or another, existed throughout the period, but the attempts by the Commissioners to relate them, in a useful way, to the grammar school were not always successful.

In many cases, neither the grammar schools nor elementary schools wished to regard the middle school as a nexus between them.

The scheme for Macclesfield, which came into operation in 1880, provided for three types of exhibition or scholarship into the various schools. Under cl. 86, two scholarships to the value of £10 per annum were to be awarded to elementary school scholars, tenable at the modern school: under cl. 84, four exemption scholarships, open to elementary and modern pupils, entitling the holder to exemption from fees, for two places at the modern school and two at the grammar school for two years: and under the same clause, eleven other exemption scholarships, for competition among boys already at the schools for one year, for two boys at the grammar and nine at the modern school, which enabled boys who were already at the latter to attend the grammar school at the same fees as they had been paying previously.

Leach, reporting on the school in 1893, strongly advocated the abolition of the modern school, and suggested that more should be done for the education of girls. He also recommended that extra scholarships should be established which took pupils direct from the elementary to the grammar schools.[95] The headmaster of the grammar school complained to Leach that the age at which boys came from the modern school – twelve years – was too old, as they possessed no knowledge of Latin and had to be placed in a lower class than was consistent with their attainment in English subjects.[96] An analysis of why good candidates were not forthcoming from the modern school was attempted by the headmaster:

> The experience of the Charity Commissioners at other places, as well as in Macclesfield, has shown that this excellent theory (i.e., scholarships) does not work properly in practice. The Masters of the Lower Schools naturally do not care for their schools to be considered merely stepping stones to the higher ones, and the valuable scholarships given at the former also tend to keep boys there till their schooldays are finished, and the loyalty to their school among boys themselves probably tends in the same direction.[97]

This is borne out in Leach's report: 'There does not seem to be any great (if any) difference of class between the boys in the modern and the Grammar School except that there are only three of the professional class in the former. But many described as manufacturers' merchants and gentlemen are in the Modern School, who I was assured could perfectly well pay the fees in the Grammar School, but are tempted by the lower scale of the Modern School.'[98] These were: £4-£8 in the latter, £8-£20 in the former. The governing body, by the time of Leach's visit, were desirous of abolishing the modern school but had made this difficult by the arrangement of the awards, which offered a premium on attending that school rather than the grammar school: and, as in the case of Ipswich School, the middle school was still very popular.

It was claimed by the elementary schools of the town, which were efficiently run and challenged the modern school in the range of subjects and standards attained, that in the system of education in the town, the modern school acted as a stumbling-block to many elementary school pupils. A headmaster in one of the schools, George Beach, raised this point with both the governors and the Commissioners. To the latter he wrote stating that in his experience many boys were quite capable of proceeding direct to the grammar school without passing through the modern school.

> It appears that the present arrangements were made before Elementary Schools had attained their present educational efficiency, and before such subjects as Algebra, French, Latin

etc. were taught. *Then* it was wise to afford large facilities to the Modern School and make that school necessarily a step to the Grammar School. Such grading is no longer necessary. Under the present system of scholarships, a clever lad from the Elementary Schools is practically shut out from the Grammar School, except in special circumstances. The *Entrance* scholarships are too few in number as compared with Exemption scholarships, the inevitable consequence being that too large a proportion of the Funds is devoted to a comparatively wealthy class.[99]

This change seems to be confirmed by the figures available for this period. An Annual Report for 1889 of the grammar school shows that six boys had been transferred from the modern school to the grammar school who, under cl. 47 of the scheme, were receiving tuition at half fees, five in 1890, thirteen in 1891, and sixteen in 1892. The entrance scholarships into the modern school, about which Beach complained, attracted fourteen candidates for the two scholarships in 1887, twenty-two in 1888, fifteen in 1889 and fourteen in 1890. For those who were successful at the examination, the award was for three years only, which was inadequate if an extended stay at the school was contemplated.

Beach's protest to the governors was met by the reply that under the scheme, they had no power to found scholarships direct from the elementary to the grammar schools. The Commissioners, for their part, whilst not agreeing with the existing pattern of schools, did not seek to alter it. In a Minute on the Commissioners' file (16 December 1895), Sir George Young noted the drawbacks at a separate modern school. He agreed with the governors that the notion 'that boys should pass through the Modern School into the Grammar School is a mistake'. Nevertheless, he supported the governors' actions, stating that 'While the Modern School remains, the Governors are right in giving the greater part of the scholarships limited to Public Elementary boys an entrance into it rather than into the Grammar School.' The value of the entrance scholarships was not increased through lack of funds,[100] and the modern school continued in existence.

Other factors affecting the admission

Besides the relationships existing between the different types of school, there were a number of other factors which restricted the numbers who could have attended the endowed schools. An important one was parental ignorance in respect of opportunities available for their children. In discussing the views of witnesses that poorer children were at a disadvantage in competing for exhibitions, the 1886 Report of the Select Committee on the Endowed Schools Acts rightly stated: 'The alleged injustice seems to arise partly from the gaps and imperfections in our educational system, but still more from the imperfect acquaintance with it possessed by the working classes.'[101]

Notices giving information as to the condition of the award of scholarships and the dates and time on which the examination was to be held, were often given little publicity. At Tideswell, Derbyshire, the notice was too legally worded for easy understanding, it being merely a reiteration of cl. 55 of the scheme.[102] Where publicity was given, the response was often poor. The Queen Elizabeth Grammar School, Barnet, had offered two or three scholarships yearly out of the endowments for free scholars at public elementary schools. Fifteen schools in the area were notified of the examination: of the five schools who ever sent candidates, only three of these did so regularly. The number of candidates was so small, an average of about two per school, that the headmaster of the grammar school considered that there were 'fewer real candidates than scholarships'.[103]

The timidity of parents when faced with a determined headmaster is seen, for example, at Wigan. Because of the growth of successful private schools in the town, the grammar school headmaster proposed to effect major alterations in the structure of the school in order to meet the challenge. The school, he suggested, should be split into two, the second grade school becoming first grade and the commercial school third grade, the latter to be conducted on the lines of a higher grade school: 'All the Free Scholars would naturally be placed at first in the Third Grade School, but on the recommendation of the Headmaster, a scholar of talent might be transferred to the First Grade School. The transfer would most conveniently take place when the boy had been six months or a year in the Third Grade School.'

Such a plan could not have hoped to have received the sanction of the Charity Commissioners and in fact was rejected by them. However, before this was known, a meeting between the headmaster and the parents of the thirty-one free boys in the school had taken place, at which the following resolution was passed:

> That this meeting of the parents of the Free Scholars elected in 1894, 1895 and 1896, having heard the Headmaster's explanation of the scheme proposed by him to his Governors for the future arrangements of the Grammar School, approves the same.

Twenty-two parents were for the arrangements, none was against and one was neutral.[104]

It was of great importance that there should be sufficient funds to meet the cost of scholarships and exhibitions, but it did not necessarily follow that when available, the funds could be fully utilized. The Solicitor to the Attorney-General in *ex officio* proceedings relating to charities in 1884, Mr. John Clabon, quoted the following instance:

> In default of the appointment of trustees, I am the honorary receiver of a large charity in Kent, and £50 a year is devoted out of the fund to the higher education of girls; and we cannot find out any school in the neighbourhood that would give them a higher education; and we cannot take them from their homes, because they are the children of poor people, living at home, and engaged in hop-picking and so on, and the result has been that, the £50 a year remaining unemployed, the Charity Commissioners have just sanctioned a new scheme under which we are going to try to devote the £50 a year to teaching cookery.[105]

As children left school early, governing bodies were reluctant to make more than minimum provision for exhibitions. At Micheldever, Hampshire, the trustees applied to the Commissioners to use such funds for building schools for poor children rather than for exhibitions and scholarships on the grounds that the present pupils left school too early to take advantage of the awards. The average total school life of boys was calculated as 4 years 3 months and girls 4 years 5 months.[106] Ex-elementary school pupils gaining scholarships to Barnard Castle County School, Durham, in 1892, stayed at the school for a period of about four terms.[107]

There is little doubt that much of the apathy of the poor shown in the securing of free places at the endowed schools stemmed from economic motives. Giving evidence before a Select Committee, Fitch stated that exhibitions of less than £25 per annum were of little use to the poor: £10 would probably be used for the payment of fees, the rest for maintenance.[108] In practice, the amounts awarded were, on the whole, some way below this figure.[109] The Commissioners were not unaware of this situation, but considered that fixing a higher value to the exhibitions also had its dangers:

> With regard to the charge that scholarships and exhibitions, though open to the poorest children, are, in fact, useless to them, because they do not repay the indirect cost of the additional education for which they provide, it must be recognised that it is difficult to fix the precise mean between a scholarship too small to maintain the child of a poor parent at a secondary school, and one so large as to excite undue competition by children of a higher rank in life.[110]

But this policy did not face up to the fact that the value of exhibitions awarded did not, as a rule, cover more than basic needs. The provision of text-books, for example, was to come out of the exhibition. At Petworth, Sussex, in 1895, a working man's daughter competed for, and won, one of the exhibitions to the value of £15 per annum for four years. The following year, the father wrote to the Commissioners explaining why the exhibition had not been taken up: 'I thought she was fortunate in winning it at the time, but found on making inquiry it was quite out of her reach simply because her Father was a working-man and not able to put his hands in his pocket for another £20 or £30 per year to take up the Exhibition.'[111]

It was reported by an Assistant Commissioner at approximately the same date that at Emanuel School, Wandsworth, the best boys with good qualifications often declined the scholarships into the school, one of the grounds being the inability to provide the necessary uniform; under the scheme the governors were empowered to assist with its purchase, but had not acted.[112]

It is clear that, in instances of poor children who were academically successful at an endowed school, further education was almost impossible because of the lack of leaving exhibitions.[113] The excellent management of Wyggeston Grammar School, Leicester, had drawn the following comment from A. F. Leach: 'I have small hesitation in saying that this is, considering all things, one of the most, if not the most, successful schools in the country under the Endowed Schools Act ... all sorts of conditions of boys flock to the school.'[114] Eighteen of the thirty-four exhibitions into the school were taken up by 'children of artisans or of those of a similar class', the rest being lower middle-class. The following extract from the Report on the school is of interest, as there are few records of the after-school careers of poor children attending endowed schools which have survived: it also illustrates the handicaps imposed by the lack of leaving exhibitions from the school:

> Of former Exhibitioners in the school numbering 66 – ten are employed as Teachers in Public Elementary Schools mostly in Leicester, several of whom have taken degrees in London University; and all but one of these appear to belong to the working classes, including in that term a Police Constable and a Sergeant in the Army: four have taken good places in the Cambridge Local Examinations and degrees at London and are Masters of Grammar Schools. These are all sons of working people.
>
> Several have been offered sizarships at Cambridge on the result of the Local Examinations but, in the absence of any exhibitions from the school, have been unable to accept the offer.
>
> One, the son of a Framework-knitter is Librarian of Watford Public Library; another the son of a dressmaker has taken an M.A. degree and Bachelor of Medicine at Glasgow University and is said to be distinguishing himself in his medical career; one, the son of a scene-shifter at the theatre is officially mentioned as the boy who ought to have gone to College but there being no Exhibitions from the school could not and is now a clerk in a shoe factory.
>
> On the whole there can be no doubt (1) that these Exhibitions fall into the hands of the poor, or the real working-classes or quite the lower middle-classes, (2) that these are of real profit in a large number of cases to the winner, but (3) that a great deal more good would have been done in many deserving cases if it were not that *There are No Exhibitions from the School.*[115]

In contrast to this, the winners of scholarships from public elementary schools to Queen Mary's School, Walsall, did noticeably better in their post-school careers than those boys who won scholarships from the lower school to the high school, and those already in the high school who won scholarships.[116] The lack of familiarity with some of the subjects of the grammar school curriculum possibly placed the elementary school boys at a disadvantage as compared with those who were already at the school and this was reflected in examination results.

An important source of information on the working of schemes and the awarding of scholarships and exhibitions with special reference to public elementary schools is contained in the *Fortescue Return* of 1883,[117] named after Earl Fortescue who requested this information in the House of Lords. Questionnaires were issued to the endowed schools, and detailed replies from twenty first grade schools, seventy second grade schools and seventy-six third grade schools were published. Table 1 (p. 115) shows the distribution of scholarships at the schools.

It can be seen that in the first grade schools 9 per cent of the scholarship holders were public elementary school boys: in the second grade, 39 per cent and in the third grade schools, 56 per cent. The policy of the Commissioners, which was to ensure that provision was made in schemes for exhibitions and scholarships, was not entirely successful: some 20 per cent of the schools under schemes in 1882 were either unable or did not wish to put the relevant clauses into operation.

As has been noted earlier, there were two dimensions of a scholarship or exhibition which were of importance to poor boys, namely (i) its value, and (ii) its duration.

(i) *Value of Scholarships*

Table 2 (p. 116), showing the value of scholarships, has been compiled from a scrutiny of the submitted returns of the 166 schools making up the Fortescue Return.

This Table should be read with a number of points in mind. Some schools did not state the actual amounts awarded and must therefore be excluded. It does not include girls, as the numbers are too small to be representative. Day scholars only are shown. The abnormally high figure for £5 scholarships is accounted for by the United Westminster Schools' award of 150 scholarships of this value. 'Exemptions' means the payment of fees only. However tentative the conclusion which might be drawn, the Table does

TABLE 1

DISTRIBUTION OF SCHOLARSHIPS
TO DECEMBER, 1880

	Secondary schools under scheme making Returns	Secondary schools in which scholarships were held in 1882	Number of Scholarships			Number of Scholarships held by children from Public Elementary Schools		
			Boys	Girls	Total	Boys	Girls	Total
First Grade	59	45	771	28	799	66	13	79
Second Grade	124	95	575	40	615	233	18	251
Third Grade	115	79	1,019	228	1,247	574	90	664
Total	298	219	2,365	296	2,661	873	121	994
Add from Returns of Schemes independent of any particular school, omitting those held at public elementary schools					185	–	–	109
Add Exhibitions held at secondary schools by scholars of elementary schools under the Scheme					42	–	–	42
					2,989			1,145

Source: Fortescue Return House of Lords, P.P. 1884, X.

TABLE 2

VALUE OF SCHOLARSHIPS
OF PUBLIC ELEMENTARY BOYS IN ENDOWED SCHOOLS
TO DECEMBER 1880

	Number of Schools	Value in £ sterling								Exemptions		Total number of boys
		1-5		6-10		11-15		16-17				
		No.	%	No.	%	No.	%	No.	%	No.	%	
First Grade	20	16	33	8	16	14	29	3	6	8	16	49
Second Grade	70	40	27	64	43	9	6	2	2	32	22	147
Third Grade	76	264	74	30	9	5	1	5	1	53	15	357

Average Value: First Grade   £8 13s.
                Second Grade £7 18s.
                Third Grade   £4 16s.

Source: Fortescue Return House of Lords, P.P. 1884. X.

show that the sums awarded to elementary school boys were inadequate to maintain a boy at an endowed school, according to Fitch's calculations (see p. 112 above).

(ii) *Duration of Scholarships*

Of equal importance was the duration of the scholarships, i.e., the period for which the award was tenable at the school (see Table 3).

TABLE 3

DURATION OF SCHOLARSHIPS
FOR PUBLIC ELEMENTARY SCHOOL BOYS IN ENDOWED SCHOOLS

	1 Year	2 Years	3 Years	4 Years	School Life
	%	%	%	%	%
First Grade	30	10	25	-	-
Second Grade	23	16	22	2	4
Third Grade	21	13	16	3	6

Source: Fortescue Return House of Lords, PP 1884.X

Again, the returns were not in all cases specific: where the duration of the scholarship is not stated it has had to be omitted from the Table. Nevertheless, some interesting facts emerge from the figures. It will be noticed that no first grade schools gave awards for more than three years, although the leaving age was eighteen; the duration of the award was hardly sufficient for an able boy to complete a course of study without outside financial help. Both second and third grade schools made liberal provision for those boys who would benefit from an extended stay at school: 5 per cent of second grade scholarships were for the duration of school life or for four years, and 9 per cent of third grade scholarships were for similar periods.

In sum, it can be said that the relationships existing between the different types of schools had the greatest bearing on the question of the poor gaining admission to the schools. The value and duration of awards were equally potent factors in determining his length of stay at the school. The Commissioners did not attempt to evaluate or interpret the Fortescue Return, but noted that 42 per cent of the scholarships were awarded to children from public elementary schools; more illusorily, it was claimed that the Return showed the existence of a system of education 'whereby children of the poorest, or specially qualified to profit by superior instruction, may find it within their reach.'[118]

NOTES

1. 27th Annual Report of the Charity Commissioners for 1879, P.P. 1880, XVIII, p. 6.
2. E. F. Hinder, *The Schoolmaster in the Gutter or a Plea for the Middle Class* (1883), p. 16.
3. F. C. Gomez, 'The Endowed Schools Act, 1869 – A Middle-Class Conspiracy? The South-West Lancashire Evidence', *Journal of Educational Administration and History,* Vol. VI, No. 1, 1974, p. 16.
   There were, however, several attempts from 1870 onwards, to provide free education in elementary schools. It was not until September 1891, after the passing of the Education Act, that children were admitted free to elementary schools on a large scale. See G. Sutherland, *Policy Making in Elementary Education, 1870-1895* (1973), Chapters 6 and 10.
4. J. C. Tarver, *Essays on Secondary Education* (1898), p. 196. Cf. letter from 'Headmaster' in *Kendal Mercury,* 7 September 1883: 'If then, the number of free scholars be greater than that of the paying scholars, or even form any large proportion of the whole number, the influence for good will *pro tanto* be seriously impaired: and the school will, as a whole, take its tone from the boys of the lower standard of moral character.'
5. *The Macclesfield Courier and Herald,* 15 January 1876.
6. For a sociological analysis of the origins of the Elementary Education Act and its subsequent impact, see Helen M. Lynd, *England in the 1880s* (Cass, 1945), pp. 365-77.
   Another factor which must be considered is that of the high cost to the middle classes of educating their sons. This caused ill-feeling towards those who obtained such an education without payment. For cost of careers in this period, see J. A. Banks, *Prosperity and Parenthood* (1953), p. 173 ff., and cost of schooling p. 188 ff.
7. Hinder, op. cit., p. 27.
8. C. S. Kenny, *Endowed Charities. The True Principles of Legislation with regard to Property Given for Charitable or other Public Uses* (1880), pp. 176-7.
9. P.P. 1884. House of Commons, LXI. For fuller details, see A. B. Robertson, 'Children, Teachers and Society: The Over-pressure Controversy, 1880-1886', *British Journal of Educational Studies,* Vol. 20, No. 3, 1972, pp. 315-23.
10. Op. cit., p. 77 of the Report. Browne's Report, which was an example of special pleading more than an objective medical report, approached the truth in the following part: 'The children want blood, and we offer them a little brain-polish; they ask for bread and receive a problem; for milk, and the tonic sol-fa system is introduced to them.' Fitch, at that time Chief H.M.I. of Schools, had unsuspectingly invited Browne to accompany him on his inspection of schools in the poorer parts of London. At the end of Browne's Report, Fitch

appended a Memorandum, strongly disagreeing with the former's conclusions. Quoting the sentence above, Fitch wrote: 'The answer to this is that a School is established for the purposes of instruction and not for the purpose of dispensing new milk. And I trust the statesmen and philanthropists who are now considering this difficult and anxious question of national education will not confuse the issue by mixing up with it the administration of food and medicine to the children of the poor. It is already a drawback to the success of the Education Act that it has unfortunately done a little to diminish the area of parental responsibility. To enforce, in regard to any human duty, a legal obligation, is to weaken, in some degree the sense of moral obligation.'

11. *Compact Dictionary of National Biography* (1975), Vol. II, p. 2574.
12. Collings' political activity on behalf of rural labourers is described in J. Collings and J. L. Green, *Life of Rt. Hon. Jesse Collings* (1920), Part II.
13. Select Committee on Endowed Schools Act 1887, Q. 7709, op. cit.
14. As a member of the Birmingham Endowed Schools Committee, he told a public meeting in the town in 1871 that the cost per head to the Grammar School foundation was £20, 'while at the same time there were 21,000 poor children about the streets, with equal rights and equal needs, who never had one farthing.' *Birmingham Daily Gazette,* 2 March 1871.
15. The full story of the Scarning School case can be followed in the following references: PRO Ed. 21/12996, PRO Ed. 49/5526; *Norfolk News,* 6 December 1879; *Daily News,* 23 September 1882.
16. For further details, see A. N. Willson, *A History of Collyer's School* (1965), pp. 142-9; PRO Ed. 27/4791; *The Horsham Advertiser,* 15 October 1881; *Sussex Daily News,* 9 August 1883; *Daily News,* 20 December 1883.
17. The West Lavington case lasted from 1883 to 1891 before it was finally settled. Amongst the many references are the following: PRO Ed. 27/5291-4; *Devizes and Wiltshire Gazette,* 11 October 1883; *Pall Mall Gazette,* 5 February 1884; *The Times,* 11 August 1885; *The Democrat,* 2 January 1886; *Morning Post,* 13 October 1886. The Dauntsey Charity, Cabinet Paper CAB 37/29, 28 January 1894. Select Committee on the Charity Commission 1884.
18. Pamphleteers had been expressing this view since the investigation into the endowed schools had begun. See, for example, attempts to explain why experiments in this field had been unsuccessful in Rev. W. Pound's pamphlet, *Remarks Upon English Education in Nineteenth Century* (1886). Section I is headed 'English Education is a Class Education according to the Social Position and Prospects of the Boy'. An interesting explanation which would account for the opposition to the admittance of poor boys into Endowed Schools is instanced in S. G. Checkland, 'Growth and Progress: the Nineteenth Century View in Great Britain', *Economic History Review,* August 1959.
19. 25th Annual Report of the Charity Commissioners for 1877, P.P. 1878, XXIV, p. 9.
20. Ware Grammar School, PRO Ed. 27/1742, Minute, D. C. Richmond, 25 April 1895.
21. Except in special cases such as the Emanuel Scheme, where it was stated that scholarships for elementary schools shall be for 'poor' children. 1884 Select Committee on the Charitable Trusts Acts, P.P. 1884, IX, Q. 3599.
22. Balshaw's School, Leyland, PRO Ed. 27/2130a.
23. The term 'Charity Commissioners' is used here with reference to the period after the transfer of the powers of the Endowed School Commissioners to the former body after 1874. In fact, an Endowed Schools Department was formed by the Commission and all officers who had been on the staff of the Endowed School Commission were continued in their respective posts in the new

Department. 23rd Annual Report of the Charity Commissioners for 1875, P.P. 1876, XX, p. 6.

24. Balshaw's School, Leyland, PRO Ed. 27/2130a.

25. In some instances, the Commissioners proposed to provide finance for elementary schools in order to improve their efficiency and produce promising scholars. One such attempt in Essex to promote a Colne District Elementary Schools Improvement and Reward Scheme was rejected by the Earls Colne Grammar School trustees on two grounds. First, that it was a misappropriation of their funds, and second, that the Grammar School was not founded for the education of the labouring classes: A. D. Merson, *Earls Colne Grammar School, Essex. A History* (1975), pp. 100-1.

26. Re G. Fisher and Jones' Reports, (1858), p. 529.

27. Ulverston Grammar School, PRO Ed. 27/2296.

28. Sir George Young in connection with the Ulverston case, 14 August 1901, wrote: 'On the decided case quoted, the drafting in these schedules was originally settled, and we have always adhered to their interpretation.'
   Hobhouse stated that up to 1872, the Commission predominantly awarded scholarships to be held in elementary rather than grammar schools. 1884 Select Committee on the Charitable Trusts Act, P.P. 1884 IX, Q.2872.

29. 1886 Select Committee on the Endowed Schools Acts, P.P. 1886, IX, Q. 879.

30. Ibid., Q. 6261.

31. Ibid., Q. 1397.

32. 1886 Select Committee on the Endowed Schools Acts, P.P. 1886, IX, Q. 881.

33. Petworth, Taylor's Exhibition Endowment, PRO Ed. 27/4815.

34. Alderman Newton's Charity, Leicester, PRO Ed. 27/2415, Minute, 15 March 1892.

35. This can be seen in a survey undertaken by Isaac Sharpless, President of Haverford College, Pennsylvania in the late 1880s, to establish the number of English public elementary school boys who, by successes in examination had worked their way through to Oxford and Cambridge. Sharpless found twenty such boys at the Universities, with slightly more at the latter than the former, making a total of 1 per cent of the students. Even this figure exaggerates the number of poor elementary boys gaining such successes. I. Sharpless, *English Education in the Elementary and Secondary Schools* (1892), p. 80.

36. This can be illustrated by the King's School, Rochester, where the Rev. R. Whiston, the Headmaster of the School at the time of the Endowed Schools Act, interpreted the statutes of the Cathedral, which provided for the education of twenty 'poor boys' at the Grammar School, to mean sons of clergymen, schoolmasters and of officers in the Army and Navy with a good education and a good knowledge of all aspects of Latin. Ralph Arnold, *The Whiston Matter* (1962), p. 89. In 1869, the inhabitants of Rochester and Strood complained to the Commissioners that the entrance examination into the school was unfair to children who had not received private coaching. The Dean and Chapter admitted that the younger and poorer candidates were at a disadvantage but did not favour unrestricted competitive examination. Rochester Cathedral Grammar School, PRO Ed. 27/1935, 16 December 1869.

37. Even in instances of an enlightened headmaster, such as W. E. Pryke of the Royal Grammar School, Lancaster, who endowed scholarships for poor boys out of his pocket and admitted more than the maximum number of Corporation scholars allowed, pressure was put to bear on the boys by middle-class parents. The current complaint in the '80s was 'who would like to be a free boy at the Grammar School? Not many people. It is the case that free boys at that Institution and assisted boys have led a life of torture on account

of the stigma.' Quoted in A. L. Murray, *The Royal Grammar School, Lancaster* (1952), p. 174. See also C. Cookson, 'The Scholarship Question', in *Thirteen Essays in Education* (1891), pp. 104-5.

38. Examples are given in J. Lawson, *The Endowed Grammar Schools of East Yorkshire* (1962), p. 30.
39. See also, I. E. Gray and W. E. Potter, *Ipswich School 1400-1950* (1950), p. 133; and Ipswich Grammar School, PRO Ed. 27/4379.
40. Walsall, Queen Mary's Grammar School, PRO Ed. 27/4323. Cl. 73 stated: 'The Master shall receive a fixed stipend of £75 per annum. He shall also receive payment according to the number of boys in the Lower School; that is to say, such sum, calculated on such a scale, uniform or graduated, as may be agreed between him and the Governors, being not less than £1 yearly for each boy.'
41. Norwich Grammar School, PRO Ed. 27/3613.
42. D. M. May, *The History of Lymm Grammar School* (1960), pp. 100-1.
43. W. Lempriere, *A History of the Girls' School of Christ's Hospital* (1924), p. 55.
44. Bryce Report, Vol. VI, P.P. 1895, XLVIII.
45. Wigan Grammar School, PRO Ed. 27/2330.
46. Emanuel School, Wandsworth, PRO Ed. 27/3375.
47. At Ashby-de-la-Zouch, Leicestershire, ten foundation scholarships were established at the Grammar School. Only if the English school failed to compete for them were they then made available for elementary school pupils in the Ashby district. L. Fox, *A Country Grammar School. A History of Ashby-de-la-Zouch Grammar School through Four Centuries 1567-1967* (1967), p. 79.
48. Sons of clerks were often mentioned by headmasters in their correspondence with the Commissioners as very 'deserving scholars', e.g. King's Lynn, King Edward VI Grammar School, PRO Ed. 27/3592, Letter 12 May 1883.
49. It would be interesting to trace the consequences of grammar school headmasters being elected to school boards. At Thorne, Yorkshire, the Governors of the Grammar School informed the Commissioners that the headmaster had been re-elected to the School Board: 'The Governors, the School Board and the Master, who acted as its clerk, are placed in a very anomalous position, giving occasion for various self-evident complications'. Brooke's Grammar School, Thorne, PRO Ed. 27/6214, 28 February 1893.
50. 1873 Select Committee on the Endowed Schools Act (1869), Q.1421.
51. Ibid., Q. 1779.
52. Ibid., Q. 1781.
53. Chertsey, Sir William Perkins' Scholarship, PRO Ed. 27/4463.
54. Stone, Alleyne's Grammar School, PRO Ed. 27/4303. Letter from the governors to the Commissioners, 6 April 1891.
55. Tideswell Grammar School, PRO Ed. 27/606. Report by Mr. Leach on state of school, July 1886.
56. Calday Grange Grammar School, West Kirby, Cheshire, PRO Ed. 27/240.
57. Fitch, giving evidence on this topic, condemned the necessity for special preparation in many entrance examinations to grammar schools. 'For the protection of the interests of deserving scholars among the poor, the examination of a higher school ought never in its requirements to go beyond the ordinary work of the school below it; it ought to be such as to pick out the most clever and diligent boy, but it ought not to require supplementary teaching of any kind; for instance, even the Latin Grammar. On that point it would be easy to collect a great deal of testimony.' 1886 Select Committee on Endowed Schools Acts, Q. 1124.
58. Bromsgrove Grammar School, PRO Ed. 27/5327, 20 July 1899.

59. Mansfield Grammar School, PRO Ed. 27/3784. A. F. Leach's Report, 13 April 1889.
60. Ipswich Grammar School, PRO Ed. 27/4381, Mr. Eddis' Report, 7 November 1892.
61. 1873 Select Committee on the Endowed Schools Act (1869), P.P. 1873, VIII, Q. 270.
62. *Journal of the National Association for the Promotion of Social Science,* Vol. 9, No. 5, 27 June 1876. The first scholarship awarded to a London School Board elementary school boy led to his subsequently becoming captain of the school and later a Fellow of Trinity. A. E. Douglas-Smith, *The City of London School* (2nd edn.) (1965), p. 202.
63. Sharp's School, Rothbury, PRO Ed. 27/3773. Letter, J. P. Ridley to Commissioners, 12 September 1901.
64. Audlem Grammar School, PRO Ed. 27/4198. Leach's Report, 13 July 1888.
65. W. E. Marsden, 'Education and Social Geography of Nineteenth Century Towns and Cities' in D. A. Reeder (ed.), *Urban Education in the Nineteenth Century* (1977), p. 69.
66. Emanuel School, PRO Ed. 27/3379. Mitcheson's Report, 5-6 February 1895.
67. L. Tripp, *Queen Elizabeth School, Barnet* (1935), pp. 135-6.
68. Bingley Grammar School, PRO Ed. 27/5704.
69. In rural schools, where economy was essential, there was even more incentive to employ monitors rather than assistant teachers, P. Horn, *Education in Rural England 1880-1914* (1978), p. 80.
70. King Edward VI Foundation, Birmingham, PRO Ed. 27/4893.
71. M. Cox, *A History of Sir John Deane's Grammar School, Northwich* (1975), p. 232.
72. 1886 Select Committee on the Endowed Schools Acts, Q. 1268.
73. 29th Annual Report of the Charity Commissioners for 1881, P.P. 1882, XX, p. 15.
74. John Morley, *The Struggle for National Education* (3rd edn., 1874), p. 31.
75. Wigan Grammar School, PRO Ed. 27/2331.
76. *The Morning News,* 18 September 1875.
77. *Birmingham Morning Post,* 14 May 1876.
78. Letter to the Charity Commissioners, PRO Ed. 27/4911, 29 December 1885.
79. 1886 Select Committee on the Endowed Schools Acts, P.P. 1886, IX, Q. 3954. For an outline history of Birmingham schools and the schemes of 1875, 1878 and 1883, see J. H. Muirhead, *Birmingham Institutions* (1911), pp. 549-53.
80. For example, at St. Olave's, Southwark, all the scholarships from the public elementary schools were taken up by children from middle-class homes. H. C. Smith, Governor of the School in Evidence before the 1886 Select Committee on Endowed Schools Acts, P.P. 1886, XI, Q.4396.
81. Ibid., Q. 1682. For background, see J. W. Kirby, *History of the Roan School and its Founder* (1929), pp. 134-7.
82. 1873 Select Committee on the Endowed Schools Act, Q. 1280.
83. King Edward VI Foundation, Birmingham, PRO Ed. 27/4893, 21 April 1871.
84. 1886 Select Committee on the Endowed Schools Acts, P.P. 1886, IX, Q. 990.
85. *Norfolk Chronicle,* 20 June 1877, Report of the Grammar School Committee.
86. 'That institution [the Middle School] though or because it was more a school of the city and more loved by the city generally, has throughout been anathema to the senior institution, and its later conspicuous successes were a cause of further irritation.' J. W. Saunders, *A History of the Norwich Grammar School* (1932), p. 380.
87. J. Sergeaunt, *A History of Bedford School* (1925), p. 93.
88. The rivalry between the schools dated back some time: R. S. Wright, reporting

on the school, 6 June 1866: 'At the present time there is no connexion between the Grammar School and the English Schools. Few boys ever rise from these into it. Their systems and books are different and the few who rise are at a disadvantage; similarly, few pass from the National into the higher English schools.'

89. Memorial, Bedford School, PRO Ed. 27/9, 10 January 1873. The Modern School assumed its title in 1877. L. R. Conisbee, *Bedford Modern School. Its Origins and Growth* (1964), p. 31.

90. See Sergeaunt, op. cit., p. 82: 'he hated Liberalism and he shuddered when he learnt incidentally that one of his boys had been reading "Essays and Reviews" '.

91. Bedford, PRO Ed. 27/9, 29 March 1873.

92. Rev. Charles Evans to Charity Commissioners, PRO Ed. 27/4911, 24 December 1885.

93. Walsall, Queen Mary's Grammar School, PRO Ed. 27/4323. Mr. Stanton's Report, February 1871.

94. Ashby-de-la Zouch Endowed School, PRO Ed. 27/2368. R. Durnford's Report, 12 May 1883.

95. Ibid., A. F. Leach, Report, 28 January 1893.

96. As Leach remarked, 'In Latin this is not surprising as the Master has only learnt it at an advanced age in life in order to teach it.' Report, 26 July 1892.

97. Darwin Wilmot, *A Short History of the Grammar School in Macclesfield* (1910), pp. 86-7.

98. According to a Return, Michaelmas 1894 (Macclesfield, PRO Ed. 27/274), an analysis of professional and 'middle class' occupations of parents in the two schools gives an almost identical percentage: 42 per cent in the Grammar School and 41 per cent in the Modern School.

Return by School, End of Michaelmas Term 1894

Grammar School		Modern School	
14 out of 100	Silk Manufacturers, Merchants or Brokers	14 out of 124	Farmers
		9	Silk Manufacturers
8	Solicitors	7	Land Agents and Surveyors
7	Bank and Insurance Managers	6	Schoolmasters
6	Clergymen	5	Chemists
4	Doctors	3	Bank Managers
2	Accountants	2	Solicitors
1	Assistant School Inspector	1	Doctor
		4	Auctioneers or Accountants

99. Ibid., Letter to Commissioners, 1 October 1893.

100. Macclesfield, PRO Ed. 27/274. See Charity Commissioners' Minute, 23 September 1895: accounts for 1894 showed a deficit for the Foundation of £413.

101. 1887 Select Committee on the Endowed Schools Acts, P.P. 1887, IX. Report, v.5.

Apathy too was important: see letter of Joseph Chamberlain to Morley, 19 August 1873: 'I have long felt that there is not force in the Education question to make it the sole fighting issue for our friends. From the commencement it has failed to evoke any great popular enthusiasm. Education for the ignorant cannot have the meaning that belonged to Bread for the Starving... the assistance of the working classes is not to be looked for without much extension of the argument.' Quoted J. L. Garvin, *The Life of Joseph Chamberlain*, (1932), Vol. 1, p. 146.

102. Tideswell Grammar School, Derbyshire, PRO Ed. 27/606. Leach's Report, July 1886.

103. Rev. J. B. Lee, *Middle Class Education and the Working of the Endowed Schools Act* (1885), p. 36.

104. Wigan Grammar School, PRO Ed. 27/2330.

105. 1884 Select Committee on the Charitable Trusts Acts, op. cit., Evidence. Q. 1720.

106. Micheldever School, Hampshire, PRO Ed. 27/1522. Letter to Endowed Schools Commission, 23 February 1870.

107. Barnard Castle North Eastern County School, PRO Ed. 27/954. E. Wells to Commissioners, 30 January 1892.

108. 1886 Select Committee on Endowed Schools Acts, P.P. 1886, IX, Q. 1224.

109. See the Fortescue Return for confirmation of this, p. 114 below.

110. 1886 Select Committee on the Endowed Schools Acts, P.P. 1887, IX. Report, v. 6.

111. Petworth, Taylor's Exhibition Endowment, PRO Ed. 27/4815. Letter from Henry Cooper to Charity Commissioners, 23 May 1895.

112. Emanuel School, PRO Ed. 27/3375. Mitcheson's Report, 5-6 February 1895.

113. But see 31st Annual Report of the Charity Commissioners for 1883, P.P. 1884, XXII, p. 19, which complained that in a large number of schemes, the scholarships and exhibitions clauses were either imperfectly carried out or disregarded by the governing body, who treated them as optional, and used the money as revenue. The Commissioners pointed out that this was unlawful and that the money was to be used to help deserving scholars.

114. Wyggeston's School, Leicester, PRO Ed. 27/2418. Report, 28 October 1889.

115. Ibid., Leach's Report.

116. Queen Mary's Grammar School, Walsall, PRO Ed. 27/4326. 'List of Careers of Public Elementary School Scholarship Holders 1877-1888.'

117. Return to an Order of the House of Lords dated 31 July 1883. Returns of Scholarships and Schemes made by and approved under the Endowed Schools Acts up to 3 December 1880, as mentioned in 13th Annual Report of the Charity Commission. P.P. 1884, X.

118. 31st Annual Report of the Charity Commissioners for 1883, P.P. 1884, XXII, p. 18.

CHAPTER 4

Governing Bodies

The composition of the governing bodies of endowed schools after the 1869 Act raised many problems. It will be shown in this chapter that the successful challenge to Church domination of such bodies by Nonconformists led to a widening of the basis of representation; that the emergence of politics in local government raised the question of the method of electing representative governors to governing bodies; and that the newly-created school boards desired to participate in the government of endowed schools: all these elements affected, in various ways, the chances of a poor boy receiving an education at such a school.

It must not be underestimated how powerful an influence the governing body was in this respect. Recalling the early days of the Commission, D. R. Fearon told a Select Committee:

> ... with regard to the principle of admitting the poor scholars from public elementary schools into grammar schools, that was a thing which was most strongly contended against. Over and over again, when I met the trustees of an old grammar school which was proud of its connections with Universities, and, perhaps, of its classical distinctions in times past, I used to have the very greatest difficulty in persuading the head master, that the school would not be ruined if working men's children, poor men's children, selected from the public elementary schools, were admitted. I can recollect rooms in which I have sat; I can see now the faces of the gentlemen sitting round, with whom I had been discussing, horrified at the thought of working men's children being admitted to the benefits of these schools.[1]

Up to 1869, the main elements of a governing body were *ex*

125

officio and representative governors, elected in a variety of ways, depending on the nature of the charity.[2] In the case of charitable institutions where subscribers possessed voting rights, votes were often purchased.[3] The Schools Inquiry Commission had proposed that the system of governing bodies should be the responsibility of Provincial Councils for Education.[4] Although the Councils never materialized, the Endowed Schools Commissioners stated that bodies constructed on a single principle were unhealthy. Section 10 of the Endowed Schools Act gave the Commissioners wide powers to alter the constitution of governing bodies and change the composition of such bodies by dismissal if necessary. Henceforth, governing bodies were to consist of three elements: *ex officio*, representative and co-optative. This would ensure that the widest possible range of representation would be secured for these bodies.

The problem of putting this ideal into practice was a difficult one, as the Commissioners at an early stage admitted:

> In many places suitable popular constituencies do not exist with any legal organisation; and they can only be organized by Scheme at great risk of complication and expense, and, if they are thus organised, it must be very uncertain how such new bodies will discharge the duty cast on them. Again, many persons are well-suited to do good service on a Trust by reason of their habits of business, or of their knowledge of scholastic affairs, or the possession of tact or judgment; qualities well-known to their associates, but not known or capable of being known to a large public constituency.[5]

Ready to hand to fill this gap was the clergy. It was an open secret[6] that Hobhouse had written the 'Memorandum as to the Legality of the Appointment of Ecclesiastical Corporations or Persons to be *ex officio* Governors of Educational Endowments not falling within s. 19 of the Endowed Schools Act 1869' as an Appendix to the 1st Report of the Endowed Schools Commissioners published in 1872. In the Memorandum, Hobhouse had enumerated the reasons for favouring the appointment, where possible, of clergy as governors:

> He is the principal parish officer; he is Chairman of the vestry; he is owner of a freehold property; he is bound by law to be upon the spot; he is, either by himself or with others, keeper of

the parish records; he is the legal representative of the Church and its appurtenances; and in these respects he is bound to perform, and does perform, duties for all the parishioners, whether they attend his ordinary ministrations or not. By the combined law and practice of the Church he (often alone in the parish) must have attained a certain amount of intellectual culture, evidenced by a university degree or some like credentials. . . . The services of such men ought not to be lost, and they should be appointed to manage endowments in their own neighbourhood in the way in which their services can best be procured, whether by making them *ex officio* or co-optative governors.

The appointment of a vicar to a governing body of a school, however, often generated a strong feeling of resentment in a locality. To many of the poor who were themselves Dissenters[7] the Church represented an unchanging and unchangeable order of things. The forces opposing Church domination in educational matters were actively led by Dissenters of all denominations who found a common meeting ground politically in the Liberal Party. This combination, in the form of the 'Birmingham Radicals', was responsible for promoting the National Education League, whose aim was to secure universal, free, secular and compulsory education. Although a great body of Nonconformists continued to oppose State education long after the 1870 Elementary Education Act,[8] nevertheless there were many who campaigned enthusiastically on its behalf. The League also worked in close association with the Trades Union movement, especially after the formation of the Trades Union Congress, whose long-term policy for education followed closely that of the League.[9] There was thus an identity of interest between the Nonconformist and the skilled working class – that of breaking down the barriers of educational privilege in order that their sons could be suitably educated.

This natural link was sensed by R. W. Dale, the militant Birmingham Congregational minister[10] who, in an address to the Congregational Union in 1869 on his favourite theme of attracting a greater number of the working classes to church, called for 'a great army of preachers [to] rise up among the working people themselves'.[11] Although the League itself failed ultimately to achieve all its aims, the support of the more articulate sections of the poor for Dissenters in their attempt to gain representation on the governing bodies of endowed schools in the 1870s naturally followed.

The 1869 Act had, in theory at least, abolished the religious qualification for governors in all except Church schools coming under s. 19.[12] In practice, it was a more difficult proposition. Before 1860, it was assumed that as scholars attending endowed schools received instruction in the religious teachings of the Church of England, the trustees should be of that denomination. Lord Cranworth's Act of that year opened the schools to all denominations, giving the pupils a claim to have their interests protected by the appointment of trustees chosen from other than Church candidates. Attempts to elect Dissenters to governorships usually ended unsuccessfully in the Law Courts, the most important case being that of Ilminster Grammar School.[13] The mood of the 1860s is caught in the following letter to a newspaper of the time: 'No doubt Dissenters are equally well-qualified as Churchmen are for the office of Trustee, but this is not the question at issue. Let Dissenters manage their own schools, and let, as a reasonable request, Churchmen superintend the schools connected with their own belief.'[14]

Edward Miall, an influential Nonconformist, in August 1871 attacked Forster in the Commons for allowing, in the greater number of schemes, the *ex officio* governors to be chosen from the incumbents of the respective parishes.[15] Under R. W. Dale's leadership, the Central Nonconformist Committee, with its headquarters at Birmingham and with some 100 associated committees in different parts of the country, waged a ceaseless campaign to bring to the public notice, amongst other matters, the lack of representation of Dissenters on governing bodies. Frank Schnadhorst, the Committee's Secretary, made an analysis of 85 schemes of the Commissioners drawn up in its first three years. Of the 431 co-optative governors appointed, 43 were Nonconformists, 385 were Church of England and 3 Roman Catholics: in over fifty schemes there were no Nonconformists among the co-optatives. The political allegiances were calculated at 313 Conservatives and 128 Liberals.[16] The link between politics and religion was clearly shown.[17] Dale's efforts were rewarded to the extent that Church *ex officio* governors were henceforth few in number.[18]

The Dissenters' determination to gain representation on the

governing bodies of schools was equally matched by the Church's opposition to the secularization of the endowed schools. Since the 1870 Education Act, the sting had, to a certain extent, been taken out of Church teaching in the public elementary schools. A dilemma confronting the Church was that the application of the funds of an elementary endowed school to form a middle-class foundation could weaken the Church's hold over the former, by leaving the support of the elementary schools to the ratepayers. At Chertsey, Surrey, for example, where such a scheme was proposed, 'Mr. Scott [the Vicar] could not disguise from himself the fact that this solution must lead to the establishment of a School Board, and consequently to the absence of any provision for the education of the children of the poor in the principles of the Church of England, which would be a direct violation of the intentions of the Founder.'[19]

A slightly different problem arose regarding the principle on which the selection of representative governors, that is, those representing the 'popular element' of the community, should be based. This involved two things: firstly, the need for popular elections, thus making the system of selection democratic: secondly, that there should be a preponderance of representative over *ex officio* and co-optative governors. What in fact happened was that three different elements laid claim to be representative of the community: the ratepayers, the town councils, and the school boards. The struggle for control over the election of representative governors between these elements lasted well into the 1880s.

It is not surprising to find the suggestion that the representative element should constitute the majority of the trustees was widely opposed.[20] James Bryce, for example, disliked the principle on the grounds that the town council had been elected for some other purpose.[21] Many governing bodies raised the objection that such a system would be 'too democratic'.[22] At Birmingham, the 1873 scheme as proposed by the Commissioners would have given the burgesses responsibility for electing two-thirds of the governors of the King Edward School. Of the 50,000 burgesses of Birmingham, 40,000 were compound householders, occupiers of houses with a net annual value of less than £10 per annum, and so were exempt from paying rates: thus, it was argued, control of the government of the school would pass to representatives of compound household-ers. 'The action of the new scheme will be to raise the education in the elementary schools.'[23] At the other end of the scale, a rural parish – Evershott, Bedfordshire – afforded an illustration of the difficulty of introducing a large representative element into the governing body, to be elected by the parish:

> A good many of the appointments made under that scheme have been objected to by someone or other on the ground of the poverty or character of the person elected. It was an unfortunate case; a case in which the local gentry were inclined to take offence at our scheme, and to some extent they withdrew from the trust; and we were hard put to it to find trustees, and therefore we had rather a stronger representative element than we otherwise should have had.

An opposite point of view was taken by Sir John Swinburne, M.P. for Lichfield, who successfully conducted a one-man campaign to obtain for the ratepayer the right to elect, directly, representative governors for governing bodies. His argument was that by such a method, ratepayers would be encouraged to take a real interest in the schools, would take care that no abuses crept into the administration and make certain that no unnecessary expenses were incurred. The ratepayers would be free to elect any outside persons if they wished. Elections should be held during the day and voting was to be by a show of hands. Swinburne claimed that he had been instrumental in securing a scheme for a school at Stamfordham, Northumberland, in 1878, by which all the governors were elected by ratepayers.[24]

His unorthodox views were brought into prominence by an incident in the House of Commons in May 1886. Earlier that month, the Charity Commissioners had produced a scheme for Lowe's Charity, one of the richest in Lichfield: it provided for seven of the governors to be co-opted and the other five places to be filled by the town council. At 1 a.m. on the morning of 18 May 1886, when the Government benches were fairly empty, Swinburne's motion came before the House: 'That, in the opinion of this House, every scheme of the Charity Commissioners ought to provide for the majority of the Trustees or Managers being directly elected by the ratepayers in the locality to which the Charity extends.' Sir Lyon Playfair, then Vice-President of the Council, was unaware that such a Motion was coming on and resisted it because of the inclusion of the phrase 'every scheme of the Charity Commissioners'; in schemes for educational trusts, he believed that men with the requisite technical knowledge should be sought. Hugh Childers, the Home Secretary, was against this method of election on the ground of cost. Yearly elections would be necessary under this system at a cost of £200 to £300 annually.[25] Swinburne's motion was carried by a majority of 14 (73 to 59), but in the event had little effect on the Commissioners' policy in this sphere.

There were sound reasons for the Commissioners' lack of enthusiasm for voting by ratepayers.[26] Some fifty years previously, the passing of the Regulation of Parish Vestries Act in June 1818,[27] known as the 'Sturges-Bourne Act', after its sponsor William Sturges-Bourne,[28] had brought about reforms in the method of electing governors to charities at vestry meetings. Under s. 3 of the Act, those inhabitants who were assessed for the poor rate on any rent or profit to the value of £50 were entitled to one vote; for every £25 above this, one more vote was given, up to a total of six votes per person.

In a debate on the Third Reading of the Bill, Sturges-Bourne had outlined what he hoped to secure:

the object in view was, to follow the analogy of kirk sessions in Scotland, so far as the very different system of poor laws in England would admit. In Scotland, the wealthier classes had the greater influence in managing the provision for the poor. By this bill it was proposed to bring back the wealthier classes to attend parish vestries. Their absence was occasioned by the numbers and the clamour of others who attended, of whom some were connected with paupers, and some were employed in trades which made it their interest to be liberal to certain paupers. . . . He would appeal to any member, whether it was reasonable that one who paid a third, and even a half of the poor-rates, should have no more influence in vestries than one who paid the very lowest sum.[29]

One result of the Act was the creation of the 'cumulative vote', by which method the votes of a person could 'accumulate' for one of the candidates.[30] The Elementary Education Act of 1870 made use of this system, in a modified form, for the election of managers.[31] The ratepayers of a borough outside London, whose names appeared on the burgesses' roll, were entitled to 'give all such votes to one candidate, or may distribute them among the candidates as he thinks fit' (s. 29). The number of votes per person fluctuated between five and fifteen, except in London, where the number given was linked with the number to be elected to a Board. Inherent in the system was the possibility of freak results if a comparatively small number of voters 'cumulated' on one candidate.

A Select Committee was set up some fourteen years after the Forster Elementary Education Act to examine the system of voting and many abuses were discovered. One example will illustrate the general state of affairs. At the Brighton School Board elections in 1884 the Chairman of the Finance Committee, a schoolmaster who had given excellent service, was rejected after receiving 2,288 votes representing 879 voters. 'Of those elected who were standing independently, one of them, Mr. William Seal, who is an itinerant vendor of coffee and teacakes, stood fourth on the list, and he got altogether 3,642 votes. You notice that he was ahead of every single one of the members of the two parties who had practically carried on the work of the board. He got those 3,642 votes from only 412 people.'[32] Another disadvantage of the system was that it encouraged religious sects to enter candidates, so turning the election into a denominational battlefield.

Witnesses before the Select Committees on the Endowed Schools Acts expressed concern lest the system be applied to the election of representative governors in endowed schools.[33] That this method could be employed for such a purpose can be seen in the election of governors for Brewood Grammar School, Staffordshire. By the scheme of 1877, a second grade school was established; the Commissioners advised that if a poll was demanded for the election of governors at the vestry meetings, the voting would be *per capita* and not under the provisions of the Sturges-Bourne Act. Ten years later, A. F. Leach found the advice given be unconvincing: 'I understand that in other cases contrary advice had been given. A Select Vestry is subject to the same rules as other vestries and there seems to be nothing to prevent s. 3 of 58 c.III c. 69 [i.e., Sturges-Bourne Act] from applying to the election of Charitable Trusts as well as to Guardians under a local Act'.[34]

Similar troubles to those which had plagued school board elections arose out of the Charity Commissioners' use of the cumulative system of voting, raising in an acute form denominational difficulties. One instance of this which achieved national prominence was that of the election of governors for Crosthwaite High School, Keswick, Westmorland.

The school, predominantly Church in character, had been remodelled by the Commissioners under a scheme of 1882. Ten of the twelve governors were to be Anglicans, the remaining two vacancies being filled by Dissenters, all holding office for five years; election of five of the governors was to be by the ratepayers. One of the Nonconformist members resigned in 1887 and at a vestry meeting, another Nonconformist was elected in his place, but he later declined to take office. A further vestry meeting was necessary and was held on 8 September 1887. Two candidates were nominated: Mumberson, a Dissenter, and Wilson, a Churchman. The chairman of the meeting, an Anglican clergyman, proposed that the election should be decided by a show of hands. No objection was made to the method of voting. Mumberson received nineteen votes to Wilson's thirteen, many remaining neutral. A poll was then demanded, which was opposed and after some discussion Mr. Mumberson and thirty-five ratepayers left the room rather than submit to the ballot which was being proceeded with; only twenty-four remained. A motion to adjourn the meeting was proposed, but was prevented being put to the meeting by the advice of the law clerk, who stated that the meeting could not be legally adjourned. A resolution that a poll of the whole parish should be taken was then proposed and seconded, but the clerk again interposed and stated that such a poll could not be taken, but that a decision had to be made at the meeting. Sheets of blank paper were then given to each of the ratepayers present who entered the name of the candidate and the number of the votes to which he considered he was entitled. With one exception there was nothing to identify the paper with the voter and therefore the number of votes was Wilson 22, Mumberson 1. The Chairman stated that counting the *cumulative* votes given, the numbers were 33 - 1, and he declared Mr. Wilson duly elected.[35] The rate books of some of the districts in which the ratepayers present held property were not available and the voter's word had to be taken on trust for the number of votes to which he was entitled.[36]

The matter was referred by Mumberson's supporters to the Charity Commissioners, who maintained that 'sufficient reason has not been shown to invalidate the election of Mr. Wilson as a Representative Governor by the Vestry of Crosthwaite under the scheme' (Board Meeting, 1 November 1887). This decision was based on cl. 69 of the scheme, which laid down that 'any question affecting the regularity or the validity of any proceeding under this scheme shall be *determined conclusively* [author's italics] by the Charity Commissioners upon such application made to them for the purpose as they think sufficient'. Following this rebuff, an application was made to Queen's Bench Division, before Mr. Justice Matthew and Mr. Justice Smith, for a grant of *quo warranto* and a reversal of the Commissioners' decision. It was held that the matter was outside the Court's jurisdiction, as cl. 69 had made the Commissioners the final arbiter in such a matter.[37]

This case drew public attention both to the inadequacies of the cumulative system and the extent of the quasi-judicial powers exercised by the Commissioners. *The Pall Mall Gazette* commented: 'It follows that the Charity Commissioners without inquiry may confirm a flagrantly unfair, if not illegal election, and that there is no legal remedy for those who have been jockeyed out of their rights. If this is not the legalization of ballot stuffing, it comes perilously near it.'[38]

One of the very few instances in which the cumulative system of voting was specified in a scheme of the Commissioners was that of Sutton Coldfield Grammar School, Warwickshire. This arose out of problems connected with the constitution of the new governing body. The Sutton Coldfield Charities were both educational and eleemosynary in character, but as the non-educational part amounted to less than half the total, the Commissioners were empowered to make a scheme.[39] The Warden and Society of the Royal Town of Sutton Coldfield, a body dissolved by the Municipal Corporations Act of 1833, had been one of the elements responsible for the appointment of representative governors to the charity. Much discussion centred round the body which was to replace the Society in discharging this function. A deputation from the existing governors of the charity saw the Commissioners on this matter. 'Different possible electing bodies were discussed: the Town Council, the Municipal Charity Trustees and the Burgesses. The deputation inclined to approve the selection of the Town Council, as securing an indirect representation of the burgesses, without entailing a biennial expense of £150, at which figure they reckon the cost of an election in Sutton Coldfield by the burgesses. There are eight Wards and must be eight Polling Stations with separate Returning Officers and Staff.'[40]

For their part, the Commissioners had suggested one board of management for all the schools of the parish, which included twelve elementary schools;[41] the election of a truly representative element on the governing body was therefore essential. The scheme, published in 1884, provided for a governing body numbering seventeen – one *ex officio*, eight co-optative (four of whom were to be women) and eight representative governors. Eventually, the town council took over responsibility for electing four of the representative governors,[42] but the interest of the scheme lay in the use of the cumulative system in the election of the remaining four governors. Cl. 6 of the scheme stated: 'The Representative Governors shall be appointed by an electing body, consisting of the persons whose names are on the burgess roll of the borough of Sutton Coldfield for the time being in force. At every such election every voter shall be entitled to a number of votes equal to the number of the Governors to be elected, and may give all such votes to one candidate, or may distribute them among the candidates, as he thinks fit.' When the scheme came into operation in 1887, a vestry meeting was called to choose four ratepayer representatives. Interest in this form of election appears to have quickly waned, twenty ratepayers being present at the second election of governors in 1892. The occupations of those elected did not differ from those of governors elected by other methods: two were manufacturers, one a Congregational Minister and one a clerk in Holy Orders.[43]

It is clear that the cumulative system, although originally intended to give the ratepayer direct participation in the electing of governing bodies, did not accurately reflect the wishes of the voter, and was not widely favoured or adopted by the Charity Commissioners. Of greater importance to the subject of this study were the attempts of town councils and school boards to gain the right to elect representative governors. It can be argued that the triumph of the former body over the latter weakened the already tentative links between the public elementary and endowed schools up to the end of the century.

Members of the school boards were not only well-acquainted with the circumstances and problems of poor children in their schools, but often possessed with a fund of experience in educational organization. They were responsible, in many cases, for sending boys to the endowed schools and appeared to be a likely source of representative governors for these schools. The presence of such an element on a governing body would have ensured that the welfare of the ex-elementary school boy would receive sympathetic attention.[44] That the personnel of the school boards were not extensively employed as governors in the endowed schools can be traced to events which took place in Birmingham in the early 1870s.

Even before school boards had been created, the town council of Birmingham, which included the leading members of the National Education League, had anticipated the Elementary Education Act in proposing that the council should be empowered to levy a rate for educational purposes. The council saw, in the setting up of a school board, a method of out-manoeuvring the governing body of the King Edward Schools which had, in the words of the town council's protest to the Commissioners in 1870, 'resisted all attempts to alter the system of self-election which uniformly resulted in confining the Governing Body to men holding the same political and theological opinions as themselves.'[45]

By capturing control of the school board, the town council with its own nominees to the governing body of the grammar schools together with staunch Liberal and Dissenter support within the school board, would be in a position to press for fuller representation on the governing body. Before the first school board elections took place, the Bailiff of the schools, C. E. Mathews, became involved in a public controversy on the subject of corrupt practices with regard to school elections; in meetings with Hammond, the Assistant Commissioner, to discuss the proposed new scheme for the school, a Resolution was put forward by the governing body to reduce school board representation as much as possible. Much depended on the voting at the board elections, then taking place. Hammond reported the outcome of the elections to Lyttelton as follows: 'While the Board [Governing Board] was sitting, the result of the School Board elections was announced. The business of the meeting was suspended which did not surprise me, considering how the Governors are affected towards the School Board. The Church Party has gained a decided victory and this may induce the Governors to regard the School Board with more favour than it has hitherto.'[46]

The consequences of this victory for the Church were far-reaching. Asa Briggs stated the subsequent events as follows:

The Liberals were goaded, as a result of 1870, into fighting local

political battles far more fiercely both for control of the School
Board and the Town Council. . . . The presence on the School
Board of an anti-Liberal majority (nine members of the
Education League had been defeated in 1870) seemed to make it
imperative to tighten the Liberal grip on the Town Council, with
which the School Board was engaged in almost perpetual
conflict between 1870 and 1873.

At the municipal elections of 1872 and 1873, therefore, party
feeling ran very high indeed. In 1872 the Conservatives contested seven of the thirteen wards, and although losing almost
everywhere, succeeded in defeating F. W. Schnadhorst. No·
defeat, except that of Chamberlain himself, could have more
riled the Liberals. Almost inevitably, the General Committee of
the Liberal Assosiation, which had already intervened in earlier
elections, decided formally in March 1873, on a motion of
Chamberlain, 'that in consequence of the recent action by the
Tory Party in Birmingham [in fighting municipal and School
Board elections] the Liberal Association, should in future take
part in such elections, and that whenever a Liberal candidate is
opposed by a Tory candidate, the support of the Association
should be given to the Liberal'.[47]

The organization of a party caucus by Joseph Chamberlain was
aimed at gaining control of the school board; but it was immediately appreciated that this method could also be used to retain power
politically in Council elections. In 1873, the Church Party was
swept from power on the school board, to be replaced by men such
as Chamberlain, George Dixon, R. W. Dale, George Dawson and
Jesse Collings.

Chamberlain combined his chairmanship of the school board
with his membership of the town council until his election to
Parliament in 1876. From 1873 onwards, Chamberlain's concept of
civic consciousness and pride led him to elevate the town council to
the position of supreme controller of all the affairs of the city. This
idea was outlined by him in a speech made some five years later:

In the first place, by unifying the work of the town – to use an
expression which offends many people – by monopolising it, by
making the leading governing local authority the authority, as
far as possible, in all the local work of the town; by making the
authority the channel through which all who had the laudable

ambition to ensure their town should fulfil that aspiration; and by securing the presence on that body of the men who were well-qualified not merely for special work, but for all the work which motivated the highest interests of the constituency there represented. . . . . . . [48]

Chamberlain's experiences on the school board with its bitter religious battles during the 1870-3 period, centring round the use of the rate for denominational schools,[49] possibly convinced him that *ad hoc* bodies such as the board were too narrow in outlook to be truly representative. Matters came to a head with the settlement of a new scheme for the grammar schools in 1878. Under ss. 4 and 6 of the scheme, the town council was required to appoint eight representative governors. This did not restrict the choice of governors to members of the council. Accordingly, George Dixon, the Chairman of the School Board, who had exchanged his seat in Parliament with his close friend, Chamberlain, P. H. Muntz, a Birmingham M.P., and Henry Hawkes, all of whom were not members of the council, were nominated, together with eight members of the town council. At a special meeting of the council on 30 April 1878, an amendment, not to confine nominations for governorships to council members, was lost by a large majority, 13 – 41, and the three school board nominees rejected.[50]

This was a cruel blow to Dixon, who offered his resignation as chairman of the board. In his resignation speech[51] to the Board, Dixon showed that school board representation on the governing body was justifiable: for example, at that time in the Boys' High School, there were about one-quarter who had been in the board's elementary schools.[52] The failure of the Birmingham School Board to secure representation on the governing body weakened the link between the elementary and secondary systems which flourished in the city. Politically, the caucus system spread to other towns, with similar results. Any hopes entertained by school boards of eventually being entrusted with the supervision of secondary education were finally crushed in 1889 when the Technical Instruction Act nominated local authorities and county councils for this task. (See chapter 5 following.)

The religious disputes of the 70s, the rise of rigid political control over town councils and the lack of comprehensive representation on governing bodies of the endowed schools were problems of too great a magnitude for the Commissioners to tackle. In retrospect, the views which were expressed by a Town Commissioner at a meeting at Walsall in 1872, to discuss the division of Queen Mary's School into an upper school, a second grade and a third grade day school for the poorer inhabitants of the town, were something of a pious wish:

> It seemed to him that by developing the Lower School, it might be made applicable to a large number of those who would want to use the school, and that as the governing body would be in the main representative, and therefore to a considerable extent under the control of the inhabitants, it would rest very much with the latter as to whether the Governors should not pay more attention to the Lower School, and leave the other pretty much to develop itself.[53]

NOTES

1. 1886 Select Committee on Endowed Schools Acts, P.P. 1886, IX, Q. 5906. Election could be by the M.P. for the county, by the vicar and churchwardens, boards of guardians, local boards and even by burial boards.
2. One writer at this time divided membership of governing bodies thus:
   (i) *Non-Resident Trustees* – 'high official personages who are more Patrons than Trustees, as they never take any interest in the duties of their appointments.'
   (ii) *Hereditary Trustees* – heirs with connections in the Army, Navy or the Bar. 'Trustees who are appointed because they are quiet unmeddling men, who let one or two active-minded Trustees and the Headmaster rule the roost, and who only attend Trustee Meetings when their votes are wanted to ratify some new regulation, whereby Boarders may compete for the Exhibitions and Prizes belonging to the Town Boys alone.'
   George Griffith, *The Endowed Schools of England and Ireland, Their Past, Present and Future* (1864), p. xii.
3. Henry Carr, 'On the Mode of Selection of Beneficiaries to Charitable Institutions', *Journal of the National Association for the Promotion of Social Science,* Vol. VII, 9 December 1873, pp. 26-32. Carr mentions three types of trafficking in votes:
   (i)   Professional brokers in votes;
   (ii) Amateur dealers offering votes for sundry considerations;
   (iii) Bartering and exchange of votes, one against the other.
4. As Lord Lyttelton wrote in a Memorandum on the Bradford Grammar School: 'In this particular case, the constitution which was suggested presumed the existence of a Provincial Board, for which at present there is no Parliamentary provision.' PRO Ed. 27/5721.
5. Report of the Endowed Schools Commission to the Committee of Council on Education, P.P. 1872, XXIV, p. 15. Cf. Roby's evidence in the following year:

'... in the present state of education and for other reasons, it is desirable to import into the management of these schools persons who would not perhaps be elected by a popular constituency, but who from their general knowledge and intelligence and social position, would be very valuable adjuncts to a trust.' Evidence, Select Committee on Endowed Schools Act 1873, Q. 2227.

6. 1884 Select Committee on the Charitable Trusts Acts, op. cit., Q. 821.

7. The popularity of Methodism, for example, amongst the working classes in the nineteenth century has been explained in the following terms: 'It captured the affections of the common people because of its religious appeal. Through its agency a panacea for all their troubles was gratuitously offered them, and they accepted it with whole-hearted enthusiasm. Having won so many by its religious appeal, it retained and utilized the majority of them by its collective and democratic customs. By offering opportunities for service it created a sense of individual and communal responsibility. That sense of accountability was never lost while the members had a share in the enterprise. Methodism indeed was much more a layman's movement than a minister's.'
R. F. Wearmouth, *Methodism and the Working Class Movements of England 1800-1850* (1937), p. 27.

8. See, for example, Arthur Miall, *Life of Edward Miall* (1884). Forster's brother-in-law campaigned against the 1870 Education Act, both as M.P. for Bradford and Editor of *The Nonconformist*.

9. For further details of this association, see M. Cruickshank, *Church and State in English Education* (1963).

10. Dale's activities are described in D. A. Hamer, *The Politics of Electoral Pressure* (1977), Chapter VII, p. 122 ff.

11. Quoted in K. S. Inglis, *Churches and the Working Classes in Victorian England* (1963), p. 104.

12. Cl. 17, s. 1, stated: 'The religious opinions of any person shall not in any way affect his qualifications for being one of the Governing Body of such Endowment.'

13. Case 8, House of Lords, Cases 495. See also: The Stafford Charities 25 Beavan; and Attorney-General v Clifton 32 Beavan 596.

14. *Stockport Advertiser*, 26 July 1867.

15. Only four out of the first forty schemes of the Commissioners did not contain provision for Church of England *ex officio* governors.

16. 1873 Select Committee on the Endowed Schools Act, (1869), op. cit., Q. 5117.

17. An article by K. M. Hughes, 'A Political Party and Education – Reflections on the Liberal Party's Educational Policy 1867-1902', in the *British Journal of Educational Studies*, Vol. VIII, No. 2, 1960, shows the interrelationship between politics, religion and education at this period. Both Nonconformists and Churchmen used Party as a means of expressing religious views on education. The Nonconformists and Philosophical Radicals were joined in the Liberal Party by the Utilitarians. Some way to the right of this group were the 'English Liberals', consisting of people such as Forster, who were predominantly humanitarian in outlook, and who would collaborate with any Party to further the education of children.

18. In 1872, Dale led a deputation of Nonconformists to the Endowed Schools Commissioners to urge objections against the appointment of 'Church' governors. An account of the interview with Lord Lyttelton is contained in A. W. Dale, *Life of R. W. Dale* (1899), p. 285.

Although Dale served with distinction on the Birmingham School Board, placing the need for education before religious controversy, his bitterness towards Forster and Gladstone over what he felt had been the betrayal of

Liberalism was reflected in his attitude to the endowed schools and his campaigning was partly responsible for the downfall of Gladstone's Government in 1874. J. H. Muirhead, *Nine Famous Birmingham Men* (1909), pp. 280-1.

19. Chertsey, Sir William Perkins School, PRO Ed. 27/4463, Report by Durnford, 29 March 1879. This attitude was an echo of the 1870 struggle reflecting the Church's attempt to oppose popular control: 'The opposition to the School Boards was led by the Bishops. The Bishop of Salisbury publicly returned thanks that there was only one School Board in an important part of his diocese. The Bishop of Chester headed the attempt to prevent the formation of a Board in his Cathedral Town.' F. Adams, *History of the Elementary School Contest in England* (1882), p. 242.

20. D. R. Fearon, giving Evidence before the 1886 Select Committee, recalled the early opposition to the reconstruction of governing bodies by vested interests: 'When I used, in 1871, 2 and 3, to meet trustees and tell them that, by a scheme under the Endowed Schools Act, it would be necessary that a headmaster should hold office at the pleasure of a governing body, and that governing body reconstituted with a popular element in it, they very frequently used to say: "Well, we shall never be able to get a good man as Headmaster of this school if he is to hold it at the pleasure of a governing body" '. 1886 Select Committee on Endowed Schools Acts, P.P. 1886, IX, Q. 5906.

21. 1884 Select Committee on Charitable Trusts Acts, op. cit., Q. 2927.

22. William Mathew, Chairman of the Board of Governors, King Edward's School, Birmingham. 1873 Select Committee on the Endowed Schools Act (1869). Q. 3082. No doubt the prospect of the unseemly behaviour associated with elections further deterred many people. An election for representative governors at Bedford, reported an Assistant Commissioner, 'creates a most undesirable strife in the town once every year, and is attended with more or less bribery and corruption: therefore, many would welcome the abolition of elections.' Bedford, PRO Ed. 27/8 A.

23. 1873 Select Committee on Endowed Schools Act (1869), op. cit., Q. 3082.

24. 1886 Select Committee on Endowed Schools Act, P.P. 1887, IX, Q. 6998. Swinburne's policy in many ways translated the recommendations of the Schools Inquiry Commission into practice. On this point, the Commission had stated: 'The real force, whereby the work is to be done, must come from the people. And every arrangement which fosters the interest of the people in the schools, which teaches the people to look on the schools as their own, which encourages them to take a share in the mangement will do at least as much service as the wisest advice and the most skilful administration.'

25. *Hansard,* Ser. 3, CCCV, House of Commons, 1886, cols. 1395-7, 18 May 1886.

26. Governors were elected by ratepayers only in second and third grade schools; 1886 Select Committee on Endowed Schools Acts, Q. 896, op. cit., P.P. 1886, IX.

27. 58 Cap. LXIX George III, s. 3.

28. William Sturges-Bourne (1769-1845) held office briefly at the Home Office, April-July 1827, as a friend of Canning. He resigned from Parliament 1831. *Compact Dictionary of National Biography* (1975), Vol. I, p. 194.

29. *Hansard* Ser. 3, XXXVIII, House of Commons, 1818, cols. 573-4, 7 May 1818.

30. See Hugh Owen, *Manual for School Board Elections* (1875), p. 49. 'The Parochial Rate Assessment Act, 1869, had given every *bona fide* household the right to vote at the annual vestry meeting when Churchwardens and overseers were appointed, and the business of the rest was generally discussed. Parish affairs, however, remained in the hands of the parson and a few of the

wealthier parishioners, and since meetings were held when labourers were normally at work, their attendance was not encouraged.' L. M. Springall, *Labouring Life in Norfolk Villages, 1834-1914* (1936), p. 106.

31. The clause relating to this system of voting did not appear in the original Elementary Education Bill, but was introduced during the course of its passage. A Birmingham League amendment to extend school boards to all districts led to 112 Liberals voting against the ministry. 'The ministry made some concessions. Dilke's proposal that the School Boards should be elected by the ratepayers instead of the town councils and vestries was rejected by the narrow majority of 150 to 145, but the Government later accepted the suggestion. The use of the ballot in School Board elections was carried by a large majority.' Asa Briggs, *History of Birmingham*, Vol. 2 (1952), p. 103. See also: W. O. Lester Smith, *To Whom do the Schools Belong?* (1945), p. 129.

32. Select Committee on School Board Elections (Voting), P.P. 1884 5, XI. Q.3985.

33. 'The avowed principle of the Act was to leave the decision of important questions of policy and administration to the judgment of localities. The effect of the cumulative vote was, in the greatest number of instances, to deprive the majority of the power of laying down any principles of action. Worse than this, in many cases, it enabled the minority, brought together by the combination of sectarian interests, to impose a policy and conditions absolutely repugnant to the view of the majority... In execution, the new franchise became a Church and Chapel franchise, giving power to a number of discordant sects which had the resources of electioneering at their command, and whose last thought was the promotion of general education.' Adams, op. cit., p. 247.

Sidney Webb, writing in 1891, placed the 'abolition of vestrydom' high on his list of pressing reforms for London. 'The arrangements for elections are primitive. A meeting of ratepayers is held on a day in May, the hour being fixed in the morning, when few persons can be present. . . . The election is not subject to the provisions of either the Parliamentary or the Municipal Corrupt Practices Act, and the Ballot Act does not apply to it. No notice of it is taken by the leading newspapers; the very slightest public interest is aroused; and practically the 5,000 members of the 78 vestries elect each other.' *The London Programme* (1891), pp. 20-1.

34. Brewood Grammar School, PRO Ed. 27/4209.

35. Keswick School, PRO Ed. 27/428. W. W. Nelson, solicitor acting for Mumberson, in letter to Charity Commissioners, 17 September 1887.

36. *Keswick Visitor and Guardian,* 11 September 1887. It is clear from an account of a later meeting that many of those present did not know the number of votes to which they were entitled.

37. Regina v Wilson, 19 January 1888. Q.B.D. *Weekly Notes,* 28 January 1888, p. 12.

38. *The Pall Mall Gazette,* 21 January 1888. Two days later, *The Daily News* launched an attack on the Charity Commissioners, claiming that the decision gave the Charity Commissioners the right to 'override Common Law and Statute Law regulating vestry procedure'.

39. Endowed Schools Act 1869, sub-s. 3.

40. Sutton Coldfield Grammar School, PRO Ed. 27/5084. Alderson's Memorandum, 2 August 1888.

41. Sutton Coldfield Grammar School, PRO Ed. 27/5085. Stanton's Report, 6 August 1883.

42. Ibid., Minute, 14 December 1888.

43. Sutton Coldfield Grammar School, PRO Ed. 27/5085. Mitcheson's Report, 23 December 1892, records complaints from the governors: the notice given for

the election, four days, was insufficient and it was poorly advertised. The rector suggested that more interest would be roused if voting took place in each of the four ecclesiastical districts of the parish, each to elect one representative, instead of one meeting to elect the four. It is interesting to note that fears expressed, that local elections would involve large expenditure, were ill-founded: at Sutton Coldfield, the only expense incurred was for printing.

44. On the other hand, the school board was often openly hostile to the local grammar school. At Hull, Humberside, in March 1876, the school board joined with the leading proprietary college and the Trades Council 'to protest at the "plundering" of a "working class" charity for the benefit of a "middle-class school".' Because of this opposition, the scheme was rejected. John Lawson, *A Town Grammar School through Six Centuries, A History of Hull Grammar School against its Local Background* (1963), p. 239.

45. Birmingham King Edward VI School, PRO Ed. 27/4891, Memorandum, 28 March 1870. Ironically, as future events showed, Lyttelton, who was the Commissioner in charge of the first Birmingham scheme, had, some ten years previously, taken the Chair at a meeting of the Birmingham Church Defence Association at Birmingham Town Hall at which Nonconformists were severely attacked. 'A Lecture on the Past, Present and Prospective Circumstances of the Church of England by the Rev. J. Bardsley', *Birmingham Church Defence Association (Pamphlet No. 1)*, December 1861.

46. Hammond to Lord Lyttelton, 30 November 1870, PRO Ed. 27/4891. The Church victory was due to the fact that the Conservatives, attempting to secure only a narrow majority, had all eight candidates returned, whereas the Liberals put fifteen candidates into the field, and had only six members returned. R. K. Dent, *Old and New Birmingham* (1880), pp. 547-8.

47. Asa Briggs, *Victorian Cities* (1963), p. 224.

48. *Birmingham Daily Gazette*, 1 May 1878. Cf. Collings: 'because these men can conduct the business of the borough they are always before their constituents and know the wants of the locality, the public have every security against misuse of resources and any faulty administration.' 1886 Select Committee on the Endowed Schools Acts, P.P. 1887, IX, Q. 7664.

49. A sample of the quality of the bitterness with which debates on religion in education was conducted in the board meetings can be found, for example, in a pamphlet, *Religious Instruction in Board Schools, Report of a Debate in the Birmingham School Board held on 8 May 1872*, National Education League 1872, in which Chamberlain and the Rev. F. S. Dale, the Conservative leader, were involved, pp. 38-68.

50. J. T. Bunce, *History of the Corporation of Birmingham*, Vol. II, (1885), pp. 529-30. See also King Edward School, Birmingham, PRO Ed. 27/4911. Minutes of the Town Council, 30 April 1878.

51. This was not accepted and Dixon remained Chairman until 1889.

52. *Birmingham Daily Gazette*, 3 May 1878. Dixon had been responsible also for securing a number of scholarships from the board schools to the King Edward Schools, see A. Briggs, *A History of Birmingham* (1952), p. 107. Chamberlain, for his part, admired the work of the Board. On taking leave of the Board in 1876, Chamberlain offered £500 for founding scholarships for board school boys to continue their education at the Midland Institute and Mason's College. Garvin, op. cit., Vol. I, 1932, p. 212, footnote.

53. *Walsall News*, 23 March 1872.

CHAPTER 5

New Opportunities: The Growth of Technical Education

In the last twenty years of the nineteenth century, the growth of technical education had a profound effect on the status of the endowed schools and the type of education offered, as well as broadening the opportunities for entry into the schools. The Industrial Exhibitions in the 1850s and 1860s had demonstrated the seriousness of foreign competition in this field. The collapse of the apprenticeship system, the growing interest in science and technology from the middle of the century and the lack of systematic provision for such education in the schools made the need for action imperative.

It was during the trade depression of the 1870s that the Devonshire Commission (the Royal Commission on Scientific Instruction, 1872-5) presented a series of reports which examined the state of scientific education in schools. Giving evidence before this Commission, Lyttelton had stated 'that it was the intention of the Endowed School Commission to insist on one branch of science being taught in all schools, and two in schools with a "modern" curriculum'.[1] In fact, the endowed schools had been little affected by the scientific movement and were continuing to stress the literary aspects of education.[2] Because of this, the Royal Commission on Technical Instruction (1881-4) which pointedly praised the continental provision of technical education in middle-class schools, put forward three main recommendations which, if followed, would have challenged the conservative nature of the endowed schools. Firstly, steps should be taken to accelerate the application of ancient endowments, under amended schemes, to secondary and technical instruction; secondly, that provision should be made by the Charity Commissioners for the establishment in suitable localities, of schools, or departments of schools, in which the study of natural sciences, drawing, mathematics and modern languages would take the place of Latin and Greek: and thirdly, that local authorities should be empowered, if they thought fit, to establish, maintain and contribute to the establishment and maintenance of secondary and 'technical' schools.[3]

The lack of suitable units of local government made the last proposal unworkable; however, the elementary schools enthusiastically took up the work marked out by the first two recommendations.[4] The Science and Art Department had from 1859 offered grants to any classes in any school devoting part of their time to the study of science and art. After the creation of the school boards, who showed great eagerness to supplement the Education Department grants, upper departments were created which could well specialize in this work, especially after 1882 when the Code had abolished payment for any scholar staying on after reaching VIIth Standard. It was but a small step to the growth of advanced or higher grade elementary schools. As early as August 1879, the Education Department had considered the situation and had laid down their policy in a letter to the Bradford School Board. The Department mentioned the enlargement of the scope of elementary education since 1875 to almost secondary level. Few children were able to take advantage of the facilities offered, and in order to meet such difficulties 'my Lords are of the opinion that an attempt should be made by School Boards of large towns to grade the different schools under their control by adjusting, as far as is possible, the quality of the education given to the fee paid, while at the same time, by exhibitions or otherwise, facilities are afforded for those who show capacity to pass from the lower to the higher-grade schools.'[5] In the North especially, Organized Science Schools, working to a science curriculum outlined by the Science and Art Department, became popular: originally functioning as independent entities, by the beginning of the present century there were 212 of them, a quarter of which were attached to school boards.[6]

In face of this competition, the third grade school gradually fell out of use. The Commissioners to a great extent associated themselves with the suggested reform of the endowed schools. Before the 1886 Select Committee on the Endowed Schools Acts, Fitch expressed the view that the Schools Inquiry Commission had

been unwise in suggesting three stages between the elementary
school and the university. There was need for but two: schools
catering for pupils proceeding to the university, and intermediate
schools, to give an education to sixteen or seventeen for those
entering business or the minor professions.[7] Instead of third grade
schools there was a need for apprenticeship or evening schools,
where an elementary education could be completed, with higher
value scholarships attached.[8] Although the Commissioners wished
to effect this change, the cost of such an education was as much as
£5 to £6 per pupil. After the Technical Instruction Commission had
reported, however, note was taken of the recommendation to use
endowments for training youths in skilled handicrafts. The Charity
Commissioners agreed that in endowed schools 'there should be the
option of learning a skilled craft by aid of proper apparatus' and
proposed that there should be schemes similar to those which 'dealt
with certain endowments in South London, by aid of which
children chosen from Public Elementary Schools may receive free
of all charge intermediate scientific education, with instruction in
the use of tools and may further by means of Exhibitions have the
opportunity of securing the higher and more complete training
which the Institute affords': it was hoped to extend such schemes to
the provinces.[9] But without adequate funds for building and
unable, unlike the elementary schools, to draw on the rates or
receive Education Department grants, any large-scale contribution
to scientific and technical training was difficult.

The 1888 Local Government Act created the county councils and
county boroughs and when in the following year the Technical
Instruction Act[10] was passed, they became the units primarily
responsible for administering its provisions. Elementary schools
were excluded from receiving aid under the Act, so the school
boards' powers in this field were weakened. County and borough
councils were able to levy a penny rate and receive grant aid in
order to promote various subjects at schools or colleges in return
for representation on the governing body of the institution
receiving aid. Two further measures increased the powers of
councils – the 1890 Local Taxation (Customs and Excise) Act made
available additional sums of money ('Whisky Money') for technical
subjects and, by an amending Act of 1891, the councils were
expressly permitted to establish scholarships at schools approved
by them. This legislation was largely the result of a pressure group,

the National Association for the Promotion of Technical and Secondary Education. A. H. D. Acland, one of the prime movers in setting up the Association, regarded the new powers of county councils as a means of bridging the gap between elementary school and the university.[11] The operating of the 1889 Act was handicapped by the fact that the technical instruction committees, who administered the scholarships in borough and county councils, were geographically limited in making awards within their own areas. The Act of 1891 changed this situation. By the following year it was reported that

> As a rule the policy of County Councils is *not* to attach scholarships to special secondary schools, but hold examinations open to pupils of all public elementary schools in the county, and to allow successful candidates to choose the secondary school at which to attend, out of a list of such schools providing technical instruction approved by the County Council.[12]

By 1901, fifteen out of forty councils providing scholarships to secondary schools were permitted to hold them in out-county schools.[13]

There was no single form of selection procedure for awards. In parts of England, either the Cambridge Local Examination Syndicate or Oxford Local Delegacy set the examinations. Some Technical Instruction Committees established their own examination board, whilst the West Riding Technical Instruction Committee awarded scholarships to candidates based only partly on performance in the examinations.[14]

The Charity Commissioners readily acknowledged that, because of the size of the amount of money now available, 'the proposed appropriation of these funds, whether in aiding existing institutions or in founding new ones, must materially affect the fortunes of these schools and the character of the education to be given in them.'[15] The widening of the curriculum which resulted often included, as at Brigg Grammar School, Lincolnshire, such subjects as bookkeeping, carpentry and shorthand and an increased allocation of time to science.[16] It should be mentioned that some county councils envisaged by-passing the endowed schools in their system of technical education. One of the most successful technical schools, the Wigan and District Mining and Technical School, desired the link to be – elementary school, continuation school, technical school.[17] Further, the Commissioners did not favour the narrow application of the funds and asked that Parliament should attempt a definition of subjects for which grants may be made available 'so as to cover the whole field of secondary instruction suitable to the class intended to benefit'.[18] It is clear that the Commissioners had hoped to play a central part in the administration of the grants, as had been the case under the Welsh Intermediate Education Act of 1889: there, County Joint Education Committees were set up, with power to initiate schemes for both new and existing foundations for presentation to the Charity Commission, and Intermediate Schools became the acknowledged secondary schools.[19]

The creation of the London Technical Education Board and its subsequent activities made necessary a clarification of the relationships existing between the endowed and other 'secondary' schools where awards could be held: this roused the headmasters of the endowed schools to defend themselves.

From the beginning of the London School Board, thanks to the energy and vision of T. H. Huxley, much attention was paid to the problem of the higher education of clever children attending elementary schools. A Committee of the Board was appointed in 1871, under Huxley's chairmanship, to consider suggestions for making this possible. A historian of the Board has written:

> The chief recommendation of the Committee was that the Board should enter into communication with the Endowed Schools Commissioners and seek to establish a system of scholarships providing maintenance grants equivalent to the earnings of children between the ages of thirteen and sixteen, tenable for the periods during which they might remain in the secondary schools. Little came of this proposal. The School Board, of course, had no money to spend on schools and the Endowed Schools Commissioners did not display any great eagerness to devote to this object any of the funds they controlled.[20]

It has been calculated that just before the London Technical Education Board came into existence, the School Board was offering twenty scholarships per annum to secondary endowed schools, a total of some nine hundred in all, which the Charity Commissioners used for needy pupils in reorganized foundations.[21] The chances of an elementary school child being assisted to pass on to any form of higher education was, for a boy 150 to 1, and for a girl 500 to 1.[22] The history of the establishment of the Technical Education Board is well known. The lack of enthusiasm displayed by the London County Council for using the powers given to it under the 1889 and 1890 Acts convinced Sidney Webb that only the Fabian policy in education would produce results.[23] Webb was equally certain that the London School Board hindered the promotion of secondary education and later, worked for its destruction.[24]

After the 1892 Council elections, Webb, leading the Progressives, commissioned Hubert Llewellyn Smith, Secretary of the National Association for the Promotion of Technical and Secondary Education, to survey London's need for such education.[25] With Liberal support and A. H. D. Acland's encouragement, the Technical Education Board was formed. Given almost complete authority by the London County Council in its activities, the Board had a unique composition for its Council: besides the twenty members nominated by the London County Council, there were fifteen members drawn from a number of parties interested in secondary education – the London School Board, the Head Masters' Association, the Head Mistresses' Association and the City and Guilds Institute, each body electing its own members.[26] One of the new Board's main concerns was to provide, on a massive scale, a series of scholarships and exhibitions at all levels, from the elementary school to the university. In 1893 alone, the Board awarded five hundred Junior Scholarships, entitling pupils from elementary schools to free education at any approved secondary or higher grade school in London, with a £10 per annum maintenance grant to compensate parents for the loss of potential earnings of the children.[27]

The new sources of revenue made available to secondary schools brought into the open the antagonism of the grammar school headmasters towards the higher and advanced elementary schools because of the latter's encroachment on their territory. The older endowed schools, many in financial difficulties, were unable to compete with these schools, whose pupils successfully sat the same examinations as the former, earned grants from the Science and Art Department on a large scale,[28] and were able to draw on the rates: now, they were able to claim a share of the scholarship children created by the Technical Education Board's scheme. Further, Webb had engineered the interpretation of the basis of awards for 'technical instruction' to include an enormous range of subjects, which the endowed schools already taught. The status of the higher grade school had been enhanced as a result of the deliberations of the Cross Commission on Elementary Education (1886-8). It had been charged with the task of enquiring into the adequacy of the provision of elementary education under the 1870 Act and the relations existing between elementary and higher education. The Commission, in its Report, regarded the higher grade schools as suitable places at which to hold exhibitions as an alternative to other 'secondary schools'.[29]

The hostility of the endowed schools was based on the assumption that elementary education was an education complete in itself and that the emergence of the higher grade school was a pale imitation of the genuine grammar school tradition. The higher grade school was attacked on four grounds:[30] that the 'higher' education offered was not catering for a specific need; that the cost to the ratepayer would be excessive;[31] that the staff were not qualified to teach the subjects to an advanced level;[32] and that the educational facilities offered by endowed schools were inadequate because of diversions of funds to these schools.

Matthew Arnold had sounded the warning that a more flexible approach to middle-class education was needed in order to exercise an attracting force upon the lower classes, whilst at the same time upholding the principle that all education above elementary must be got at the citizen's own expense.[33] By the 1890s, the situation was almost reversed. At the Conference on Secondary Education convened by the Vice-Chancellor of Oxford in October 1893 and which led to the setting up of the Bryce Commission, the damage done to the endowed schools by the higher grade schools, in attracting middle-class children in order to win scholarships, was demonstrated.[34] Similar doubts were raised on the wisdom of the extensive scholarship system at the Cambridge Conference in 1896. One headmistress stated:

> The reasons given for advocating state or local control of all secondary education are various and mostly mistaken. Some advocate it in order that Elementary School children may receive higher education. These forget or shut their eyes to the fact that the work procurable in business or in the professions is exceedingly limited, and that already there are thousands who,

having passed through Higher-Grade Board Schools, have no other prospect before them than an ill-paid clerkship: for they consider themselves too well-educated for even skilled manual work.[35]

It was claimed that the high cost of elementary education to the ratepayer would prove fatal to the establishment of a parallel system for secondary education.[36]

In London, however, the picture was rather brighter. Webb, as a result of his own educational experiences, wished to erect 'two educational ladders for every Londoner', one for climbing by day, the other available in the evening, to rise to educational heights. This was to be achieved without building new institutions, and the needy endowed schools would benefit from this policy: fifty out of the ninety applied to the Board for financial help.[37]

Webb also hoped to bridge the gulf between the two parties by eliminating the overlapping jurisdiction between the Technical Education Board and the London School Board and thus achieve a new unity under the aegis of the former. He argued that 'this cleavage between elementary and secondary education was bad for both teachers and scholars: it made elementary teachers feel they belonged to a lower grade, and it prevented scholars from seeing that there was an organic connection between elementary and the higher schools'.[38] For their part, the endowed schools resisted suggestions for 'dilution' as advocated by reformers on the ground that this would not meet the real educational needs of the working classes and they defended this view at all levels.[39]

The headmasters of public endowed schools had formed an Association in 1890 'for the purpose, as opportunity arose, of taking combined action and of making corporate recommendations in professional, or public, matters affecting secondary education'.[40] In fact, it hoped to combat school board intrusion into the field of secondary education, win back middle-class children attending these schools and, at the same time, encourage the intelligent working-class elementary school child to enter the grammar school and thus help to raise academic levels.[41] R. P. Scott, the lively Secretary of the Association and Headmaster of Parmiter's School, London, devised a scheme to aid the endowed schools by initiating and administering an entrance examination for scholarships taken in the elementary school for entry to the secondary schools: in this way, not only could standardization be achieved, but it was particularly hoped to attract county scholars, whose fees were paid by the sponsoring authority.[42] Llewellyn Smith was called in to advise on a draft scheme and, after a conference with the Executive of the National Union of Teachers, arrangements were made for holding a uniform examination throughout the country on the same day.[43] In 1892, a sub-committee was formed to study the relations between secondary schools and the County Council Technical Committees: a study of the Headmasters' Association's deliberations shows that it aimed at asserting the secondary schools' independence of technical education whilst at the same time making out a case for benefiting from County Council grants. Secondary and technical education, the Association stated, cannot be separated in the sense that secondary schools lay the foundations of real technical instruction: therefore it recommended that immediate steps should be taken by means of grants for scholarships, buildings and masterships to make the former schools more efficient.[44]

The establishment of the Technical Education Board was welcomed by the Association, but it protested at the limitation of the award of scholarships to attendance at elementary schools, in view of the fact that there were many parents 'who, while they may fairly claim assistance, prefer that their children should receive their early education elsewhere than in a Public Elementary School.'[45] Llewellyn Smith's suggestion of helping governing bodies of London's endowed schools by awarding annual grants, based on the number of pupils coming from the public elementary schools to be admitted at a low fee, was much criticized by the Headmasters' Association. It was finally agreed that no one method of award would be suitable and that each school should be considered on its merits. A Technical Education Board Minute of March 1894 laid down the conditions for receiving assistance; it helped to some extent to democratize the character of the schools accepting the conditions. In the Board's first year, no fewer than thirty-seven schools accepted and received grants totalling £12,200.[46]

The success of the Association's scheme for administering the scholarship examinations can be judged from the fact that by 1894, the Technical Education Board and two-thirds of the secondary schools in London used their examinations, and in the following year so did eleven county councils. By 1896, there were 6,675 candidates for the examinations,[47] which were praised by the Bryce Commission for their fairness.[48] The Association's pressure for widening the field for candidates yielded results in 1895 when, for the first time, the Board offered scholarships not confined to elementary schools, to pupils already in attendance at endowed schools; but, as the Association complained, 'the maintenance of a somewhat low income-limit has shut out a large field of competitors', and it strongly deprecated the poverty test for those entering for the examinations.[49] In 1895, the successful venture was handed over to a Joint Scholarship Board, which was officially independent of the Association.[50]

Outside London, the 'Whisky Money' had not, by the mid-1890s, been applied on as liberal a scale for the benefit of the needy. In 1894, twenty out of the forty-nine county councils and forty-seven out of the sixty-one county boroughs made no grants to secondary schools,[51] although of those authorities giving awards, many of the scholarships went to the children of poor parents.[52]

The Charity Commissioners, after some initial apprehension, enthusiastically welcomed the county councils' plans to benefit the existing schools with the money placed at their disposal by the Local Taxation Act. Plans were drawn up to co-ordinate the work of county councils and the Charity Commissioners: the schemes prepared by the Commissioners from 1892 onwards increasingly assumed they would receive help from the councils.[53] As with the Technical Education Board's schemes and those under the Welsh Intermediate Act, county council representation on the governing bodies of schools was provided for. The main difference between the policies of the Charity Commission and the Headmasters' Association lay in the former's concern with the overall provision of secondary education in England, whereas the latter's interest was in retaining control over the secondary schools already established.[54] By the time of the Bryce Commission, ten county councils had received representation on the bodies of seventy-four different schools.[55] With the passing of the Local Government Act in 1894, co-operation at a local level was facilitated. The policies of the Charity Commissioners and the Headmasters' Association were identical in one respect: the public secondary school should, where an already ancient endowed grammar school existed, be the sole recipient of aid from the new public sources rather 'than that its usefulness should be crippled and its existence imperilled by the competition of a rate-supported Higher Grade Elementary School or a Technical School, for boys of school age, subsidized by the Town Council'.[56]

Two important enquiries – the Select Committee on the Charity Commission 1894 and the Bryce Commission 1894-5 – examined the educational work of the Charity Commission. The first was appointed to enquire into the measures necessary in order to make the Commission more effective in dealing with the business before it: the second considered the best methods of establishing a well-organized system of secondary education in England. Whilst recognizing the good work done by the Commission, the Select Committee reported: 'The position of the Charity Commission has now become somewhat analogous to that of the old Poor Law Commission, which it was found necessary to dissolve in 1847 and replace under a Minister.'[57] Briefly, the Bryce Commission favoured the unification of central authority in secondary education with the county councils and county boroughs as the two units of educational administration. The Charity Commissioners were criticized on two counts: that their functions were too narrowly circumscribed and that they were too divorced from educational policy.[58]

In anticipation of legislation which would follow the Bryce Report, the scheme-making activities of the Commission slowed down,[59] but two important principles were adopted in these late years. Encouragement was given to schools to apply for amended schemes in order to become recognized as science schools under the terms of the Science and Art Department; and exhibitions and scholarships provided out of the endowments were increased in value and reduced in number, to enable those who could benefit from secondary education to complete a full course of study.[60] The necessity for a form of maintenance grant, which had for some years been an important element in county scholarships held at endowed schools,[61] was thus acknowledged by the Commissioners.

A clumsy attempt to implement the findings of the Bryce Commission in making county councils the supreme educational authorities, failed in 1896,[62] when an Education Bill was rejected in the House of Commons. But in 1898, the Duke of Devonshire, then Lord President of the Privy Council, introduced two Bills into the Lords – the first concerned with the Registration of Teachers, the second to unite the Science and Art Departments and the Education

Department, and to provide for closer working between the Education Department and the Charity Commissioners. In the following session, a single Bill was brought in in place of the two. Under the Board of Education Bill, the educational functions of the Charity Commissioners were to be transferred to the newly-created Board of Education, thus bringing the endowed schools under central supervision.[63]

In a speech in the Lords introducing the Bill on 1 August 1898, the Duke of Devonshire somewhat imprudently, as he admitted later,[64] undertook to reorganize secondary education as a distinct entity from the Elementary and the Science and Art branches. This was due to the systematic lobbying of the Headmasters' Conference Committee and the Incorporated Association of Headmasters, formerly the Headmasters' Association, both of whom had urged the Duke to keep secondary education distinct from technical education.[65] Rumours had begun to circulate upon the retirement of the Director of the Science and Art Department, Major-General Sir J. F. D. Donnelly in 1899 and the appointment of Sir George Kekewich, the Secretary of the Education Department, as Secretary also of the other Department. It appeared to many headmasters that what would probably happen was that elementary education would be treated as a separate branch, and Science and Art and Secondary lumped together.

Before a decision could be reached on the most profitable grouping, a Departmental Committee known as the Walpole Re-organization Committee, after its Chairman, was charged 'to consider and report what changes in staff and organization of the Education Department and the Science and Art Department were necessary in order to bring into effect the Lord President's Minute of 29 June 1899 and to bring these Departments into closer relation to each other'.[66] Its personnel included Kekewich, Captain W. de W. Abney, Principal Assistant Secretary to the Science and Art Department, and W. Tucker, Principal Assistant Secretary of the Education Department. No representative of the Charity Commission was included until, as an afterthought, Spring-Rice, at the Treasury, wrote to Kekewich

If someone has to be added to our Committee to 'represent' [save the mark!] Secondary Education, would not Fearon be a good choice? He is thoroughly sensible and practical, and the contemplated transfer of educational work from him to you would be a good pretext. It would never do to have on a business committee some educational theorist or advocate of a doctrinaire idea.[67]

Fearon submitted a closely reasoned 'Memorandum on the Transfer to the Board of Education of power to make Schemes under the Charitable Trusts Acts' at a meeting (1 December 1899) of the Committee; it was agreed that if the educational work of the Endowed Schools Acts were transferred, then the Charity Commissioners' staff would still be required.

Fearon's advocacy for the retention of the Charity Commission's powers by the Commission rather than handing them over to the new Board of Education found ready agreement with Devonshire,[68] whose knowledge of educational matters was slight.[69] For three years after the establishment of the Board of Education, the administration of the Endowed Schools Acts and the Commissioners' powers to make schemes for educational endowments under the Charitable Trusts Acts remained with the Commissioners. The Board took over the exercise of powers to regulate the administration of endowments in Wales and Monmouthshire, the supervision of the Treasury grant to schools established under the Welsh Intermediate Education Act, and the enforcement of educational inspection of secondary schools, as distinct from administrative inspection, which the Commissioners had undertaken from 1888,[70] although under s. 2 (sub-s. 2) of the Act, power had been given by Order in Council to transfer to the Board of Education *any* of the powers of the Charity Commission relating to education.

Notwithstanding the headmasters' opposition to linking technical with secondary education, the overlap between the work of the Science and Art Department and the endowed schools was recognized by those responsible for framing the 1899 Act. Spring-Rice noted that about seventy of the institutions receiving grants from the Science and Art Department were endowed schools.[71] Abney pointed out that the Charity Commissioners had provided in their schemes 'for the small Grammar School where the middle-classes have to obtain their secondary education, the modern or science side is much better suited. Their students do not go into the professions, but into commerce or industry and it is some of these schools which have been aided by the Science and Art Department. . . . This action of the Charity Commissioners, wise in itself, had also been the means of saving some schools from absolute bankruptcy. The potential severance of these schools from the control which has been exercised over them by the Science and Art Department would be most harmful. One of two things would happen. The schools would drift away from modern to literary education, or the grant would be fruitlessly expended.'[72] Abney was eventually appointed as Principal Assistant Secretary to the new Secondary Branch.

During the months following the passing of the Act, the opposition by endowed school headmasters was modified: the adoption of science and art instruction in the grammar school as part of general education, in addition to classical and literary instruction, was acceptable provided that a Secondary Branch of the Board completely distinct from the Technical Branch[73] could be established.

The 1902 Education Act, under Morant's direction, marked the beginning of the real work of reorganizing the different branches, but it was not until 1907 that the Secondary Branch was established on a territorial basis of three divisions. One of the reasons for the long delay was that the Secondary Branch inherited the heavy legal work from the Charity Commissioners. Morant solved this problem by forming a separate Legal Division within the Secondary Branch.[74]

Almost the entire personnel of the Charity Commission who dealt with educational endowments, and who were since 1900 part of the new Branch, played prominent parts in the work of secondary reorganization after 1902. At the transfer of the Endowed Schools Department to the Board of Education, the Hon. W. N. Bruce, an Assistant Charity Commissioner, became Principal Assistant Secretary of the Secondary Education Branch. He was joined by four other colleagues— W. C. Lefroy and A. F. Leach as Assistant Secretaries, and A. C. Eddis and R. E. Mitcheson as Senior Examiners. Thus by 1904, the key posts of the Secondary Branch were occupied by men who had had wide experience of dealing with the endowed schools, and who were now able to undertake a study of their problems with the full resources of a Government Department behind them.

At the time of the transfer, Mitcheson, Leach, Bruce and Eddis were involved in the administrative inspections of North London, Essex, Herefordshire and Devonshire respectively. Mitcheson had earlier contrasted the meagre supply of scholarships available in England with those of Wales since the Welsh Intermediate Act had come into effect and which Bruce had been responsible for administering since 1889.[75] Out of a total of 6,912 scholars inspected in Wales, no fewer than 4,974 or 70 per cent had proceeded to the county schools from public elementary or higher grade schools: the Charity Commissioners remarked at the time (1899): 'This preponderance of scholars drawn from the lower or middle-class is a salient feature of the Welsh Intermediate Schools. It presents a striking contrast to the minority of such scholars who, as a rule, obtain admission by means of competitive scholarships, to the English Grammar Schools.'[76]

Nevertheless, the achievement in England was not to be underrated. The absorption of the Charity Commission into the Secondary Branch of the Board of Education ensured a continuity of policy and a carry-over of the long-established principles of the Endowed Schools Commissioners. Not the least important of these was the securing of wider access for all classes to the new secondary schools. A ladder of education, however frail, had been established. As a Permanent Secretary to the Board of Education wrote some years later:

> On the whole there can be little doubt that statutory powers over educational endowments have been exercised, whether by the Charity Commissioners, or the Endowed Schools Commissioners or the Board, conscientiously and with no kind of indifference to the interests of the 'poor' and no kind of preference for the interests of the rich.[77]

NOTES

1. Quoted in Archer, op. cit., p. 138.
2. Philip Magnus, a Commissioner of the Technical Instruction Commission, put forward a plan for intermediate technical schools and higher secondary science or non-classical schools on the ground that 'the education given in the majority of our middle-class schools was not of that character which was best adapted to fit children from the elementary schools to become skilled mechanics: that the education was, by far, too literary, and that even the literary education was not of the kind best adapted to their requirements.' 1886

Select Committee on Endowed Schools Acts Evidence, Q. 3133. Magnus' views on technical education are seen in full in 'Manual Training in School Education' in *The Contemporary Review*, November 1886.

3. F. W. Edwards, *Technical Education, Its Rise and Progress* (1885), p. 41.

4. The work of Sir Lyon Playfair (1818-98) must be mentioned in this connection. Playfair had been Chairman of the Select Committee of 1886 enquiring into the working of the Endowed Schools Acts. He was appalled by the low standards of education offered to elementary school children as compared with middle-class schools. See his *Subjects of Social Welfare* (1889), pp. 284 ff.; pp. 306-36. To combat this, Playfair advocated scientific instruction in those schools: 'If the educational endowments of this country were not to be freely opened to the miserable minority of the talented poor, let them give in the elementary schools such instruction as would enable the pupils to know what was the object and purpose of the elements there taught, so that they might not fling away those elements like their worn-out boyish small clothes as soon as they begin to win their daily bread, but that they might use their knowledge acquired in school to further their advancement as intelligent beings in whatever position and occupation they might be placed'. Quoted in T. Wemyss Reid, *Memoirs and Correspondence of Lyon Playfair* (1899), p. 214.

5. E. Eaglesham, *From School Board to Local Authority* (1956), pp. 33-4.

6. Adamson, op. cit., p. 413.

7. 1886 Select Committee on Endowed Schools Act, P.P. 1886, IX, Q. 1115.

8. Ibid, Q. 1160.

9. 32nd Annual Report of the Charity Commissioners for 1884, P.P. 1884-5 XXI, p. 13. This arose out of the City of London Parochial Charities Act which extended the scope of these charities to the Metropolis as a whole. By means of *cy-près* applications, it was possible to apply the charities to a variety of objects, especially, in the words of the Act, 'to improve the physical, social and moral condition of the poorer inhabitants'. *Nathan on the Charities Act, 1960* (1961), p. 6.

10. The Technical Instruction Act of 1889 and that of 1891 were largely the work of Henry Roscoe, a German-trained Professor of Chemistry at Owen's College, Manchester, who became an M.P. and Secretary of the National Association for the Promotion of Technical and Secondary Education. This growing respect for science was shown by Gladstone's recommendation of a knighthood for Roscoe in 1884. H. Ausubel, *In Hard Times* (1960), p. 200.

11. W. H. G. Armytage, *Four Hundred Years of English Education* (1964), p. 172. Much of the success was due to Acland's work in the House of Commons, even though the Liberal Party was in opposition at this period. He gleefully reported to his father in 1890: 'We managed to persuade Goschen (the Chancellor of the Exchequer) that County Councils might use the whole residue (£750,000 for England and Wales) of this money under the Technical Instruction Act if they wish.' Acland Papers, A. H. D. Acland to T. D. Acland, 9 August 1890, Bodleian Library, MS. Eng. Lett. e. 100.

12. G. R. Benson and H. Llewellyn Smith, 'Recent Progress in England' in *Studies in Secondary Education* (1892), p. 88. A reviewer of Llewellyn Smith's contribution to the book took up Smith's remark that the majority of London endowed schools were filled with middle-class children and that in very cheap endowed schools, there was a sprinkling of children of working men. 'In consequence of this, we are asked to remember that we must legislate, first for the larger number – the children of small shopkeepers, and next for those children of the working classes who are at present excluded from all *but the*

very cheapest endowed schools. These children, it seems, are to be the special care of Mr. Smith and his friends. Any organization of secondary education, or our existing secondary schools, is to be, first and foremost, framed for the special wants of these classes.' *Educational Review,* July-August 1892.

13. Quoted in P. H. J. H. Gosden, 'Technical Instruction Committees' in History of Education Society, *Studies in the Government and Control of Education since 1860* (1970), p. 30. Full details of awards of scholarships and exhibitions are given in *The Record,* a quarterly journal published by the National Association for the Promotion of Secondary Education from 1891, devoted to the progress made by county and local authorities in awarding exhibitions and scholarships.

14. P. R. Sharp, 'The Origin and Early Development of Local Education Authority Scholarships', *History of Education,* Vol. 3, No. 1, 1974, pp. 38-9. In 1900, the 'Technical scholars' at Bristol Grammar School were described by its headmaster as 'amongst the best prepared of all the school's entrants'. C. P. Hill, *The History of Bristol Grammar School* (1951), p. 132.

15. 38th Annual Report of Charity Commissioners for 1890, P.P. 1890-91, XXVI, p. 20.

16. F. Henthorn, *The History of Brigg Grammar School* (1959), p. 153.

17. Mr. A. Hemlett, at a meeting of the Executive Committee of the school (1 October 1896), said that 'it would be greatly to the advantage of the students and the school if, when a scholar left the Elementary School, he was not able to come to that school [i.e. Technical School], that he should attend the continuation school, so that when he came to that school his mind would be thoroughly prepared to take up the higher system of education which was given there. That would free them from doing any elementary work at all, because that school was not for elementary purposes.' Wigan Grammar School, PRO Ed. 27/2340.

18. 38th Annual Report of Charity Commissioners for 1890, P.P. 1890-91, XXVI, p. 21. The Commissioners also asked that sums appropriated from the funds for educational purposes should be declared 'educational endowments' within the meaning of the Endowed Schools Acts.

19. In many ways, the Act led the Commissioners to apply similar principles to English schools. An Intermediate Education and a Technical Education were defined. Local endowments could be used and county councils could insert a rate clause into schemes for secondary education. Parliamentary grants were also available. Where rate-aided, representation on governing body of school by the county council or county borough was obligatory. See Welsh Intermediate Education Act, and J.E.G. de Montmorency, *The Progress of Education in England* (1904), pp. 215-16.

20. H. B. Philpott, *London at School, The Story of the School Board 1870-1904* (1904), p. 54. By the time the first Board went out of office in 1873, there were only three scholarships under the Board's control. For an account of Huxley's work in this connection, see Cyril Bibby, *Huxley* (1959), p. 157. His famous speech of 15 February 1871 also included references to establishing continuation schools, and ultimately a scheme of technical education in London. For the text of the speech, see Leonard Huxley (ed.), *Life and Letters of T. H. Huxley* (1913), Vol. 2. An appreciation of Huxley's work on the Board is to be found in T. A. Spalding, *The Work of the London School Board* (1900), p. 212.

At Sheffield, the school board and other interested persons managed to form a Scholarship Committee in November 1874: although unable to raise funds from the rates, by 1877, £280 had been privately subscribed to sending 'exceptionally clever youths' to continue their studies. J. H. Bingham, *The Period of the Sheffield School Board* (1949), p. 156.

21. Kenneth Lindsay, *Social Progress and Educational Waste* (1926), pp. 35-6. Lindsay names Parmiter's School, a fee-paying school, as still retaining its local character, and the United Westminster Schools, which offered more than half the London scholarships then (1892-3) available, as 'continuation' schools. The other schools assumed that pupils had been educated from an early age at secondary schools and catered exclusively for their requirements.

22 G. Gibbon and R. W. Bell, *History of the London County Council, 1889-1939* (1939), p. 248. It has been calculated that in 1894 the chances were 270-1 for a boy in England as a whole to gain admission. Lowndes, op. cit., p. 10.

23. For an account of the aims and policy of the Fabian Society, see, for example, M. Beer, *History of British Socialism* (1924), Vol. II pp. 284-5, and *Fabian Tract No. 70*, Report on Fabian Party, July 1896.

24. See Webb's attack on the London School Board in *London Education* (1904), pp. 12-17, and *Fabian Tract No. 106*, '*The Education Muddle and the Way Out*' (1897), p. 8, on a number of grounds.

25. See Smith's Report to the Special Committee on Technical Education; especially p. 72. G. D. H. Cole pointed out that the Fabians did not originate London Progressivism, which had been developed by the London Radical Reform Movement long before the County Council was set up. 'The Second International 1889-1914', in *A History of Socialist Thought* (1956), Vol. III, Part 1, p. 119.

26. Webb's skilful handling of the Committee and an account of its emancipation from the restrictions of other Committees of the Council, see Beatrice Webb (ed. B. Drake and M. Cole), *Our Partnership* (1948), pp. 78-80.

27. Gibbon and Bell, op. cit., p. 248. For further details, see B. M. Allen, *William Garnett: A Memoir* (1933), pp. 59-61.

28. The Birmingham School Board's Seventh Standard schools' income in 1886 was £1,431, of which £963 represented receipts from the Science and Art Department and £238 from rates. Eaglesham, op. cit., p. 38, quoting from the Cross Commission's figures.

29. For a full account of the Cross Commission, see C. Birchenough, *History of Elementary Education* (1935), pp. 134-6.

30. One writer has explained the situation in these terms: 'The motives of the secondary teachers and their supporters were both personal and professional. The secondary teachers wished to maintain their status and their monopoly of middle-class education. They were constantly complaining that the normal development in the numbers attending secondary schools has been checked by the erection of lavishly equipped Board Schools. They were supported by Conservative politicians who wished to reduce the amount spent on the education of the working class. They were supported by the advocates of the voluntary school system who could not compete with the attractions of higher grade education offered to the working class.' Tropp, op. cit., p. 176.

31. See, for example, W. R. Lawson, *John Bull and His Schools* (1908), pp. 52-3.

32. P. W. Musgrave has shown that by the time of the Technical Instruction Acts, there had been a shift away from the principles of technical and scientific subjects to *practical* instruction applicable to specific industries, a process encouraged by the setting up of the City and Guilds Institute and the London Polytechnics. 'The Definition of Technical Education 1860-1910' in *Vocational Aspects of Secondary and Further Education*, Vol. XVI, Summer 1964, pp. 105-11.

Opposition also arose from the connection of higher grade schools with the

Science and Art Department, whose examinations were intended for industrial and operative classes. See A. Abbott, *Education for Industry and Commerce in England* (1938), Chapter III, passim. Mention should also be made here of the lesson which the grammar schools learned from the struggle for monopoly of higher education in Prussia, Bavaria and Austria in the 1880s and 1890s. By this time, the 'Trade School' movement had swamped the academic opposition. In 1890, Latin was curtailed in the *Gymnasium,* drawing was made compulsory in middle-class schools and leaving examinations were simplified. G. Kerchensteiner, *The Schools and the Nation* (trans. C. K. Ogden) (1914), pp. 251-2.

33. W. F. Connell, *The Educational Thought and Influence of Matthew Arnold* (1950), p. 267. See also his speech at Dulwich College, *The Times,* 30 July 1885.

34. Miss Blackmore, Roan School, Greenwich, *Report of the Oxford Conference on Secondary Education* (1893), p. 108. This tendency was also apparent in confining scholarships in the larger endowed schools to public elementary scholars. A scheme for St. Paul's by the Charity Commissioners proposed that 51 places should be reserved for such scholars. Colonel M. Clementi, *St. Paul's and the Charity Commissioners,* 1896. One comment on this ran: 'It is easy to argue that poor gentle people may make their boys eligible for the closed scholarships by sending them to a school that falls under the 75th clause. But to argue this is to admit that it is desirable to lower the standard of teaching at St. Paul's. . . . It is to admit that it is advisable to encourage the lowering of the professional class to the social level of workmen, and thus to level down instead of levelling up.' F. C. Marshall, 'St. Paul's School and the Charity Commissioners' in *Educational Review,* June 1893.

35. Miss J. Allen Olney, Private Schools Association, *Report of the Cambridge Conference* (1896), p. 65. In discussing opposition to State Secondary education, it must be remembered that the 1897 Return of Public and Private Secondary and Other Schools (not being Public Elementary Schools or Technical Schools) in England, P.P. 1897, LXX, showed that two-thirds of secondary schools were 'private venture', often of low calibre and with a vested interest in maintaining the *status quo* in education. See R. H. Tawney (ed.), *Secondary Education for All* (1922), p. 25.

The prospects of the 1896 Bill to give local authorities control over secondary education moved a speaker at a Teachers' Guild Meeting to remark: 'It was difficult to say why, but the L.C.C. seemed in absolute fear of the British workman, and if the secondary schools got into their hands there would be an unreasonable desire to swamp them with elementary scholarship children, by no means, in a large proportion of cases, to the ultimate benefit of these children.' *Cheltenham Ladies' College Magazine,* July 1896.

It is interesting to note that the universities were engaged, on a different level, at this time in a 'Science v Humanities' battle. See, D. S. L. Cardwell, *The Organization of Science in England* (1957), p. 127.

36. F. Smith, *A History of English Elementary Education 1760-1902* (1931), pp. 311-12.

37. E. J. T. Brennan (ed.), *Education for National Efficiency: the contribution of Sidney and Beatrice Webb* (1975), p. 28.

38. Quoted in A. M. McBriar, *Fabian Socialism and English Politics 1884-1918* (1962), p. 212. Webb was not alone in expressing these sentiments. An enthusiast of co-ordinating the two systems, whilst admitting that the primary schools had much to learn from the secondary schools, went on to say: 'On the other hand, in the Secondary Schools the teachers, though in themselves better

cultured than Elementary teachers usually are, are far inferior to the latter both in the art of teaching, and in the art of handling numbers. . . . In all these points, the two systems, if closedly connected, would tend to correct each other.' E. M. Howe, *The Organization of Secondary Education. Address to the Liverpool Philomathic Society,* (1896).

39. O. Banks, *Parity and Prestige in English Secondary Education* (1955), pp. 15-19, discusses this point. The National Union of Teachers supported the claims of the higher grade schools for parity with grammar schools and considered the 'ladder' to be an important agent of social change. See Bryce, Vol. V, Evidence, P.P. 1895, XLVII.

It is worth noting that the more articulate members of the Labour movement showed little enthusiasm for technical education, apart from the skilled craft unions, who were mainly concerned with the decline in apprenticeship in the nineteenth century. S. Cotgrove, *Technical Education and Social Change* (1958), p. 23. Keir Hardie, speaking at the International Workers' Conference held in London in July 1896, attacked Webb's assumption that only those working-class children capable of profiting by secondary education should be provided for and thought 'that to have a competitive spirit in education was as immoral as having it in the capitalist organization of society'. E. J. T. Brennan, 'Sidney Webb and the London Technical Education Board, II – The Board at Work', *The Vocational Aspects of Secondary and Further Education,* Spring 1960, Vol. XII, No. 24. Similarly, the Labour Representation Committee opposed the Bill of 1902, which led to a Fabian Executive Committee sending a resolution to the L.R.C. 'that it was acting *ultra vires* in poking its inexpert nose into questions of education'. Margaret Cole, *The Story of Fabian Socialism* (1961), p. 105.

40. Report of the Committee of the Headmasters' Association for 1891, p. 3.

41. I am indebted to Professor G. Baron for this suggestion.

42. See G. Baron, *The Secondary Schoolmaster 1895-1914,* Ph. D. Thesis, London University (1952), p. 122.

43. R. P. Scott, 'The Scholarship Link between Elementary and Secondary Schools' in *The Educational Review* (October 1892). The scheme would do two things: base examinations on the elementary education Code and thus attract elementary head teachers; and by holding the examination on the same day, allow adequate preparation time for the teachers.

44. Report of the Committee of the Headmasters' Association for 1892, p. 5. One endowed school headmaster wrote to Kekewich, the Education Department Secretary: '*They* must do the purely technical work and one of the most urgent things yet to come is a departmental enquiry into the way these large sums of beer money are being *wasted* on "hygienic lectures" and "first aid" and "ornamental bent ironwork" etc., and winter recreations, to the great delight of the country clergy and the Ladies Bountiful on Local Committees.' PRO Ed. 24/64, 10 July 1899.

Some enlightened headmasters disagreed with such a view. J. Lewis Paton, High Master of Manchester Grammar School, for instance, favoured the 'continuation schools' on a compulsory national day-time basis. C. Norwood and A. H. Hope, 'The Secondary Education of the Working Classes' in *The Higher Education of Boys in England* (1909), p. 544 ff.

45. Report of the Committee of the Headmasters' Association for 1892, p. 14.

46. Report of the Committee of the Headmasters' Association for 1894, p. 24. The grants were made on the following conditions:

(i) the school could be legally aided under the Technical Instruction Act;

    (ii) one or more Representatives of the Technical Education Board could be added to the governing body of the school;

    (iii) open to inspection by representatives of the Board;

    (iv) school curriculum to include drawing and science as well as normal subjects;

    (v) free place scholars – no charge to be made for entrance fee, books, etc. Grant of £5 for each scholar by the Technical Education Board;

    (vi) examinations for awarding scholarships by governing body to public elementary schools were to be held in conjunction with Technical Education Board Junior County Scholarships.

For further details, see P. H. Andrews, *Post-Elementary Education in the Area of the London T.E.B. 1893-1904,* M.A. Thesis, London University, 1959, Chapter V.

47. Reports of the Committee of the Headmasters' Association for 1894-5.

48. Bryce, Vol. I, General Report, P.P. 1895, XLIII, pp. 171-2.

49. Report for 1895 Headmasters' Association, p. 27.

50. Philip Magnus, Chairman of the Joint Scholarship Board, 1895-1906, has left an account of the scientifically precise methods used in the examinations to test sound instruction rather than acquired knowledge. *Educational Aims and Efforts 1880-1910,* (1910), p.39.

    How successful the venture was may be judged by reference to the organization of the examinations at Palmer's Endowed School, Gray's Thurrock, Essex. In 1897, twenty-four boys competed for four places and twenty-five girls for two places. A preliminary examination was held to reduce the number of candidates. Palmer's Endowed School, Gray's Thurrock, PRO Ed. 27/1155, A. F. Leach's Report, 31 May 1897.

51. Fleming Report, op. cit., p. 30. By 1901, thirty-three county councils and twenty-five county boroughs possessed an organization for the promotion of secondary education recognized by the Board of Education. See Return for every County Borough, etc., P.P. 1901, LVI.

52. J. H. Yoxall, M.P., *Secondary Education* (1896), p. 87. As a strong N.U.T. man and one of the Royal Commissioners for the Bryce Commission, Yoxall's statement can be taken as authoritative.

53. It is noticeable that the Charity Commissioners' Reports of the 1890s use the term 'Intermediate Education' possibly as a result of the Welsh Act, to denote the schools coming under their jurisdiction. 'It seems likely that many of the minor Grammar Schools which have hitherto escaped reform for no other reason than that their resources were too small to serve any effective purpose may, under the new scheme, become valuable centres in a system of Intermediate Education.' 40th Report of Charity Commissioners for 1892, p. 32. P.P. 1893-4, XXV.

54. In evidence before the Bryce Commission, Fearon listed eleven towns, including eight county boroughs without endowed schools. Bryce Report, Vol. VI, P.P. 1895, XLV, Q. 11006.

    H. J. Roby agreed that endowments were either too large or too small for the locality and in need of redistribution at the local level. P.P. 1895, XLV, Bryce Report, III. Q. 16509.

55. 41st Report of the Charity Commissioners, 1894, P.P. 1895, XXVIII, p. 37.

56. Report of the Charity Commissioners for 1897, P.P. 1898, XXI, pp. 28-9. Sir George Young, the Commissioner for administering the Endowed Schools Acts wrote, 'I am afraid the large sums placed in England in the hands of County Councils for technical instruction are likely to have a prejudicial effect upon the schools where sound general culture is now obtainable by the

middle-class. Special institutions for technical instruction appear hardly to belong to the region of secondary education; they rather correspond to Universities, in respect of their relation to the other institutions we are considering.' *Educational Review,* September 1892.

The relationship between endowed grammar schools and higher grade schools as such is not involved in this study; but it should be noted that the 1897 concordat agreed upon by representatives of the Headmasters' Association and the higher grade schools demarcated the work to be attempted by each type of school. R. P. Scott played an important part in this work and helped to draft the 'Lockwood' Bill to settle this issue. However, the Cockerton judgment and the intervention of Morant led to the abolition of the school boards, thus leaving the grammar schools as the sole representatives of 'true' secondary education. Baron, op. cit., pp. 126-8.

57. 1894 Select Committee on the Charity Commission, P.P. 1894, XI, Report, p. v.

58. Bryce Report, Vol. I, P.P. 1895, XLIII, p. 95.

59. An earlier attempt to merge the Endowed Schools Department of the Charity Commission in 1893 into the work of the Commission as a whole, failed. See the Report of the Departmental Committee appointed by the Treasury to inquire into the Charity Commission, P.P. 1895, LXXIV.

60. 46th Annual Report of the Charity Commissioners for 1898, P.P. 1899, XIX, p. 29.

61. Return showing the extent and manner in which local authorities in England, Wales and Ireland applied funds to the purposes of Technical Education. P.P. 1899, LXXXIII.

62. Sir John Gorst, the Vice-President, campaigned for the county becoming the chief authority in education. See his 'Prospects of Education in England' in *North American Review,* October 1896.

63. Elie Halévy, *History of the English People, Epilogue 1895-1905* (1939), Book 2, pp. 101-5.

64. PRO Ed. 24/64. Memorandum to Cabinet 31 May 1900.

65. Dr. Edmond Warre, headmaster of Eton (7 July 1899) had met the Duke and made it clear that any move that would sever the school's University connections and which would put the schools on the same level as technical schools would be fiercely opposed. T. C. Fry, of Berkhamsted, on the same day, claimed that his experience on the technical committee of a county council had shown that the committees were largely ignorant of the distinctive features of secondary education and were largely in the hands of their secretaries. PRO Ed. 24/64.

66. Return (to the Order of the House of Commons, 12 February 1900) of the Minutes of the Lord President of the Council Relating to the Reorganization of the Education and Science and Art Departments.

67. PRO Ed. 24/62, 25 July 1899.

68. Fears had been expressed in the Commons, on the Report Stage of the Bill, that the impartial quasi-judicial body dealing with endowments was to be handed over to a new authority, in no sense judicial and entirely dependent upon the Party vote. James Bryce admitted that at that stage of the Bill, no further safeguards could be written in. It was probably such criticism which led to the acceptance of Fearon's plans for the future of the Commission. *Hansard,* Ser. 4, LXXV, 1899, cols. 1073-5.

69. See Sir George Kekewich, *The Education Department and After* (1920), Chapter X.

70. Administrative inspection was concerned with the educational application of

the endowments, as distinct from educational inspection. For details of inspection, see John Leese, *Personalities and Power in English Education* (1950), p. 206, and 36th Annual Report of the Charity Commissioners for 1888, P.P. 1889, XXVIII, p. 25.

71. PRO Ed. 24/63. Proposed paragraph for 3rd Report of Walpole Committee.
72. PRO Ed. 24/64. Abney to Kekewich (January?) 1900.
73. Ibid., Devonshire to Gorst, 26 March 1900.
74. P. H. J. H. Gosden, 'The Board of Education Act 1899', in *British Journal of Educational Studies,* Vol. XI, No. 1, November 1962.
75. 39th Annual Report of Charity Commissioners for 1892, P.P. 1892, XXVII, p. 38. Bruce's enlightened attitude towards education is seen in, for example, 47th Annual Report of Charity Commissioners for 1900, P.P. 1901, XVIII. He stresses three essentials for secondary education: (i) girls' as well as boys' education to be fully catered for; (ii) day scholars rather than boarders to be encouraged at rural grammar schools; (iii) grammar schools should be centres of advanced work of technical instruction, and, in rural areas, centres for evening instruction under the Technical Instruction Acts.

   Bruce had gained the goodwill of headmasters and headmistresses as a result of his tactful handling of the post of Secretary of the Bryce Commission. Morant became Senior Examiner under him in 1900. B. M. Allen, *Sir Robert Morant* (1934), p. 141.

   See also Bruce's Evidence before the Royal Commission on the Civil Service. P.P. 1912-13, XV, Q. 9700-12.
76. 46th Annual Report of Charity Commissioners for 1898, P.P. 1899, XIX, p. 23.
77. Ibid.

CHAPTER 6

The Free Place Regulations

During the eleven years 1895 to 1906, the number of scholarships provided by local authorities increased from about 2,500 places to over 23,500. By 1907, more than half the pupils in secondary schools were from elementary schools, those paying fees and those who did not being roughly equal in number. On the face of it, these figures indicate considerable progress towards providing access to post-elementary education. In fact, much dissatisfaction was voiced concerning the small scale provision made for those parents unable to afford the fees of these schools.

Politically, the organized Labour movement from the 1890s showed its opposition to any plan which did not result in secondary education for all. At the 1897 Trades Union Congress, a resolution condemned a system which provided secondary education 'only for the very small proportion of the workers' children who can come to the top after severe competition with their school fellows'.[1] Such a view did not take into account the state of the secondary schools at the time. By 1903, there were only 407 schools on the grant list, 61 of which were local council and 346 endowed schools. The distribution of secondary schools across the country remained extremely uneven. A further complication was the nature of the provision. Although the number of schools had increased to 575 by 1904, only 99 of these were for girls, 292 were for boys and a mere 184 mixed.

Matters were not made easier after the 1902 Education Act by the tensions which existed between the newly created local education authorities and the Board of Education on secondary education policy. Now, these authorities were in a position to aid existing secondary schools and to establish new ones. The Board, who looked to the traditional independence of the public and endowed secondary schools, was confronted by powerful Directors of Education who challenged this concept of autonomy.[2]

In addition, as we have already seen, many of the old foundations were in financial difficulties, being obliged to compete with the grant-aided science schools. Furthermore, many authorities were niggardly in helping able pupils. Michael Sadler reported that in Liverpool during the six years preceding 1904, not more than eight junior city scholarships had been awarded in any one year.[3] To avoid having to shoulder a growing financial burden which would inevitably occur as the secondary population expanded, the Board of Education by the 1904 Regulations refused to allow schools to charge fees below £3 a year.

For the first time, an official definition of a secondary school[4] was made: a school which offered a four-year course of general education up to and beyond the age of sixteen, with a certain minimum amount of time being allocated to English language and literature, geography and history, a foreign language and mathematics and science.[5] To ensure that standards were maintained, a new Chief Inspector, W. C. Fletcher, and four staff inspectors, all public school men, were appointed in 1904, to oversee a team of HMIs who carried out 'Full Inspections' of municipal secondary schools every three to five years.[6]

One critic of the new Regulations must stand for many. Dr. T. J. Macnamara, a Liberal MP and editor of *The Schoolmaster*, considered that secondary education was now obviously being organized on 'class' lines and that the imposition of a limit of scholarships on local education authorities was unjustified. As for the £3 fee, 'the working-class parent will throw up the sponge in despair'.[7] Previously a form of cheap advanced education had been available at the higher grade schools, but since the Cockerton Judgment of 1900 had declared such education to be illegal, many of these schools had been turned into secondary schools by the new authorities. The gulf between the social classes in respect of schooling therefore was widening.[8]

These matters were taken up direct with the Board by the Association of Education Committees, who sent a deputation to meet Sir William Anson, Parliamentary Secretary to the Board, Robert Morant, the Permanent Secretary and other officers. The point was strongly made that, without prejudice to existing grants from the Board, Education Committees should have local option in fixing the fees to be charged as well as in deciding the proportion of free scholarships[9]. The Board, in reply, conceded that they were prepared to consider the special circumstances of each school in which a local authority desired to vary the arrangements as regards fees, or the absence of fees or the number of free places.[10]

A stimulus to increasing the number of scholarships followed the Board's Regulations of 1905 which required boys and girls intended for the teaching profession to receive a sound general education in a secondary school for three or four years. Up to then, the route had been attendance at elementary school followed by a spell of time at a pupil-teacher centre. The London County Council Education Committee, which succeeded the Technical Education Board in 1904, offered as many as 1,200 such scholarships in 1905 to boys and girls of elementary, higher elementary or secondary schools who, at the age of 14 or 15, desired to become pupil teachers.[11] There was a further consequence of this new policy. Over 3,400 junior county scholarships were awarded to pupils of between the ages of 11 and 12, tenable till the age of 14 and renewable for a further two years. These were given in a 2:1 ratio for girls, with a view to increasing the supply of teachers,[12] and seven new or converted secondary schools were earmarked for girls.[13] It is interesting to note that the authority was unable to adhere to this rule without unduly lowering the standard for girls or fixing an unreasonably high standard for boys. From 1909, this quota system was dropped and a fairly equal number of boys and girls were chosen.[14]

A Return compiled by the Secretary of the County Councils Association in November 1905 gives details of the award of scholarships at this date in all the English administrative counties except London.[15] The term junior or minor scholarships covered all awards to pupils from public elementary schools, though in a few cases candidates already at secondary schools (e.g. Leicestershire, Yorkshire, North Riding) were eligible. Several counties had not as yet adopted a complete scholarship scheme and there were wide variations relating to the conditions attached to the awards. For instance, in Durham, Lincolnshire (Lindsey), Middlesex, Northamtonshire and Northumberland, scholarships were only tenable during residence in the county. The number awarded ranged from seven each in Devon and Dorset to 150 in the West Riding of Yorkshire. The age limit was usually 11 to 13 but Oxfordshire

allowed pupils up to 15 to enter. Perhaps the widest variation lay in
the value of the scholarships. Some, such as Rutland, awarded a
fixed sum of money, in this case £15. Most authorities spelt out
different categories of assistance: Durham gave general grants for
fees, books (up to £2), fares and maintenance, whilst rural counties
(e.g. Berkshire and Buckinghamshire) made boarding allowances.
Only eight of the counties allocated places specifically for boys and
girls. 'Other conditions' imposed included, in Wiltshire, 1,050
attendances at a public elementary school within the previous three
years; in Nottingham the stipulation was that 'parents must need
help', whilst in Shropshire, preference was given to intending
pupil-teachers.

New Policies

The return of a Liberal Government headed by Campbell-
Bannerman in 1906 saw the introduction of an Education Bill
which would have redeemed their election pledge to establish
public control over all schools maintained out of public money and
to abolish religious tests for teachers. One clause of the Bill
approved by the Commons provided for scholarships for elementary school pupils to enable them to extend their full-time
education. The Bill, which met with virulent opposition from the
former Prime Minister A. J. Balfour, and the Church of England
interests, was sent back to the Commons, in the words of Augustine
Birrell, the President of the Board of Education, 'with clouds of
Amendments',[16] including the deletion of this clause, and the Bill
was eventually dropped.[17]

By the beginning of the following year, the combined forces of
the National Union of Teachers, the Trades Union Congress and
many Members of Parliament had pressed the Government to pay
regard to the higher educational interests of the working classes.
The last straw was the intention of the Board to raise fees at
secondary schools.[18] Reginald McKenna had replaced Birrell as
President of the Board in January 1907;[19] on May 15, he
announced a new policy, enshrined in Regulations for Secondary
Schools, which went some way to meeting the demands of the
Government's critics. Secondary schools would in future offer up to
25 per cent of their places free to pupils from public elementary
schools and thus make for wider access and counter the notion

that secondary schools were, in Macnamara's phrase, 'class institutions'.

The reactions of some of the grammar schools at the time have been recorded as displaying at the least a lukewarm attitude and at the most intense hostility towards the Free Place Regulations.[20] Much of this arose from the changing system of grants following the Regulations. Previously, schools making special provision for science had been awarded grants at double the rate received by others. These grants were assessed at different rates on pupils in different years of the course. The new Regulations swept all this away and grants were assessed at a uniform rate of £5 for all pupils in the school. No longer was there a temptation to distort the curriculum in the quest for earning higher grants. The Regulations, therefore, placed the responsibility directly on the school without regard to the school's ability to meet the cost.[21] As a Board Minute on the matter put it,

> The proposed new rule as to free places for ex-Public Elementary School scholars is presumably intended to secure that the Board's grants are not paid to schools which are in a real sense exclusive class schools used chiefly by those who ought to pay for the education of their own children.
>
> It is obvious that no single test can effectually distinguish such schools and the test proposed has the serious drawback that it puts a very heavy financial burden on Schools and Authorities which in many cases the Schools cannot and Authorities will not carry: either the rule will be whittled away in prejudice or there will be a serious loss of efficiency in the schools.[22]

In fact the Board attempted to alleviate these difficulties by adjusting the percentage of free places required to rates ranging from the normal 25 down to 10 per cent. No definite age of entry was laid down. To counter the financial objections to transferring pupils from the elementary to the secondary school between the age of 10 and 12, grants of £2 per head were made payable to the former school.

Two important consequences followed these Regulations. First, it took the individual school as the basis of allocation, making all grant-aided secondary schools equally accessible, and avoided the segregation of free place holders into particular schools.[23] Second, it repudiated in theory rather than in practice the doctrine that free secondary education should be restricted to the particularly able working-class child. The aim was not, as many nineteenth century critics had feared, for children to rise into a different social class, but that education 'should be open to children of all classes as near as possible upon equal terms'.[24] The Board refused to acknowledge the view of one local authority which questioned 'providing academic education for scholars who were more fitted for industrial than for clerical or scholastic pursuits, and had the effect of encouraging boys to become inferior clerks instead of good artisans'.[25]

In introducing the Free Place Regulations, McKenna stressed the fact that pupils would be expected to pass an 'attainment test' which was not, like the scholarship examination, competitive in nature. The only prerequisite for taking the test was that the boys and girls had been attending a public elementary school for at least two years. Shortly after the announcement of the Regulations, McKenna discussed several matters arising out of them with a deputation from the Incorporated Association of Headmasters, which included the heads of Charterhouse, Chigwell and Christ's Hospital. The question of the admission test featured largely in the discussion. McKenna admitted that there would be 'certain difficulties' as regards the qualifying examination. It would be competitive only amongst the scholars from public elementary schools.

> The examination ought to be one which would show whether the child was up to the general average standard – not scholarship standard – of the Secondary School. The examination should be the same as for ordinary fee-paying scholars. It was not in the least his intention that the standard of the secondary school should be lowered in order to admit a different type of intelligence.

The opinion of the deputation was sought as to the age these children should be admitted. McKenna stated that 'he thought the Elementary School boy who was, on entering the Secondary School, on the same level of intelligence as the ordinary fee paying scholar was really better qualified naturally because he had had fewer opportunities.' It was agreed that foreign languages should be omitted from the examination, and that the scholars should be tested only in the subjects in which they had received instruction.[26]

When it came to operating the Regulations, however, a number of difficulties of interpretation became obvious. The key paragraph of the Regulations was Article 20, which laid down the conditions of higher grants. The exact wording is as follows:

> In all schools where a fee is charged, arrangements must be made to the satisfaction of the Board for seeing that a proportion of school places shall be open without payment of fee to scholars from Public Elementary Schools who apply for admission, subject to the applicants passing an entrance test of attainment and proficiency . . . . The proportion of school places will ordinarily be 25 per cent of the scholars admitted, but this requirement may be reduced by the Board on sufficient grounds in the case of any particular school.[27]

This Article was generally suspect in at least three respects. First, whilst 'ordinarily' the proportion was to be 25 per cent, the percentage of free places could be lowered indefinitely at the discretion of the Board. For the first year only, i.e. 1907-8, schools were allowed to admit as low as 12 per cent free places, though this was not to be repeated in subsequent years. Second, the freeness of the free places was subject to continued liability to payments in addition to the fee. This had been one of the burning questions in the early administration of the 1891 Free Education Act[28] and as one official who had been involved in carrying out this Act, J. W. Mackail[29] noted, 'the whole matter must necessarily be seen in a somewhat different light by those who have and those who have not had that experience'.[30] The Chief Inspector of Secondary Schools, W. C. Fletcher, had clear views on this matter, being strongly against attempts to interfere in regulating financial arrangements between parents and schools.

> I see no good – but much harm – in prescribing rules for all if the object is to secure full privileges for free place holders. If the latter are to have books, dinners &c provided I think we should say so straight out (pay for it as well!) and leave schools free as they have been hitherto to conduct the rest of their business as they think best.
>
> For the Board to prescribe for instance that the use of books must be granted to fee paying boys is to fly in the face of a great mass of educational opinion which holds that boys should own their own books.[31]

The third weakness of the Article was that while the Government grant to schools was uniform, it was left to the individual schools or the rate-aid tendered by local education authorities to decide the scale of help given to free placers. One of the main points of contention under this heading was the extent to which authorities interpreted the term 'free place'. In his speech to the Commons introducing the Regulations, McKenna had announced that the twenty five per cent free places were to be additional to scholarships already conferred, and that such free places were not to be confused with scholarships. He further said that 'where the schools were provided by the local education authority he trusted they would all be free'.[32] Article 20, which came into force on 1 August 1907, naturally caused much disappointment. McKenna had not taken into account the fact that secondary schools had been founded under varying schemes, that there were in existence at the time many different scholarship systems and that rural areas presented features markedly different from those in urban areas.

One result of this was that in many schools, scholarship, free place and fee-paying candidates sat for the same examination for entry to the grammar schools but each group was required to achieve different standards.[33] Lancashire County Council counted as free places exhibitions offered by Co-operative Societies and individual benefactors. Out of 21 free places at Accrington, for instance, only ten were provided by the County Council. Further, the County Education Committee's Scholarships Sub-Committee reported that by providing 25 per cent of free places in every secondary school, this could lead to 'a lower standard of quality and attainments of the students to whom they were awarded'. Of the 350 junior exhibitions available for public elementary school children in the county in 1908, only 300 were awarded.[34] A deputation of Labour MPs to the Board protesting at the interpretation of Article 20 was sympathetically received. One official minuted, 'the working classes are in fact very imperfectly informed of their rights, and in order to secure them these, stringent administrative action and widely diffused publicity are often necessary.' Initially, W. N. Bruce had been charged by the President with three tasks: the direct responsibility for co-ordinating the actions of the three territorial divisions within the Department; the securing of adequate uniformity of treatment as regards the percentage of free places; and also dealing with questions relating to the curriculum under the 1907 Secondary Regulations.[35] At the end of the first year's operation of the Regulations, Bruce was pessimistic about the attempts of the Board to obtain 25 per cent free places in addition to local authority scholarships or out of endowments. Neither schools nor ratepayers, he believed, would be prepared to accept such a burden; at the same time, the modest proportion of the Board's grant put them in a weak position to force the issue.[36]

The loose wording of Article 20 caused problems for both the Board's officials and the Inspectorate. It was not clear whether free places were to be restricted to children from public elementary schools within the local authority area in which a school was situated; whether the responsibility for seeing that free place candidates satisfied the requirement as to two years in an elementary school fell on the governing body or an HMI; and whether free places were offered termly or annually.[37] By March, 1909 the Board had clarified, to the satisfaction of educationists and trade union leaders, the term 'free place'.[38] But progress in increasing the number of places up to the outbreak of the First World War was slow. Although, by 1909, 865 of the 926 secondary schools were on the Board's list, only 746 were required to offer 25 per cent free places. The following Table gives an indication of the total numbers involved. (1908-9 was the first year of the new Regulations' operation.)

	Total No. of FP pupils	% of total admissions	No. of FP admissions	% of previous year's admissions	
1908-09	42,200	31.2	15,558	31.8	
1909-10	50,146	31.8	15,311	29.6	
1914-15	65,799	33.1	17,111	28.5	[39]

The absence of a statutory starting age at secondary schools proved to be a handicap. As in the previous century, teachers at elementary schools looking to their own interests, held on to their abler pupils as long as possible, often opposing their transfer. Although London had fixed the maximum age limit for its junior scholarships at twelve, others continued to choose ages ranging up to fourteen. This lack of uniformity not only made for inefficiency in the secondary schools, but it presented organizational and curricular difficulties. One reason for pupils starting at a later age was that they were unlikely to enter as fee payers until their last chance of a free place was gone. Lancashire eventually fixed the age limits at ten to twelve in 1913 and other authorities took similar action in due course. In the year 1910-11, disregarding entries below the age of eleven, the relative age distribution of the entry was as follows.

Age	%
11-12	26
12-13	38
13-14	21
14+	15

Employers placed relatively little importance on the age at which educated boys and girls started work and the financial loss entailed by parents in leaving their children at school was often considerable. Two factors helped to change this situation before 1914. One was the need for more teachers in elementary schools as well as in secondary schools – the introduction of the new pupil-teacher system made the prospects of the profession more attractive and acted as an inducement to staying on. Second, local authorities began to demand 'school life undertakings' before pupils were admitted to secondary schools. Such an undertaking bound a child to staying for three years, sometimes less, and in some cases to the age of fifteen. Leaving out school life below the age of twelve, the average school life of boys was slightly shorter than that of girls.

	Average School Life			
	1908-9		1912-13	
	Yrs.	Months	Yrs.	Months
Boys	2	7	2	9
Girls	2	7	3	0

Similarly, girls tended to stay on at school somewhat longer.

	Average Leaving Age				
	1908-9		1912-13		
	Yrs.	Months	Yrs.	Months	
Boys	15	5	15	7	
Girls	15	11	16	0	40

In 1910 W. N. Bruce expressed his concern that in every year since 1907, the number of free places awarded in state-aided schools had fallen substantially short of the number offered. This was mainly due to the poor take-up rate in rural areas, where access to schools was difficult, a factor which told especially against girls. It is clear too from the statistics that the number of ex-public elementary school pupils who paid tuition fees was not much below that of the children whose fees were paid for them (50,625 as against 56,000), though no analysis of this latter category was attempted. Bruce stated in 1910 that if any distinctions within schools were made between the two categories, then this was unjustified, as the free placers made no more demands financially on the school than fee payers.[41]

The average fee at this date did not exceed £7, and as the cost of maintaining an efficient secondary school rarely fell below £14 a head, fee-paying parents were relieved of a half or more of the cost of their children's education.

Bruce saw the need for internal scholarships for free placers who needed maintenance allowances to enable them to stay at school after the age at which they could find suitable employment. It is a significant fact, though, that in spite of the difficulties, the average school life of a free placer was substantially longer than that of a fee-paying pupil, many of whose parents found the strain of paying tuition fees too great after two or three years.

Since the Technical Instruction Acts had first awarded scholarships, there was a tendency for local authorities to spend too much on scholarships and too little on enabling schools to give efficient instruction to the holders. Although by 1916 the balance had been largely redressed, there were still a large number of secondary schools where able pupils were unable to realize their talents to the full. As Bruce put it bluntly, 'At present the prospects of a really clever boy depend greatly on the School he happens to attend'. Although the Board had not any clear policy on the matter, it emerged in its gathering evidence for the Royal Commission on the Civil Service (1912) that except in the immediate neighbourhood of university towns, only a minority of schools sent their pupils on to universities.[42] Bruce floated the idea which had been discussed at a recent meeting of the Headmasters' Conference, of transferring potential university candidates to public schools. The difficulties involved in such a scheme, namely the provision of boarding facilities and the reluctance of schools to part with their most promising students early in their course, were recognized. To correct these anomalies, Bruce suggested a number of remedies. Suitable means of transit should be provided where necessary: 'the motor may play a great part in rural education'. Travelling allowances should be instituted, as in Lancashire, where every pupil living more than five miles from a secondary school received assistance. Maintenance grants, full boarding scholarships and the provision of hostels restricted to children from rural areas were also suggested.[43] This ambitious plan was not commented on within the Board, and the matter proceeded no further. As in so many other spheres of public welfare the stimulus of war was needed to bring about change.

NOTES

1. Quoted in B. Simon, *Education and the Labour Movement, 1870-1920* (1965), p. 202.
2. G. Baron and D. Howell, *Research Studies 6. School Management and Government* (1968), pp. 23-30.
3. M. E. Sadler, *Report on Secondary Education in Liverpool* (1904), p. 164.
4. The imprecision of this term was admitted by Morant in the 1904 Regulations. Both the Spens and the Norwood Committees found difficulty in making an authoritative definition. J. H. Higginson, 'Evolution of "Secondary Education" ', *British Journal of Educational Studies,* Vol. XX, No. 2, June 1972, pp. 174-5.
5. See P. Gordon and D. Lawton, *Curriculum Change in the Nineteenth and Twentieth Centuries* (1978), pp. 22-3.
6. J. Leese, *Personalities and Power in English Education* (1950), p. 263.
7. T. J. Macnamara, 'The State and Secondary Education', *Independent Review,* May 1905, pp. 53-4.
8. R. Barker, *Education and Politics 1900-1951. A Study of the Labour Party* (1972), p. 22.
9. PRO Ed. 24/368. Association of Education Committees. Fees and Scholarships in Secondary Schools, 8 March, 1905.
10. Ibid. R. L. Morant to J. Tudor Walters, 12 March, 1905. Morant noted, next to this point, 'This is new ground for the Board'.
11. London County Council, *Report of the Education Committee on the New Scholarship Scheme, Feb. 1905.* EO/PS/3/1, Greater London (London) Record Office. (Hereafter GLRO)
12. One critic of the scheme wrote:

    'To put it briefly, the proposals of the Education Committee practically amount to asking the County Council to spend £180,000 a year in order to induce a few thousand middle-class girls to come into the elementary schools so as they may eventually be trained as pupil teachers without cost to themselves. No! It is not a "great scholarship scheme" nor an "educational staircase" nor a "capacity catching net". It is really a scheme for catching teachers.'
    The Schoolmaster, 17 Dec 1904.

13. S. Maclure, *One Hundred Years of London Education, 1870-1970* (1970), p. 88.
14. London County Council, Education Department, *Report of the Education Committee. Revision of Scholarship Scheme,* EO/PS/3/1, 30 June 1909, GLRO. The nature of the tests varied from authority to authority. In Northumberland, the County Council Education Committee resolved that after 1905, candidates for Minor and Pupil Teachers' Scholarships, who had to be under 13 years of age, should take papers in English and arithmetic and two of the following:

grammar, geography, history, drawing, needlework and knowledge of the common phenomena of the world. Northumberland Education Committee, Curricula and Examinations Advisory Sub-Committee, 26 Jan 1906. Minute Book Vol. II 1904-15, Northumberland Record Office.

15. 'Scholarships in the English Administrative Counties, excluding London', Supplement to *Education*, 26 Jan 1906.
16. A. Birrell, *Things Past Redress* (1937), p. 191.
17. See J. A. Spender, *The Life of the Rt. Hon. Sir Henry Campbell-Bannerman* (1923), Vol. II p. 274ff; and S. Dark, *Bishop Davidson and the English Church* (1929), pp. 182-4.
18. For full details, see Board of Education, *Regulations for Secondary Schools (in force from 1 Aug 1907)* (1907), pp. 1-17.
19. McKenna, an able administrator, remained in the post for only a year, transferring to the Admiralty in February 1908. S. McKenna, *Reginald McKenna. A Memoir* (1948), pp. 46-7.
20. G.A.N. Lowndes recalled the alarm and misgivings aroused by the new regulations.

> A few of those governing bodies who felt themselves to belong to the socially superior order of 'armigerous gentlemen' hastened to shelter behind the school's coat of arms. Some successfully resisted the acceptance of free place scholars for several decades to come... Secondary school masters and mistresses serving at the time remembered that the sole question they were asked at the visit of one of their governors was 'How many girls in your class have nits in their hair?'

G. A. N. Lowndes, *The Silent Social Revolution* (1969 edn.), p. 88.

21. One consequence of low income was that secondary school staff were on the whole overworked and underpaid. See memorandum on 'Scale of Salaries' 1907, PRO Ed. 24/370.
22. Memorandum, 'The Proposed Free Place Rule' 1907, PRO Ed. 24/372.
23. *Report of the Departmental Committee on Scholarships and Free Places* (1920), p. 4.
24. Report of the Board of Education for 1909-10, quoted in O. L. Banks, *Parity and Prestige in English Education* (1955), p. 66.
25. London County Council Education Committee Report of a deputation of the Council to the Board of Education, 22 Dec 1909. EO/PS/3/26, GLRO.
26. Report of a meeting between the President of the Board of Education and a deputation of the Incorporated Association of Headmasters, 13 June 1907. PRO Ed. 24/373. A précis of this discussion was issued as a Memo to Inspectors S. No. 72.
27. Board of Education, Regulations for Secondary Schools. Free Scholars from Public Elementary Schools. W. N. Bruce, 10 July 1907. Form 4cS.
28. See, for example, *The School Board Chronicle,* 11 July 1891, p. 37, and the Minute Book of the Secretary of the Education Department, 1889-99, 'Provision of Books', G. W. Kekewich, pp. 39-42, PRO Ed. 9/5.
29. For Mackail's work at the Board, see C. Bailey, 'John William Mackail, O.M.', *Proceedings of the British Academy,* Vol. XXXI (1947), pp. 1-3.
30. J.W. Mackail to W. N. Bruce, 30 July 1908, PRO Ed. 24/377.
31. Memorandum by the Chief Inspector of Secondary Schools on the proposed changes as to Free Places, 9 March 1908, PRO Ed. 24/378.
32. *Hansard,* Ser 4, CLXXIV, House of Commons, 15 May 1907, col. 1054.
33. J. F. Chadderton, *Barrow Grammar School for Boys 1880-1960* (1964), p. 58.
34. Lancashire Education Committee Schools Sub-Committee Minute Book No. 1, 1903-15, 20 June 1908. ESM 1, Lancashire Record Office.

35. R. L. Morant to W. N. Bruce, 3 July 1907, PRO Ed. 24/375.

36. W. N. Bruce to J. W. Mackail, 30 July 1908, PRO Ed. 24/377.

37. Notes of Inspectors' Conference, 5-6 July, 1907, PRO Ed.24/374. McKenna himself attended the second day of the Conference. There was some ambiguity, as local education authorities were quick to point out, on whether the present number of pupils in a school was to be taken as a basis for reckoning the percentage. See for example, T. L. Papillon, 'The Free Places System', *Morning Post,* 10 August 1910.

38. B. Simon, (1965) op. cit., p. 272. At its annual general meeting of January, 1909, the Headmasters' Association accepted the 25 per cent requirement, whereas a year previously they had not. A. M. Kazamias, *Politics, Society and Secondary Education* (1966), p. 178.

39. Board of Education Pamphlet No. 50, *Some Account of the Recent Development of Secondary Schools* (1927), p. 15.

40. Ibid, pp. 16-17.

41. Minute, W. N. Bruce, 16 July 1910, PRO Ed. 24/379.

42. For Bruce's Evidence to the Royal Commission on the Civil Service, see Evidence, Q 9527-9739, P.P. 1912-13, XV.

43. Memorandum on provision for assisting boys and girls to attend secondary schools in England, W. N. Bruce, 27 March 1916, PRO Ed. 24/1637.

CHAPTER 7

Administrative and Political Changes
1918-45

The inter-war period witnessed a dramatic change in the conditions governing selection for secondary schools. One result of the First World War was an immediate increase in the demand for secondary education. Thanks to higher wages and salaries, the payment of fees presented much less of a problem to parents than hitherto. The average size of schools on the grant list rose by over 40 per cent in the five years between 1914-15 to 1919-20; competition for places became fierce, and the total number of pupils went up from 307,862 to 359,621. The growth of sixth forms and the establishment of the Secondary School Examinations Council in 1917 to supervise the administration of the new School Certificate Examination for pupils at 16 and 18 also swelled the numbers.[1]

If these structural factors would seem to have had a depressing effect on the free place system, the Education Act of 1918 looked to restore the balance. This Act, the outcome of wartime idealism, was steered through the Commons by H. A. L. Fisher, President of the Board and previously Vice-Chancellor of Sheffield University, who had been drafted into the Cabinet to direct educational reform. There were two vital sections of the Act relating to the question of access to secondary education. Section 1 required all local authorities, with a view to the establishment of a national system of education, to submit schemes to show how this might be best achieved. Section 4(4) provided that in such schemes 'adequate provision shall be made in order to secure that children and young persons shall not be debarred from receiving the benefits of any form of education by which they are capable of profiting through inability to pay fees'.[2]

Although the Act was in many respects an emasculated version of the original Bill, its provision for continuing education and the plan for a national system was a bold one. Economic and political events resulted in the dropping of many of its provisions, but the school leaving age was raised to 14. Fisher was anxious to extend the benefits of secondary education and in July 1919 ordered the setting up of a Departmental Committee to inquire into the existing arrangements for the award by local education authorities of scholarships tenable at secondary schools and for the provision of free places, 'with a view to improving such arrangements and thereby rendering possible facilities for higher education more generally accessible and advantageous to all classes of the population'.[3]

The Report of the Departmental Committee on Scholarships and Free Places was issued in the following year (1920). Its terms of reference were confined to a consideration of admission to secondary schools, but, in fact, it dealt more fully with the problems of transfer.[4] The Committee remarked on the variety of 'free place' admissions which constituted the 25 per cent necessary to satisfy the Board's requirement. In 1918-19, of the 246,000 pupils in the 961 grant-aided secondary schools, there were 72,386 free places. These were made up of 53,460 awarded by local authorities, 16,548 by school governors and 2,378 by other endowments, usually local trusts. Fisher had made it clear that 'if only on political grounds, the reference must not exclude maintenance allowances': the Committee therefore classified free places into three groups according to the holder receiving free tuition only, or free tuition plus cost of books, travelling expenses and so on, or in addition an actual grant of money.

This arbitrariness stemmed from the different bodies responsible for making the awards, with the local authorities providing three quarters of the places. To enable a child to be 'capable of profiting' by a secondary school course, some changes in the system were necessary. It was recommended that local education authorities should assume financial responsibility for the provision of free places and that the age of admission should normally be between 11 and 12. Maintenance allowances should be available from public money to enable pupils to complete the full secondary course.

In discussing the implementation of Section 4(4) of the Act, the Report dealt at length with the question of free education. Whilst the obvious solution was to make secondary schooling available to all capable of profiting by it, the need for national economy ruled this out.[5] Instead, the Committee recommended raising the total of free places, as a first step, from 25 to 40 per cent, hopefully to increase to 75 per cent within ten years. It also pointed out that this section's inclusion of the terms 'inability to pay fees' raised a new principle. The Committee did not believe that this limited the granting of free places to ex-public elementary pupils only, but should also include children educated elsewhere.

The post-war economic slump and the political changes which characterized the 1920s and 1930s naturally affected attitudes towards the Committee's proposals. By 1922, in the last year of the Coalition Government's life, Fisher, anxious to safeguard the balance between fee and free scholars, canvassed headmasters of the more prestigious secondary schools to ascertain if the contribution of fee payers could be raised. A typical reply was that the 'proportion of parents who could comfortably pay larger or much larger fees is *none* per cent.'[6]

These enquiries were in connection with the activities of the Geddes Committee, appointed by Lloyd George in August 1921 to investigate departmental estimates for the coming year, in order to recommend economies.[7] In a masterly Minute, E.H. Pelham, the Deputy Secretary of the Board, showed that any restriction on the award of free places would act adversely on the efficiency of the schools. The percentage of free places was fixed in relation to an area as a whole, the excess of numbers in one school being compensated for by a shortage in another and rural schools were likely to suffer unduly in free competition with urban schools.[8] An Interim Report of the Geddes Committee had recommended a limitation of 25 per cent on free places, but the Cabinet Committee concerned with acting upon these recommendations declared that the savings would be small 'and having regard also to the importance attached to those free places in the industrial areas of the country, we are not prepared to accept their recommendation as it stands.'[9]

It was due to Fisher's representations that the Committee's original proposal of limiting the grants paid was dramatically altered. This would have been a severe blow to authorities who, taking advantage of Article 19 of the 1907 Regulations, offered free or nearly free secondary education, such as Manchester, Bradford, Sheffield and Halifax; other authorities, Durham in particular, had pledged themselves to its gradual introduction. Nevertheless, the Regulations were altered in 1922 so that a closer scrutiny could be made of authorities wishing to make increases in free places. Selby-Bigge as Secretary of the Board, commenting on possible measures to restrict free places, saw little advantage in further restrictions:

> I think myself there is an overwhelming case for relaxation of our practice in respect of expenditure on free places in secondary schools. It is pretty certain that all the children who get them are good material for education, and we get both the advantage of educating good material and keeping it out of the competition for juvenile employment.[10]

Political changes were reflected in changing attitudes towards selection for secondary education. R. H. Tawney had been largely responsible for drafting the Labour Party's policy document *Secondary Education For All* (1922).[11] He attacked the Geddes mentality and called for the implementation of the 1918 Education Act relating to continuation schools, which had been killed off in the intervening period. Although Tawney advocated greater public expenditure on good primary schooling, no clear policy was defined. He suggested a variety of schools, some technical and vocational, alongside the traditional grammar schools, as well as the central or intermediate schools established by the Act. Three quarters of elementary school children would be admitted to them free of charge and receive maintenance grants. However, the ambiguity of thinking contained in this policy document did little to advance the cause of the common secondary school or directly assist free places in existing schools.

After a brief Conservative interlude, the first Labour Government was elected to office in January 1924, destined to fall within the same year. The new President of the Board, C. P. Trevelyan, a former Liberal MP who had had extensive Parliamentary experience in education,[12] initiated several important changes during his short time in office. The most notable was contained in Circular 1340, which was largely his authorship[13] and issued on 4 September 1924.

Although local education authorities were encouraged to discuss the implications of raising the school leaving age to 15, the Circular's main aim was to extend the number of places in secondary schools. Trevelyan suggested that authorities should take as their objective a provision of 20 places per 1,000 of population.

As an inducement for authorities to increase the proportion of free places, a special grant was awarded, based on the free places in excess of 25 per cent of the aggregate number of pupils in the schools on 1 October 1924.[14] Trevelyan pressed for a £3 grant, but after a clash with Philip Snowden, then Chancellor of the Exchequer, he had to settle initially for £2[15] and from 1925, £3. Higher maintenance allowances were also given. Besides the 40 per cent maximum which was now permitted, the Board's officials re-examined the Report of the Departmental Committee on Free Places and made further suggestions. E. H. Pelham saw as an alternative to the 40 per cent limit a policy based on allowing local education authorities to provide as many free places as ratepayers would tolerate.[16] Sir Hugh Orange, Accountant-General of the Board, on the other hand, warned Trevelyan that the extent to which secondary education was free raised important policy questions in which Parliament could claim to have a say; and on practical grounds 'it might be rather an alarming proposition to propose to abandon a source of revenue which at present is worth £3,000,000 per annum'.[17]

With the turn of the wheel in political fortune, a new Conservative President, Lord Eustace Percy, replaced Trevelyan in November 1924. One of Percy's earliest concerns was the future of the 'supergrant' awarded by Circular 1340 two months previously.

An autocratic politician,[18] Percy came to the conclusion that although it would mean a reversal of policy, the operation of the Circular so far had convinced him that the new grant was unfair, and ill adapted for the purpose it was meant to serve; it was best to terminate it before local authorities began to rely upon its indefinite continuance.[19] Selby-Bigge, the Secretary of the Board, reminded Percy that the grant was never intended to be temporary and that, before the election, the Conservative Party, in the person of Stanley Baldwin, had pledged itself to greater access to secondary school irrespective of ability to pay.[20]

Selby-Bigge outlined two ways in which such access could be increased. The choice was either a) maintain a system under which substantial fees were charged to those who could afford them, whilst making a liberal provision of fees for those who could not, or b) arrange a system charging very low fees or no fees irrespective of

ability of parents to pay, on the assumption that every citizen had a
right to demand free education. Trevelyan, according to Selby-
Bigge, 'was trying to ride two horses pulling different ways' and he
had criticized Trevelyan's scheme of supergrants ('I never wanted
to establish this grant', he wrote) on the grounds that it was
unsound to use funds in order to develop one particular aspect only
of education. Obviously alternative a) was more congenial to a
Conservative Government than b), but Percy and Selby-Bigge
agreed that the sudden withdrawal of the grant would be seen as a
breach of continuity and would be regarded with dismay by local
authorities.[21]

In February 1925, Circular 1352, entitled Free Place Grant,
announced the ending of the special grant from March 1926. Using phraseology similar to Selby-Bigge's, it mentioned that the
grant stressed only one branch of the higher education service. It
also pointed out that the grant was intended to further the education of juveniles between the ages of 14 and 16 as an alternative
to paying them unemployment insurance benefits and had not
proved to be an effective one. Local authorities were still permitted
to award free places up to 40 per cent but they were not to
give this priority over developing higher education facilities in
general.[22]

In this climate of economic stringency the Consultative Committee on the Education of the Adolescent was set up. Its terms of
reference did not include the established secondary schools, but it
did consider the relationship between the primary and secondary
stages of education and also suitable courses of study for pupils up
to the age of 15 in other types of school. The Committee's
recommendations on selection procedures will be discussed later
(see p. 207). Here it is sufficient to mention that it recommended the
age of 11 as a natural point in a child's development for transfer to
secondary education,[23] and that other forms of post-primary
schools, such as selective, central, junior technical and trade
schools, offering a truncated 'secondary' education, were to be encouraged. Without doubt, the alternatives to secondary schools in
the post-Hadow era drew off previous aspirants for free places.[24]
Kenneth Lindsay's study Social Progress and Educational Waste,
published in 1926, showed that at Bradford, where the refusals of
free places exceeded the number of acceptances, many of the abler
children preferred the shorter course at the central school to the

full secondary school course.[25] The central school, which had developed from the higher grade schools and the schools of science, normally had either a commercial or industrial bias. As a contemporary description of the school ran, 'Its practical utility in securing permanent and comparatively well-paid employment has been a powerful attraction both to pupils and parents'.[26] In London, Manchester and other large towns, these schools occupied an important place in the general system. Hadow had recommended that the school leaving age should be raised to 15; although Percy and his colleagues favoured a reorganization of senior elementary schools to provide four year courses, there would be two parallel systems of primary education which would be kept apart.[27]

Trevelyan's return to office in the second Labour Government in June 1929 was a foregone conclusion. The day after his appointment, he wrote to his wife: 'the two big jobs ahead are raising the school age and a denominational school settlement – the first will come off, the second may not come off'. In fact neither was accomplished during his term of office. Regarded as a militant leftist by his colleagues and personally disliked by the Prime Minister, Ramsay MacDonald, Trevelyan was defeated on the school leaving age issue in the Cabinet even before Parliament assembled.[28] However, after much hesitation and prompting by outsiders, and encouraged by Tawney's leaders in the *Manchester Guardian*, Trevelyan promised a Bill to raise the age to 15 by 1 April 1931, a hope which was not fulfilled.

Faced with these difficulties, Trevelyan turned to exploring the possibilities of extending free secondary schooling and increased maintenance allowances, though Treasury resistance against such a move was strong.[29] By February 1930, Trevelyan was able to announce that the total number of free places in a school was to be increased from 40 per cent to 50 per cent.[30] This came into effect on 1 August.[31] Circular 1412, issued in the following April, anticipated that there would be a large increase in the numbers seeking admission to secondary school in 1931 and 1932.[32]

Events once more were overtaken by crises in other places. Trevelyan had already resigned before MacDonald split the Labour movement by heading a Coalition Government, largely Conservative in composition, and which lasted from August 1931 to June 1935. This had come about in response to a deepening economic crisis of world wide proportions and the Government saw as its task the seeking of remedies which would shield the country from the worst effects of the situation.

The May Committee, an equivalent to the Geddes Committee of 1922, was appointed to seek out areas of national expenditure which could without excessive hardship be reduced. The Report, issued in July 1931, recommended a saving of almost £100 million: after unemployment benefits, the education service was the second largest target. Almost £14 million was to be saved by careful reductions, especially cuts in teachers' salaries and the postponement of the raising of the school leaving age.

It was natural that the free place system should also come under scrutiny. The Cabinet considered a memorandum on Fees and Free Places in Secondary Schools prepared by the President of the Board, Lord Irwin (later Viscount Halifax), drawn up on 25 August 1932, on possible economies. Some three years previously, a Labour Government White Paper had recommended a strict means test for maintenance allowances for the needy, a proposal which had met with much disapproval. Irwin now suggested introducing a means test for the award of free places, a course first discussed in Cabinet on 4 August. Immediate approval of the proposal was essential: it would result in a saving of £50,000 for the Exchequer and an equal amount for the rates in 1933-4; within four years the amount would rise to £200,000 under each heading.[33] The Cabinet approved the proposal on 27 August, authorising the issuing of a circular which 'while safeguarding the interests of the clever child of poor parents in obtaining free secondary education, would ensure that adequate fees are charged to parents who can afford to pay them'.

Circular 1421, dated 15 September 1932, introduced the means test for all entrants to secondary schools. Fees between £9.9s. and £15.15s. were to be charged with 'remissions where necessary'. Complete remission was available for a family with one child on an income of £3 to £4 a week (or 10s. more per week for each additional child). Open competition replaced the existing condition that candidates would have been previously in attendance at a public elementary school. The name of the award was changed from 'Free Place' to 'Special Place', though no reduction in the number of places available was contemplated.

The storm which broke when the contents of the circular became known was widespread. Within a few weeks, 1,600 resolutions were received at the Board's office. Leading public figures, politicians, trade unionists and teachers' organizations protested at the implications for secondary education. Selby-Bigge, writing to the President shortly afterwards, raised some doubts:

> As regards secondary school fees, on which you have taken action, the means test for special places seems to me to be perfectly sound in principle. But the position would be much stronger if it were applied all round and all admissions to secondary schools were governed by merit. I expect, however, that admission by merit, coupled with a means test for remission of fees would mean a loss of fee revenue to the L.E.A.s and therefore you and they can't afford it.[34]

The abolition of free places affected the lower middle-class parents as well. In Harrow, for instance, where the County School had a good record, the Chairman of the Higher Education Sub-Committee attempted to walk the difficult tightrope between disappointed parents and grudging ratepayers.

> On the one hand I would like to assure parents that facilities for higher education will not be less, or more, restricted on financial grounds that hitherto. On the other hand I would assure ratepayers that any fear as to increased expenditure arising out of these changes is groundless.[35]

In view of the widespread objections to the Circular, two significant changes were made. Irwin announced in the Lords on 27 October that an authority was at liberty to admit all pupils, not merely special place pupils, by examination and that the Board would be willing to sanction a higher percentage of special places 'where it was represented that otherwise, through the filling of special places by children whose parents could afford to pay fees, the chances of poor children will be prejudiced'.[36] Both these concessions had their drawbacks. By granting local authorities permissive powers to impose a standard entrance test, inevitably different patterns were operated over the country. On the second point, the reaction of the Essex Education Committee, a largely rural county, was typical. The fees at this time ranged from £10.10s. to £16.10s. per annum. The Committee stated that if a larger number of special places were to be offered, this would involve either a loss of income or the deficit having to be made up by fee payers.[37]

In London, where the first Labour Council was elected in 1934, consideration was given to establishing the principle of 100 per cent special places in secondary schools. Already 22 authorities were operating such a scheme.[38] The difficulties which such a proposal would entail can be seen by listing the schools in London into which pupils passed (or remained) at 11. Of the 50,000 in this age group in 1934, the following categories were identified:

Secondary	4,800
Trade & Junior Technical	1,800
Junior Art and Domestic	300
Central	8,000
Reorganized Senior	24,500
Elementary (Unreorganized)	10,600
	50,000

Of the 33,000 in aided and maintained secondary schools, 54 per cent paid full fee, 1 per cent part fee, 15 per cent were free place holders and 30 per cent were free place holders with maintenance grants.[39]

The whole question of the abolition of fees in secondary schools had been the subject of considerable correspondence within the Board of Education shortly after the second Labour Ministry was returned to office. It was noted by one official that although the Party's official programme contained a commitment to securing equal educational opportunities for every child and to raising the school leaving age to 15, it did not specifically include the abolition of fees at grant-aided secondary schools. It had, however, appeared as a recommendation in the Labour Party pamphlet *Labour and The Nation,* published in 1928.[40]

The Education Officer for the London County Council, E. M. Rich, was by no means convinced that it was in the best interests of the more able children from elementary schools to give the majority a grammar school education. Rich favoured the central school type of post-primary education and also looked to them to fill the 13 + junior technical and trade schools.[41] Even Tawney, in response to this memorandum, admitted that 'as long as facilities for secondary education are limited, there must be some method of selecting children for admission to it'.[42] The proposal for 100 per cent special places was not in the end adopted.

Towards a common secondary school

One solution to the problem of selection which began to be advocated was to end the segregation of children into different types of schools at the secondary stage. In 1934, the newly elected Labour-controlled London County Council's Education Committee recommended a 'multi-bias' school where children could be transferred without difficulty, after the first few years, from one type of course to another according to their interests and abilities. In the same year and up to the outbreak of war, successive Trades Union Congresses passed resolutions also advocating the multilateral principle. An opportunity for airing these views came with the appointment in 1934 of a Consultative Committee of the Board, chaired by Sir Will Spens on secondary education with special reference to grammar and technical high schools.[43]

The terms of reference of the Spens Committee included a consideration of the organization and the interpretation of schools other than elementary providing education for pupils beyond the age of 11. The Committee's findings are well known and need not be discussed at length here.[44] Starting from the assumption that there was already sufficient secondary provision, the main problem concerned its distribution. The Report recognized that 'many benefits would accrue when children after the age of 11 were educated together in the same sort of buildings', but rejected the solution of multilateral schools largely on the ground of the size of such schools, and the effects on existing grammar and technical and modern schools.[45] At the same time, the Report welcomed the multilateral idea which they considered should be inherent in the whole of secondary education and approved of the experiment where it seemed a safe one. Although the modern school was outside the Committee's terms of reference, it considered that it was necessary to take it into consideration as 'there is no clean line of demarcation, physical, psychological or social, between the pupils who attend grammar schools and those who attend modern schools'. Transfer between the three types of school and parity of esteem was also recommended. Although it was not possible to lay down for the country as a whole the amount of provision of grammar school places, 15 per cent of the secondary school age group should be regarded as a standard.[46]

By the time the Spens Report appeared in 1938, there had been a change of party in office. The National Coalition Government had given way to a Conservative administration with Stanley Baldwin as Prime Minister. Economic recovery had allowed some of the more drastic education cuts to be restored. An Education Act in 1936 promised to raise the school leaving age to 15 on 1 September 1939, a provision postponed with the war imminent. A declining birth rate during the 1920s and 1930s encouraged this policy. By the outbreak of war, although there had been a large fall in the elementary school population, the numbers in secondary schools continued to grow.

Circular 1444, issued early in the life of the new government, whilst retaining special rather than restoring free places, removed all maximum limits on the number which could be offered, though much still depended on the financial circumstances of local authorities as to how far these would be implemented.

During the war, the Secondary School Examinations Council was given the remit of considering changes in curriculum and examinations in secondary schools. The Report, issued in 1943 under the signature of its chairman, Sir Cyril Norwood, went much further than the Spens Committee in recommending the retention of the *status quo*. Norwood, a former Headmaster of Harrow School, had made known his views on the transfer of elementary school pupils to secondary schools in his book *The English Tradition of Education* (1929).

> It used to be assumed that everybody was capable of profiting by a full secondary education in the full academic sense: all that would be necessary, it was thought, would be to pour children into the schools and the rest would follow. Yet only a small proportion of the possible entrants have been promoted to the secondary schools, and already there are signs that the course of study is not well-suited to them – nor really within their intellectual power.[47]

Unlike the former committee, Norwood looked less to evidence and more to unscientific and unsupportable statements. Three 'certain rough groupings' of pupils were identified which corresponded with the three types of schools: the grammar, for the pupil interested in learning for its own sake, the technical, for the pupils whose interests and abilities were in the field of applied science or applied art, and the modern for the pupil who dealt more easily with concrete things than with ideas. These groupings became the basis of the tripartite system after the war and they had important effects in curriculum and organization.

Just before the Norwood Committee reported, the Government's White Paper on Education Reconstruction denied that the three types of school 'will necessarily remain apart'. After stating that 'there is nothing to be said in favour of a system which subjects children at the age of 11 to the strain of a competitive examination on which, not only their future schooling, but their future careers may depend', it suggested that different types may be combined in the building or on one site 'as considerations of convenience and efficiency may suggest'. Unlike previous official documents, it also questioned the high prestige of the grammar school. If the nation wished to offer an education which prepared primarily for the university and for administrative and clerical professions, then this would be at the expense of the needs of industry and craftsmanship.[48]

For some time before this, an Education Bill was in the process of being debated in Parliament. Its sponsor, R. A. Butler, then President of the Board, was responsible for piloting it successfully through. Committed to the notion of free secondary education for all, Butler was able to secure a broad definition of the three progressive stages of education, namely, primary, secondary and further.

Distinctions within the category of 'secondary' education officially disappeared and it became the duty of local authorities, in the context of national policy, to provide an education suitable for each pupil in terms of age, ability and aptitude. Each child was entitled to a full secondary course of four or five years. Fees for maintained secondary schools were swept away and thereafter such education became free.[49]

How this policy was to be effectively carried out remained uncertain. As one writer has described the post-1944 scene, 'If the force of tradition was not necessarily sufficient to keep the Ministry attached to the idea of tripartitism, the evidence of contemporary psychology certainly ensured it'.[50] Given the fact that local education authorities were submitting development plans based on tripartitism and that a rapid rise in the birth rate would stretch existing war-depleted resources, pupils would have to be allocated to the most appropriate type of schooling for some time to come. It had long been considered that the methods of selection, taking into account the abilities of children, could be relied on to ensure this. Even in 1945, in the new Ministry of Education's Pamphlet No. 1 *The Nation's Schools*, it was clear that selection was to continue, even though, as it was admitted, methods 'have not yet been so perfected that it is possible in any way to dogmatise about the best means to employ'.[51]

The reasons for the persistence of testing or its justification in other than administrative terms were not spelt out. These points will be examined in the following chapter.

NOTES

1. The growth of so-called 'Advanced Courses', i.e. sixth-form work, can be estimated from the following number of recognized courses in the different years. Between 1917-18 and 1925-6, science and mathematics courses tripled (82 to 233). Modern studies increased eightfold (25 to 189) and classics doubled (20 to 38).

2. Fisher remarked on the opposition within the Labour Party from colleagues such as J.R. Clynes and Philip Snowden. On the question of the abolition of the half-time system, 'they were not enthusiastic devotees of the change. It was not part of their old North Country world and they, being good Conservatives, were a little sorry to see it go'. H. A. L. Fisher, *An Unfinished Autobiography* (1941), p. 111. See also D. Ogg, *Herbert Fisher* (1947), p. 79.

3. L. A. Selby-Bigge to Sir Hugh Orange, 10 July, 1919, PRO Ed. 23/119.

4. Joint Advisory Committee of the Association of Education Committees and the National Union of Teachers, *Examinations in Public Elementary Schools* (1930), p. 25.

5. Shortly after the Act had been passed, Sir Henry Hibbert, M.P., an influential member of the Lancashire Education Committee, suggested that the county should make secondary schools free. Fisher, however, considered that such a proposal was 'undesirable'. Hibbert to Fisher, 9 September, 1918 and N. D. Bosworth-Smith to Hibbert, 12 September, 1918, PRO Ed. 24/1640.

6. F. R. Dale to Fisher, 18 January, 1922, PRO Ed. 24/1622.

7. For the effects of the 1918 Act, see D.W. Dean, 'H.A.L. Fisher, Reconstruction and the Development of the 1918 Education Act', *British Journal of Educational Studies*, Vol. XVIII, No. 3, October 1970, pp. 274-5.

8. E. H. Pelham, 6 February, 1922, PRO Ed. 24/1644.

9. Extract from the Third Report of the Cabinet Committee on the Geddes Committee recommendations, 28 February 1922.

10. Selby-Bigge to Edward Wood, 20 December, 1923, PRO Ed. 24/1645.

11. R. Terrill, *R. H. Tawney and His Times* (1974), p. 63.

12. Trevelyan had been Parliamentary Secretary to the Board of Education from 1908-1914. For fuller details, see *The Compact Dictionary of National Biography* (1975), Vol. II, p. 2933.

13. 'Your freedom from the vanity of authorship is very pleasant – we don't encourage it in this office and when the President sets the example of lighting his torch at his Officers' candles, it conduces to cheerful and disinterested co-operation and complete candour.' Selby-Bigge to Trevelyan, 23 August, 1924. Trevelyan MSS, CPT 108.

14. Board of Education, Circular 1340, 4 September 1924, para. 7.
15. Snowden to Trevelyan, 22 August, 1924. Trevelyan MSS, CPT 108. Snowden's parsimonious attitude as Chancellor of the Exchequer can be gathered from C. E. B. Roberts, *Philip Snowden. An Impartial Biography* (1929), p. 191.
16. E. K. Chambers to Selby-Bigge, 29 January 1924, PRO Ed. 24/1647.
17. Orange to Selby-Bigge, 29 January 1924, PRO Ed. 24/1647.
18. See B. Simon, *The Politics of Educational Reform, 1920-40* (1974), pp. 87-8. For Percy's own views on education, see E. Percy, *Some Memories* (1958), pp. 102-9.
19. Memorandum, 16 December 1926, PRO Ed. 24/1648.
20. Wood, later Viscount Halifax, the Conservative President of the Board of Education in the 1922 Government, told the House of Commons that no child 'possessed of the adequate intellectual merit and ability, should be debarred, by reason of his or her poverty, from obtaining the best education that the State is able, right the way up, to afford.' *Hansard*, Ser 5, CLXXVI, House of Commons, 22 July, 1924, col. 1177.
21. See Selby-Bigge's Note on the President's Draft Memorandum, 17 December, 1924. PRO Ed. 24/1648.
22. Board of Education, Circular 1352. The Free Place Grant, 9 February, 1925. Selby-Bigge wrote later that 'the Conservative Government of 1925 .... obsessed presumably by the tendency of services to expand and grants to increase .... revived the old idea of fixed grants, subject to periodical review'. L. A. Selby-Bigge, *The Board of Education* (Second edition, 1934), p. 113.
23. Following the 1918 Education Act, a number of authorities, notably Essex and Middlesex, had organized their education provision into primary, up to the age of 12, and secondary thereafter. B. A. Yeaxlee, *Working Out the Fisher Act* (1921), p. 16.
24. W. H. Hadow, who was Vice-Chancellor of Sheffield University from 1919-30, in a lecture, 'Liberty, Equality and Fraternity', made the distinction between equality of desert and equality of opportunity. W. H. Hadow, *Citizenship* (1923), p. 52. For the recommendations of the Hadow Committee, see H. C. Dent, *Secondary Education for All* (1949) pp. 60-9.
25. K. Lindsay, *Social Progress and Educational Waste* (1926), p. 11.
26. Viscount Haldane, *The Next Step in National Education* (1927), p. 104.
27. Simon (1974), op. cit. p. 139.
28. A. J. A. Morris, *C. P. Trevelyan, Portrait of a Radical* (1977), p. 175. MacDonald's dislike of Trevelyan at this time was described by Snowden in *An Autobiography,* Vol. 2 (1934), p. 600.
29. *Compact Dictionary of National Biography* (1975), Vol. II, p. 2933.
30. *Hansard*, Ser 5, CCXXV, House of Commons, 17 February 1930, col. 937.
31. Board of Education, Grant Regulations No. 10 (1930). Ss. 15 (c) and 27 (b).
32. Board of Education, Circular 1412, 2 April, 1931.
33. Cabinet Memorandum by the President of the Board of Education in regard to Fees and Free Places in Secondary Schools. PRO Ed. 24/1652. Irwin's sudden appearance for the second time as President of the Board of Education in 1932 was a surprise. Faced with financial cuts, the teachers were told by Irwin that they 'should regard their salaries as Christian missionaries regarded theirs'. Irwin also believed that the working man no longer desired more education as a thing desirable in itself. S. Hodgson, *Lord Halifax. An Appreciation* (1941), pp. 50, 150. In his autobiography, Irwin devotes only one sentence to his first spell at the Board in 1922 and the second receives no mention. The Earl of Halifax, *Fulness of Days,* (1957), p. 100.
34. Selby-Bigge to Irwin, 17 October, 1932, PRO Ed. 27/1652.

35. Quoted in T. May, *The History of the Harrow County School For Boys* (1975), p. 10. The consequences of the new policy were spelt out in R. H. Tawney, *The Children's Charter* (1932), pp. 3-9.

36. *Hansard*, Ser 5, LXXXV, House of Lords, 27 October, 1932, col. 915.

37. Essex Education Committee, *Board of Education Circular 1421* (1932), p.2.

38. I.e. Barrow-in-Furness, Birmingham, Bolton, Burnley, Bradford, Doncaster, Durham, East Ham, Essex, Huddersfield, Manchester, Middlesex, Newcastle, Norwich, Nottingham, Oldham, Plymouth, Portsmouth, Sheffield, Smethwick, Stoke-on-Trent and Wiltshire. *Secondary Schools – 100% Special Places. Memorandum by Mr. R. H. Tawney*, EO/PS/3/30, p.3, GLRO.

39. Memorandum on 100% Special Places for Programme 1935-38. C. N. Simpson, 23 Oct. 1934. EO/PSβ/30, p..1, GLRO.

40. A. W. Maudslay to Selby-Bigge, 3 September, 1929, PRO Ed. 24/1651. The official party programme included the following statement:

> The Labour Party had always been committed to securing Equal Educational Opportunities for every child. It will raise the school-leaving age to fifteen with the requisite Maintenance Grants and at once develop facilities for Free Secondary Education. Labour will open the road, to whosoever is able to take it, from the Nursery to the University.

> *Labour's Appeal to the Nation. Official Programme of the Labour Party at the General Election, 1929.*

41. E. M. Rich to Chairman of the Education Committee, 18 October 1934. EO/PS/3/30, p. 3, GLRO.

42. *Secondary Schools – 100% Special Places. Memorandum by Mr. R. H. Tawney*, EO/PS/3/30, p. 4, GLRO.

43. See M. Hyndman, 'Multilateralism and the Spens Report: Evidence from the Archives', *British Journal of Educational Studies*, Vol. XXIV, No. 3, October 1976, pp. 242-52.

44. G. Bernbaum, *Social Change and the Schools 1918-1944* (1967), pp. 66-7.

45. J. Graves, *Policy and Progress in Secondary Education 1902-1942* (1943), pp. 158-9.

46. Report of the Consultative Committee on Secondary Education (Spens) (1938), pp. 319-22.

47. C. Norwood, *The English Tradition of Education* (1929), p. 184.

48. Board of Education, *Educational Reconstruction* (1943), pp. 6-11.

49. Lord Butler, *The Art of the Possible* (1971), p. 123.

50. M. Parkinson, *The Labour Party and the Organization of Secondary Education 1918-65* (1970), p. 50.

51. Ministry of Education, Pamphlet No. 1. *The Nation's Schools, Their Plan and Purpose* (1945), p. 26.

CHAPTER 8

Methods of Selection

Procedures from 1907

One of the effects of the Technical Instruction Acts in the late 1880s had been to publicize the availability of awards at post-elementary level. The headmaster of one Midlands grammar school in 1889, where the foundation offered twelve scholarships annually, wrote to the Charity Commissioners:

> Up to quite recent times the persons who entered their sons for these Foundation Scholarships were the sons of professional men and better class tradesmen in the town, who desired their sons to have a University education. This was doubtless an abuse of the trust, but at any rate it did not prejudice the school: the sons of such parents did often do exceedingly well and by their performances they raised the reputation of the school. But of late years, our candidates have come from the public elementary schools, or from a social grade distinctly lower than formerly; and the result has been that the lower end of the school has been cumbered with boys of no ability and small industry, who have everything to learn in diction, manners and many of the qualifications of gentlemen.[1]

It was partly to meet this sort of criticism that the 1907 Regulations stipulated that candidates must take and pass an attainment test before entering on a secondary school course (see Chapter 6, p. 172). Initially intended as a qualifying examination, in reality it quickly became a competitive one. One aspect which exercised the mind of many authorities was the question of equalising the chances of able pupils in the poorest part of large cities. Superior education, it was agreed, would be given by elementary schools in more prosperous districts. A few authorities, such as Brighton, attempted to overcome this by allocating a limited number of places to particular elementary schools. The furthest this experiment was taken was at Newcastle-upon-Tyne, where headmasters nominated pupils without an examination of any kind.[2] The difficulties, as well as the undesirability, of this system led many authorities such as London, Bristol, Lancashire and Somerset to make awards based on written tests alone. In London, experience had shown that the scholarships granted by the Technical Education Board had been won by pupils from all types of home, variations in success by no means corresponding to the poverty of a district. As one report pointed out, the local distribution was affected by the character of the school, regardless of its location.[3]

Of the available forms of test, the written one was the most popular. To avoid the effects of skilful coaching, authorities, notably Kent, Northumberland and the West Riding of Yorkshire, combined written and oral testing, which proved helpful in borderline cases. Local panels carried out this task in these areas, but in Cheshire and Warwickshire, further oral tests were made at the secondary schools which pupils hoped to attend.

The Board of Education's Report for 1911-12 underlined the fact that, however efficient a combined written and oral examination might be, it was obvious that those best qualified to furnish an all round picture of pupils' abilities were the teachers. Written reports based on school records were important and ought to carry some weight.[4] In London, committees at local and central levels, composed largely of teachers from elementary and secondary schools, made the final selection; other areas also adopted this pattern, but some continued to employ the Oxford Local Examinations Delegacy or the Joint Scholarship Board. Governing bodies of endowed schools still often assigned the marking of the examination to the headmaster or headmistress.

The lack of a standard age at which the examination should be taken produced further difficulties. Circular 569, setting out the conditions for entry, merely stated that candidates 'as a rule' should be under 12. Candidates over 13 could be subjected to a severer test and those over 14 need not be accepted.[5] Whilst candidates between 10 and 13 were only required to qualify in English and arithmetic, some authorities also demanded proficiency in, amongst other subjects, history, geography and elementary science.

In Nottingham, two elementary schools were reserved for children intending to proceed to secondary education. Their curriculum included French, geometry and algebra, and more liberal staffing was allowed for this purpose. In order to enter these schools, candidates had to take an entrance test at the age of 9 or 10 and they remained at the school for two or three years before taking the secondary school examination. This form of streaming by ability had had its origins in the previous century, as in the example of Wigan, cited in Chapter 3, and was a feature from the time of the Technical Instruction Acts.[6] The original intentions of the Free Place Regulations – that awards must not be regarded as scholarships given for exceptional merit – was thus ignored. Reviewing the history of the free place examinations in 1927, an official document admitted that 'competition to get places, and the quality of the holders has been in general very good; in fact, though it was not so intended, free places have largely become scholarships'.[7] These arrangements which were designed to assist abler pupils distorted the organization and curriculum of the elementary schools, although teachers were not happy with this situation. Following a meeting between the Director of Education for Lancashire and the headteachers of elementary schools in November 1918 on the award of junior exhibitions in the county, the Scholarship Sub-Committee strongly deprecated 'the formation of scholarship classes or special coaching of any kind, and desire the award of these Exhibitions to be based in reality upon the work done as part of the normal school curriculum'.[8]

Two further aspects affecting selection which were explored during this period concerned the proportion of boys and girls gaining scholarships and the question of age allowance. Unless artificially manipulated, the number of girls with free places by 1912 almost equalled that of boys, a far cry from the pre-1902 position. An investigation carried out in London schools by the Chief Examiner for the entrance examination, G. F. Daniell, in 1913 had shown that in the previous year's competition, the work from the mixed departments was of higher average merit than that from separate ones. Repeated in 1914, an analysis of the results confirmed this finding. Boys gained distinctly, especially in English, from being in a mixed department, though there was little difference in the girls' results as between mixed and separate departments. Daniell concluded that he was favourably disposed towards mixed departments 'as an indication that the separation of the sexes is made at too early an age'. In the next sentence, Daniell drew back from the implications of this policy by adding, 'I would hesitate to draw the inference that co-education should be extended beyond the age of 9 or $9\frac{1}{2}$'.[9]

The Committee had also in 1914 drawn attention to the fact that there was marked inequality in the ages of the candidates generally and also in the ages of successful candidates, children born at the beginning of the year having a greater chance both of nomination and of success than those born towards the end of the year. This difference amounted to between one-fifth and one-sixth of the child's school life. The situation was further complicated by the fact that there was a discrepancy between the dates for calculating scholarship ages (August to July) and in connection with school promotions (April to March). To overcome both these sources of inequality it was recommended that two competitions a year, instead of one, should be held and that the period for calculating the ages of scholarships should be made from October to September instead of August to July.[10]

Added to these problems was the growing scale of the examining procedures over the years. In 1906, 23,500 elementary school pupils with scholarships had proceeded to secondary schools. By 1914, there were 63,274 and by 1924, 126,219.[11] This had come about largely as a result of the 1918 Act. The situation had been exacerbated by local authorities using the same examination for those intending to go on to selective central schools, which were becoming increasingly popular.[12] At the same time, the number of authorities conducting free place examinations grew. A Board Memorandum, issued in 1928, mentioned that a quarter of these examinations originated between 1900 and 1918, nearly a half were established between 1919 and 1921 and the rest since that time.[13] Another difficulty was the grave imbalance in secondary provision between urban and rural districts. Unlike Scotland and Wales, which had recognized this problem in the late nineteenth century, there had been no policy for rural areas until the 1930s, when the Board of Education finally abandoned the principle that the main object of country schools was to prepare children for agricultural work and life in the countryside.[14]

Lindsey Education Committee, Lincolnshire, a rural county, offered 110 free places in 1923; of these, 35 qualified candidates were unable to obtain admission, as they were too far away from schools with vacancies.[15] In 1933, a neighbouring authority, the East Riding of Yorkshire, conscious of the disparity between the number of scholarships gained by urban and rural children, changed the nature of the examination. Of the 60 annual places, one half was allocated on the written examination, while for the remaining 30 places, a bonus of 10 marks was to be given to borderline candidates from 'Grade I' schools, i.e. those which had not more than three adult teachers and an average attendance not exceeding 100.[16]

The policy of local authorities towards the award of maintenance grants throughout this period was often a crucial factor in the selection procedure. From the time of the 1907 Regulations, no clear policy was pursued. In the year 1912, about 60 per cent of the free places carried with them allowances of some sort. Some authorities, including London and Liverpool, awarded throughout school life, whilst Lancashire and the West Riding postponed the allowances to the third and later years of school life.[17] In many cases, such as the East Riding of Yorkshire, awards for school uniform, lodgings and dinners, were made on an *ad hoc* basis as late as 1935. Rural children incurred greater expense, especially in respect of travel and meals.[18] Means testing of parents' income was common in authorities such as London and Leeds. Maintenance allowances became a key issue when Trevelyan insisted, in the Labour Government of 1929, that it would be possible to raise the school leaving age only if maintenance allowances were available for those staying on.[19] This suggestion ran into heavy opposition from all three parties, and the proposed Bill was never proceeded with. Although the Spens Report later recommended a general extension of maintenance allowances, this suggestion was not taken up.

When the Departmental Committee on Scholarships and Free Places reported in 1920, it made a number of far-reaching recommendations on ways in which selection arrangements could be improved. It suggested that local authorities should take over responsibility from individual schools for administering the entrance examination, which would be common to the whole of their area. On the question of standards, the Committee affirmed that these should be fixed in relation to capacity, not attainment, the yardstick being whether the candidate was capable of passing the First Examination, i.e. the School Certificate, at the age of 16 or 17. It was urged that all pupils, except the least promising, who had reached the age of 11 should be tested because 'a great many excellent fish slip past the net'. Hopeless cases might be eliminated by a preliminary qualifying test. As to the form of the test itself, the Committee approved of the system most commonly in use, written tests confined to English and arithmetic, supplemented by an oral examination.

The Report raised a number of new principles. The basis for selection was now officially recognized as tested capacity and promise rather than attainment. The variety of entrance tests, it hoped, would now be terminated and the establishment of overall standards put in their place. In addition, since the majority of the elementary school population was to be externally tested, this was likely to affect schools in several ways. In a note of dissent to the Report, four members of the Committee feared the 'devastating effects' of reintroducing global competitive examinations.

Teachers were unanimously opposed to the change; it would give children a distaste for learning, cramp the curriculum by giving undue importance to subjects which could be mechanically treated, affect teaching methods and lead to overpressure.[20]

The growth of psychological testing

One other form of examination helpful to the discovery of capacity which was considered, but not overtly recommended, was that of psychological tests. Only a single paragraph (67) was devoted to a discussion of it, but the case for its application was forcefully put. Such tests 'would constitute the best method if they could be applied easily and give trustworthy results'.

Modern mental testing had begun some 15 years earlier by Binet, a French psychologist. Working with his colleague Simon, he had evolved a scale for measuring intelligence based on a child's performance which could be expressed in numerical terms.[21] The intelligence quotient (I.Q.) of a child consists of his or her mental age divided by chronological age, the result being multiplied by 100; on the Binet-Simon scale, those with an I.Q. of 100 are average, over 120 are able and those below 70 are mentally defective in some way. Their work was largely concerned with this last category of children.

A British psychologist, Carl Spearman (1863-1945) took the matter further, distinguishing between general and specific aspects of intelligence. The general or 'g' factor underlies, for example, all school activities, but there is also a specific or 's' factor which relates to particular skills. A hierarchy of correlations occurs when the two factors are combined for each tested ability. Spearman showed how the 'g' factor could be measured. He developed booklets of tests which required simple underlining of correct answers and which could be statistically analysed. Although Spearman's two-factor theory of intelligence was challenged by others, his work led to the construction and application in Britain of tests for general intelligence.[22]

So far, research was concerned with individual children, but from 1908 American psychologists developed objective tests across a range of subjects where standards of performance could be obtained between different schools. These might be in the form of, for example, word completion or true-false choices. It was the development of these group tests, which could be administered on a large scale, which held promise for selecting for secondary schools.

Lewis Terman in the USA had been a leading figure in this field and was one of a group of psychologists, employed after that country had entered the war in 1917, who devised group tests for measuring the general level of ability of volunteer soldiers. Earlier, in England in 1913, Dr. Cyril Burt had been appointed as the first educational psychologist to the London County Council, developing a range of tests for its schools. Shortly after the war in 1919, Bradford became the first English local authority to use psychological tests as part of the entrance examination. The interest in these developments in England can be gauged by the statement made by J. J. Findlay, Professor of Education at Manchester University, in an introduction to Terman's book *The Measurement of Intelligence* published in 1919, that 'if, five years ago, it had been proposed to issue an English edition of the book now before us, the proposal would have been rejected as impracticable'.[23] Another strong advocate in Britain of the application of group testing to schools was P. B. Ballard, an inspector for the London County Council and author of a number of tests. In his book *Group Tests of Intelligence*

(1923), Ballard explained the state of the art at that time by quoting the letter sent by the editor of *The Journal of Educational Psychology* in the USA to 13 leading investigators, in which they were invited to give their own definitions of 'intelligence'. Their replies, which appeared in the issues for March and April 1921, revealed that no common nucleus of memory was discoverable. Ballard ventured his own definition: 'the relative general efficiency of minds measured under similar conditions of knowledge, interest and habituation'. Further, 'the intelligence quotient is so often found to be nearly constant that the deviations from the rule, when not due to imperfections of measurement, are probably due to accidents of health, intuition, or fatigue'.[24]

Group tests were taken up with enthusiasm. London had already carried out an experiment called 'a special investigation'[25] under Burt's guidance in 1917, but had not incorporated the tests into the free place examinations. In 1921, Godfrey Thomson, Professor of Education at Newcastle-upon-Tyne, published an account of his own intelligence testing, which had as its primary object the discovery of gifted children in those elementary schools of Northumberland which had not sent in any candidates for the English and arithmetic tests on which free scholarships were awarded. These became the Northumberland Mental Tests which were thereafter widely employed. Thomson continued with this work after he became Professor of Psychology at Edinburgh University and Director of Studies at Moray House in 1925 and developed the Moray House Tests. In the same year, Cyril Burt published his influential *Mental and Scholastic Tests* and the movement quickly gained momentum.

In 1921 and 1922 whilst Fisher was at the Board, the Secondary Inspectorate had reported on the national use of entrance tests and were 'practically unanimous in saying that the standard for free places is distinctly higher than for fee payers'.[27] Because of this, the 1922 Regulations stipulated that the minimum standard of qualifications should be the same for both groups: it also sanctioned the use of intelligence tests to supplement the written ones.[28]

In July 1920, two years after the war, the Board of Education Consultative Committee was reconstituted. It was given two remits. The first was to investigate the differentiation of curriculum between boys and girls in secondary schools, a task completed by 1923. The second reference was to answer the question, 'What use can be made in the public system of education of psychological tests of educable capacity?' As this was a highly technical matter, a sub-committee of experts was appointed which met from October 1920 to May 1922. Its members included Ballard and Spearman with Burt supplying evidence and writing 'invaluable memoranda' which became important appendices for the final Report. The sub-committee not only gave advice to the main committee, which did not meet until 25 May 1922, but its report served as the basis of the work for the full committee.[29] Chaired by Hadow, the Consultative Committee on Psychological Tests of Educable Capacity and their possible use in the public system of education, to give it its full title, included amongst its members R. H. Tawney and Ernest Barker.

The Committee's Report cast some doubt on the validity of entrance tests at this age. 'Any system of selection whatever, whether by means of psychological tests, or by means of examination, which determines at the age of eleven the educational future of children is, and must be, gravely unreliable', and again, 'we are convinced that if selection is to be intelligent and its results trustworthy, it should come at as late a stage as possible in the educational career of children, and that any system of selection for higher education at so early an age as eleven is unsatisfactory' (para. 72).

Nevertheless, the Committee had to interpret the 1922 Regulations for Secondary Schools which required that preference be given to free placers of 'higher capacity and promise'. There was wide variation in the methods used by local authorities for selecting such candidates. The Report suggested that ' "intelligence" tests might usefully be employed to supplement and check the data obtained from the papers in English and arithmetic which form, as it were, the core of the existing examination' (para.77). It might also assist nervous pupils, test personal qualities not apparent in free place examinations and help the child affected by poor home circumstances.

These tests could be used in three ways. First, if given in the elementary school shortly before the free place examination was held, they would serve a double purpose of providing more information on pupils' abilities, and helping to eliminate those not suitable to proceed to the examination itself. Second, within the free place examination, group tests could be used as an indication of the child's ability, but should not compensate for poor perfor-mance in the English and arithmetic papers. Third, oral interview-ing was recommended as a useful supplement to the examination. This should be in the hands of a qualified person and the questions designed 'to discover mental alertness and certain aspects of character essential to success in a secondary school, such as the promise of continued attention and concentration' (para. 78).

The Inspectorate, who were monitoring free place examinations whilst the Committee was sitting, circulated their findings to colleagues. In 1923, at Leeds, where intelligence tests, as in other parts of the West Riding, were already in use, group intelligence tests correlated well with written examinations. This was an oral test and it was noted that the boys gained a large and apparently quite unwarranted advantage. It was suggested that interviewers should not be encouraged to try to detect specialised abilities. 'How far character and vigour can be judged I am personally doubtful – innate histrionic talent is widely but very unevenly distributed.'[30] Some authorities misleadingly used the term 'intelligence' in the title of examination papers which added to the confusion when calculating the incidence of use of such tests. At Wallasey, Cheshire in 1924, a paper set entitled 'General Intelligence' in effect amounted to a second paper in English and it was discontinued after only one year.[31] In Sheffield free place examinations, the term 'Intelligence Test' was used for one of the arithmetic papers to distinguish it from the Accuracy Test in the same subject.[32] The attitude of one of the pioneers in intelligence testing, the London County Council, probably influenced other authorities in deciding whether to adopt these tests. A suggestion to repeat Burt's original enquiry of 1917 was reviewed at a Conference on Junior County Scholarships held on 20 March 1925. This consisted of four inspectors, two of whom were F. H. Spencer,[33] the Chief Inspector, who was chairman, and P. B. Ballard. Other members included the Chief Examiner, B. C. Wallis,[34] the Education Officer, E. M. Rich, and his assistant. A memorandum drawn up by Wallis suggested the introduction of an intelligence test as part of the entrance examination, but this was turned down. Instead, tests in about a quarter of the schools, representing some 2,000 children, were to be given after the examination itself had been taken.

The results were to be reported to the Educational Committee 'as a piece of educational research'.[35] Financial constraints made a postponement of the experiment necessary, but interest was revived when in 1926 the findings of the Consultative Committee on the Education of the Adolescent (the Hadow Report) appeared. Recommending a definite break at eleven years of age, based on psychological evidence, the committee considered at length the best means of selecting for secondary education. After surveying different practices between authorities, it favoured the written examinations and, whenever possible, an oral test. 'A psychological test might also be specially employed in dealing with borderline cases, or where a discrepancy between the result of the written examination and the teacher's estimate of proficiency has been observed.' The Report left local authorities to decide on the most appropriate form of the examination.

The London tests were carried out in Ballard's division, Chelsea, in November 1927 and it was reported that there was a considerable measure of agreement between those who did well in the written tests and in the intelligence tests. The committee of experts asked for further and larger scale testing, though meanwhile the Brighton local authority had already purchased 800 copies of the new test for its own candidates.[36] The '1929 Experiment' consisted of a 40 minute test and was taken by 1,107 boys and 1,083 girls who had previously sat for the Junior Scholarship. A report from the committee to the Council showed that about 55 per cent of the Junior County Scholarship winners in 1927 and 1929 would have been successful if the examination had consisted solely of an intelligence test. In both years, there were a number of instances where the assessment of a candidate given by the intelligence test was markedly different from that given by the written examination.

It also noted that the results of the latter were in closer agreement with the expectations of the elementary school teachers than were the results of the intelligence test. The Sub-Committee as a matter of choice between the two systems had no hesitation in choosing the Junior Scholarship examination.[37] R. H. Tawney and L. Silkin, both influential Labour members of the Education Committee, expressed their opinions on the experiments. Both believed that the real solution lay elsewhere than in the modification of the machinery itself. As Silkin wrote, 'The real way to remove the hardships under which the children of very poor parents suffer is to remove their poverty . . . . no system of tinkering with minds will in fact do much to help the very poor and may do much harm by suggesting deficiencies in our examination machinery which do not in fact exist'.[38]

In spite of the widespread interest shown in intelligence tests before the Second World War, the practice of applying them to entrance examinations for secondary schools did not assume large proportions. By 1927, only 21 out of 75 authorities in England investigated by the Inspectorate included them. The Board of Education Pamphlet No. 63, *Examinations for Scholarships and Free Places in Secondary Schools* of that year devoted only two of its eighty-one pages to the topic. It gave nothing more than lukewarm support to its employment, quoting from the 1924 Consultative Committee on Psychological Tests that their efficacy should be investigated by means of adding group tests to the customary written examinations, and that the relative merits of the two sections of the examination should be estimated by calculating the correlation between the separate results and the subsequent development of the pupils.[39]

Even though the official pronouncements counselled caution in using intelligence tests, they were employed in a variety of ways. At Halifax, this test completely replaced the written one, with repercussions on school work which were 'highly encouraging'.[40] Kent included intelligence tests as an essential part of the selection examination, framing the written papers in accordance with the technique of intelligence testing. The task of working out the correlations between the group test and totals for the English and arithmetic tests was so great that only a small sample was attempted. An investigation by Kent in 1926 concluded that there was some correspondence between the two types of examination, but that it 'is not sufficient to suggest that they are testing the same things, and that therefore one or other could be dispensed with'.[41] In 1927, Lancashire introduced tests, by Godfrey Thomson, alongside written papers; where pupils were found to have done well on the tests and had not secured the requisite marks on the written papers, they were given an oral examination.[42] On the other hand, in the West Riding of Yorkshire, border line candidates in the written tests who, up to 1932 would have been given an oral examination as a determining factor, were obliged to take an intelligence test, again set by Thomson.[43]

By 1929, 22 county boroughs and 23 county councils, out of the 146 authorities, included mental tests in some form in their entrance examinations.[44] Although the number slowly increased in the 1930s, the total proportion remained small before the Second World War. A sampling of English boroughs carried out by Plymouth in 1934 showed that 50 out of 62 did not use intelligence tests. Of the 12 who did, seven who held only one examination included intelligence tests; those authorities holding a second examination accounted for the other five.[45]

Some of the reasons for this general lack of enthusiasm to use these tests are apparent. C. W. Valentine's book, *The Reliability of Examinations* (1932) showed that border line candidates were very close together in their marks. This meant that a repetition of the tests might have put a very different group of pupils among the 'just passed'. The tests also failed to detect specific abilities needed for the wider curriculum of the secondary school. This was confirmed, according to Valentine, by the fact that once the pupil had been tested in all branches of study in the secondary school, the order of merit was very steady from year to year.[46] There was, too, little financial incentive for local authorities to adopt this newer method. Perhaps most important was the different interpretations of Section 4 (4) of the 1918 Act's phrase 'capacity to profit'. The Labour Government's Parliamentary Secretary to the Board, Morgan Jones, a former elementary school teacher, writing in 1929 on the policy the Office should pursue, suggested that 'a Secondary Education of the academic type is really suitable for not more than about 15 per cent of the school population'.[47] Tawney, commenting on the purpose of a secondary school four years later, believed that 'a school is not to be judged by the "successes" it wins by selecting children likely to "succeed", but by what it makes of average human nature, which (thank Heaven!) is concerned with more important things than scholastic "successes".'[48]

Finally, as we have seen, as the tests were devised and administered by outside experts who were detached from the schools, it was not easy to enlist the enthusiasm of teachers. As early as 1912, the Board of Education, in a review of the free place system, stated that

> both in theory and in practice, there is a general tendency to regard any system as defective which does not allow teachers to play a large part in the final selection. No examination, whether written or oral, can hope to be in itself a satisfactory test of

ability. Its results need to be reviewed in the light of a long acquaintance with the individual candidates, and of a knowledge of the special qualities which will be most valuable in their future education, if a sound judgement is to be formed. It is obvious that the persons best qualified to furnish this information are the teachers themselves.[49]

Nevertheless, in practice, faith was placed in the efficacy of psychological testing. Whereas the Memorandum of the Board on Free Places in 1928 had cautioned that a general use of such tests would be premature, by 1936, the supplementary Memorandum advised that the intelligence test and each of the attainment tests should be assigned equal weight.[50]

Attainment tests between the Wars

Although much of the discussion of the free and special place examinations in the 1920s and 1930s inevitably referred to the use or non-use of intelligence testing, most of the free places offered were still based on attainment tests.

The form which they took varied from authority to authority, but four main patterns may be discerned:

1) The most common test was two obligatory papers in English and arithmetic.

2) Some authorities, in addition, attempted to discover ability as well as testing acquired knowledge by setting a general paper.

3) An oral test was included, either for all candidates or for border line cases.

4) Some authorities set papers in additional school subjects, and as a supplement to the English test an oral reading test was given to candidates.

The supervision of the examination was normally entrusted to an external examiner. He or she was responsible for setting the papers, standardizing and correlating the marks (where this was undertaken), was present at oral examinations and compiled a report, which was usually in published form. J. A. Green, Professor of Education at Sheffield University, who was Chief Examiner for

Sheffield in the 1920s, may serve as a typical example. Besides making detailed comments on the examination as a whole and an analysis of responses to individual questions, Green took the opportunity offered by a large sample of pupils to carry out statistical investigation into the relative successes of boys and girls in the examinations.[51] At the same time the Director of Education at Sheffield, among his other tasks, personally marked many of the examination scripts for a number of years. After 1929, the authority handed over this work to local inspectors to carry out during office hours. 'This', wrote the Director, 'is to me quite a satisfactory arrangement even though it denies me the opportunity of gaining an intimate insight into the development and improvement of the work of individual scholars.'[52]

The investigation by HMIs of the 75 areas where free places were awarded reported that in 1928 45 of these used examinations conducted by local authorities; in 23 of them, separate examinations were held at the schools (these included non-provided schools). Essex had, perhaps, one of the most elaborate schemes, one which continued to operate well into the 1940s. Three categories of candidates were identified: those who were successful in the written examinations and were offered a secondary school place, those who were definite rejects and, finally, those in between who were known as 'pool' candidates. When the numbers in the first category had been settled, heads of secondary schools were asked to state the number of pool candidates they would be prepared to accept. A 'pool examination' was then set by this school and the successful candidates were decided by the headmaster, together with an elementary school headteacher who was not acquainted with the candidate.[53]

There were difficulties between the authorities on the compulsory or voluntary nature of the examinations. In Northampton in 1923, headteachers were allowed to exclude not more than 20 per cent of eligible scholars who were considered to have no chance of success. Accordingly, 230 out of 1,505 candidates were withdrawn. However, the Primary Education Sub-Committee recommended that from the following year, the whole of the age group should be entered.[54] This pattern became more common and by 1928, it was calculated that nationally the number of children taking the examination compulsorily was about five times as large as that of those taking a voluntary examination.[55] The main reasons advanced for this policy were that children should not miss their chance through parental neglect or a headteacher's obstruction and that it was desired to make known the facilities available for higher education as widely as possible.

Another reason for entering the total age group, which roused the suspicions of teachers, was that the results could be used as a means of assessing the degree of efficiency of individual schools.[56] In 1924, the Bradford Authority, sensitive to this issue, made known 'that it is so keenly aware of the existence of this feeling and so anxious to avoid an inquisitional taint, that they have abstained in the past, more than appears to have been necessary, from drawing general or particular statistical deductions from the ample records accruing annually'.[57]

Some authorities dealt with this situation by imposing a preliminary examination which eliminated the poorer candidates and allowed the remainder to compete for secondary places. In all cases, this consisted of written English and arithmetic papers, both of which were set centrally, but marked within the candidates' elementary school or by a panel with a council inspector as chairman. Inconsistency in marking was a problem. At Exeter, children rejected for secondary education at some schools were better than those accepted at others and girls fared badly compared with boys. Durham presented an even worse case in the 1920s. Over half of the pupils were not allowed to enter for the preliminary examination because of their low classification by teachers. Great variation in standards was noted in the marking of the papers, which resulted in little more than 20 per cent being allowed to go on to the second examination. Inspectors considered that a group intelligence test could have been employed here to ensure that no able children were overlooked.[58]

The 1931 Hadow Report on the Primary School recommended that any parent who so desired should be permitted to present his child for the final test, regardless of the child's performance in the preliminary test.[59] Parental support, however, was sometimes lacking: in the West Riding in 1931, in spite of the issue of application forms to parents of recommended children, 1,300 were not presented and in 1932 nearly 1,200.[60] However, success in the final examination was only 1 in 60 of 'open' candidates as compared with 1 in 8 for recommended candidates.

With the Final Examination, there were considerable differences in the organization for setting the papers. An Examining Board set or suggested the questions, which were approved by the Director of Education or a Chief Examiner. Whilst the Board was representative of secondary and elementary schools, the examiners were frequently exclusively secondary school teachers and there was a tendency to exclude their elementary colleagues from the actual setting of papers. A second variant was for the Board to appoint individuals who may or may not have been members of the Board, to set the papers, subject sometimes to the final approval of the Director of Education. A third and rarer variant was for the Director to set the papers himself. One of the most elaborate procedures occurred at Leicester County Borough. Here, the Board appointed two chief examiners and two moderators, one from a secondary and one from an elementary school. The headteachers of schools suggested the questions which were then sifted separately by examiners and moderators and the Director made the final choice.

By 1928, four-fifths of the authorities followed the advice given in the 1907 Regulations and confined the written examination to English and arithmetic. A general criticism made by inspectors, in published and office reports, was that the material was geared, as at Liverpool, primarily to test the few exceptional candidates, and not sufficiently to test the others. This was probably due to the predominance of problem-type questions and the comparatively rare use of mechanical tests. Mental arithmetic, where included, was set as a separate paper. The wordiness and ambiguity in the phrasing and level of reading difficulty of the arithmetic paper required, it was stated, to be balanced by mental tests where facility in short calculations could be displayed.

The English examination came in for greater criticism. Most authorities made use of the essay. The Senior Chief Inspector of the Board of Education expressed the view that such a test was 'obnoxious' and was 'simply inadmissible as a test for young children'. To provide matter-of-fact subjects under examination conditions was very difficult, leading children to 'either rebel or write rubbish, or take refuge in insincerity'.[61] This criticism was ignored in the 1928 Memorandum, where the importance of composition in the examination was emphasized. Comprehension of extracts from books or responses to pictures were common. Dictation tests were popular in the East Midlands particularly.

Paraphrasing was not very successful. At Wolverhampton, it was reported, 'children were asked to write out in their own words the sense of a poem so simple in its wording that the best they could do was to use the same words'.

Formal grammar and analysis tests were found more in 'voluntary' free place examinations, as at West Ham. This procedure was not encouraged, as formal grammar was not part of the curriculum in some elementary schools. Darlington and Leicester included this aspect in their examinations.

At Leicester

> One question asked candidates to split up two sentences into Subject, Predicate, Object and Extension. By 'Predicate' it is presumed that 'verb' was meant, but it was evident from the papers that some candidates had been taught, quite justifiably, to consider the Predicate included whatever in the sentence was not in the Subject, and for such an analysis, quite right upon their own lines, these candidates received no marks.[62]

Fletcher remarked that 'at Darlington the same phraseology was used: Subject, Predicate, Object and Extension, though the sentence set contained no object'.

In addition to the arithmetic and English examinations there were intelligence tests (dealt with above) and oral tests. The latter could be used as an integral part of the examination, for border line cases or not employed at all. They were commonly used by secondary schools where the number of candidates was high. At Ipswich, secondary heads and their staff interviewed boys who had expressed a preference for a particular school and had reached the minimum standard in the final examination. The questions included arithmetic, English and general knowledge.

A point already noted was that the different examinations set by the authorities often failed to differentiate properly between candidates. Writing in 1926 on the Kent free place examinations, an investigator specially commissioned by the authority declared:

> One thing that the new type of testing has taught us is that the setting of a paper is very often as much to blame for the failure of a candidate, as that candidate's lack of knowledge or his inability, and sometimes the setting is wholly to blame. There is only one way to test the efficacy of a question, and that is to

try it out on the type of pupil for whom it is intended to set it.

This suggestion, the investigator claimed, was perhaps not feasible.[63]

A further factor which affected the continuance of selection tests was the different relative weightings given to subjects. Quite commonly, English and arithmetic had equal weight, as in Wiltshire, Somerset, Huddersfield, Cheshire, Liverpool and York. In a few cases – Darlington, Ipswich, Leicester Borough, Wallasey and Wolverhampton – a third paper which was either specifically or practically English made the English maximum anything up to double that for arithmetic. At West Ham alone, the arithmetic maximum slightly exceeded the English while at Birkenhead, Durham and Cambridgeshire, the English was half as large again as the arithmetic. The extreme case was Leicestershire, where the English marks counted as two and a half times the value of the arithmetic; the reason given was that this proportion corresponded roughly to the time allocated to the subjects in the elementary school time-table.[64]

Allowances for age became necessary as candidates ranged from ten years upwards, though the range differed across the country. By the end of the 1920s one-third of authorities, including Birkenhead, Bradford and Exeter made no such allowance. Where the age range extended over two or more years, a few areas set separate papers. School records, in the form of reports, were supplied by the elementary schools in two-thirds of the authorities. These ranged from formal written reports to the listing of examination results. Practices also differed in the extent to which they were seriously considered. Some authorities ignored them, others consulted them during oral tests. Sometimes they were used for border line cases only; there is also evidence that they could influence the final order of merit.

The actual procedure for making the awards was complex. Besides weighing offers of admission between secondary schools, candidates may have been required by an authority to sign a 'school life undertaking', a formal assurance that the pupil would remain at a secondary school up to at least the age of sixteen. (This had been sanctioned by the 1926 Regulations for Secondary Schools.) Administrative procedures concerning parents' income and eligibility would also have taken some time. In many cases, on the other hand, candidates were admitted directly on the results of the examination. Boys and girls were not usually in competition; numbers of places were fixed for each sex, even in mixed schools. (Surrey allowed open competition.) The right balance between free and fee payers was problematic, depending largely on the number of candidates coming forward and the willingness or ability of parents to afford fees. In Plymouth in 1922, the shortage of fee payers was so serious that the qualifying standard had to be relaxed. No special arrangements were made for the distribution of awards between urban and rural parts, a point mentioned earlier.

Effects of selection tests on schools

Sir Graham Balfour, as Director of Education for Staffordshire, told his Education Committee in a report of the county's examinations in July 1921, 'What we seek to avoid is allowing children, for payment or otherwise, to receive a special preparation to enable them to outwit the examiners and to outstrip their less fortunate rivals – not by ability but by mark catching'.[65] This optimistic statement was not borne out in practice. As one anonymous inspector commented, 'whatever the intention, reflexes in the Public Elementary School are inevitable'. Given the widespread adoption of the two stage examination, and the official encouragement of the policy of entering the entire eligible age range, it would have been suprising if the nature of elementary school testing had not been affected.

We have seen that the requirements of the examination often included items which were not included in the elementary school curriculum. At Kesteven, Lincolnshire, an Absurdity Test employed for three years had to be abandoned in 1924 'as it very soon defeated its own ends (supposing it to have any value) by stimulating teachers to be constantly practising it'.[66] Whilst the tests had the beneficial effect of focusing attention on the importance of the teaching of English and arithmetic in schools, this aim was negated by the sentiments expressed by such authorities as Darlington, who asserted that the examination was 'to provide an objective for work for teachers'. There was an incentive to teach potential secondary school pupils to the requirements of the examination and to display the efficiency of the school by the number of successes gained. As headmasters were sent, in confidence, the candidates' results from each school, it was not difficult to construct a 'league table' within an authority. At promotion interviews, teachers were asked about the number of scholarships obtained. Parental pressure also made itself felt.

The effects of 'cramming' and ways to avoid it in preparing for the tests were widely discussed. As early as 1912 Lindsey (Lincolnshire) Scholarships Sub-Committee considered 'whether a syllabus can be devised which will protect, or at any rate reduce, the amount of cramming of candidates for the Junior Scholarships Examination'.[67]

The Committee of Psychological Tests of Educable Capacity quoted examples by secondary school headteachers of pupils who had passed the examination with distinction and yet who were failures in their subsequent school career. This was assigned to special preparation in the elementary school.[68] The commercial sales of 'Scholarship Books', consisting of items culled from past selection examination papers, testified to this observation.[69] Various methods were employed by authorities to circumvent narrowness in the curriculum and undue concentration on the two main subjects. Surrey included in its test a general knowledge paper which did not actually affect the results, but the teachers were never informed of this. At Wallasey, Cheshire, the authority and teachers collaborated by prescribing a minimum curriculum in English, arithmetic, history, geography and science, and teachers undertook to observe it.

By 1936, it could be written:

The Special Place Examination has become a national institution. It winnows elementary school children into three distinct classes: the best of all (rarely more than 5 per cent) go to secondary schools; the second best (roughly about 15 per cent) go to some such institution as a central school, or a technical school; the remaining 80 per cent stay on at the senior elementary school.... It is difficult, therefore to over-estimate the importance of the Special Place Examination. Every year, the fate of about a half a million children hangs upon its results. In sheer magnitude it dwarfs every other public examination in the Kingdom.[70]

The impact of selection on school organization was, as a result, significant. 'Streaming' by ability was officially advocated as in the influential Board of Education *Handbook of Suggestions* issued in 1937. Psychological testing had created the notion of 'mental age' equated with ability as a method of classification rather than formal attainment or age. The *Handbook* favoured promotion by ability, considering the range of mental ages in a junior school: pupils should be arranged in at least two streams, A and B, with the brightest forming the potential 'Junior Scholarship' class.[71] Even infant schools, free from the constraints of formal academic work, were affected. Ambitious heads and equally ambitious parents pressed for premature promotion from these schools so that a longer spell of time was available for preparing for the examinations. Only a year earlier, the Board's Memorandum on Special Places had concluded that 'the free development of the Junior School must not be jeopardised and the taking of the examinations must not be looked on as the aim and end of the education given there'. Accordingly, the examination should be framed so as to ensure that every child who had been through the ordinary curriculum should have a fair and equal chance. The Memorandum was clear that any single examination involved a certain amount of chance, but was unable to recommend a suitable alternative.[72]

This uncertainty as to the most suitable form of examining was detectable in the Spens Report on Secondary Education in 1938. Whilst parity between the three types of secondary schools was desirable, it was recognized that no method of choice could work satisfactorily without an adequate supply of grammar school places. (It was assumed that 15 per cent of grammar school places should be regarded as standard.) Group tests of intelligence were to supplement the written tests and school records consulted for border line cases.[73] What was valuable in the Report was the recommendation that at about the age of 13, a review of all children was to be made. This was to be based, not on the results of further examinations, but on the opinion of the headteacher. Such a move would have restored to schools some of the ground lost in the previous decades to externally imposed tests.

These recommendations were flatly contradicted by the Norwood Report on Curriculum and Examinations in 1943 (see p. 192 above). It was described by a contemporary educationist as presenting 'a striking illustration of the principle that history waits for no-one. Those who are unwilling to take the forward way out of their difficulties find themselves compelled to step backwards'.[74] At the very beginning of the Report, a return to the Hadow-type thinking was contemplated. Under the heading 'Variety of Capacity', it claimed that children could be classified for educational purposes in three categories, serving as a justification for the separation of academic and practical activities in and between schools. The relationship between types of curriculum and types of occupation was translated into grammar, technical and modern schools. This followed logically from the 'cast of mind' argument. School records were considered as 'the best single means at present available of discovering special interest and aptitude and the general level of intelligence'. For this reason, intelligence and performance tests and internal qualifying tests of attainment were regarded as valuable supplementary evidence of fitness. Curiously, in a section of the Report which was not fully developed, in discussing the age at which children would pass into one of the three types of secondary education, it was stated, 'Eleven plus is a term of art; it means that the able child would go on at 10 plus, the average child at 11 plus and some children would more appropriately go on at 12 plus'.[75] This confident correspondence of ability, selection procedures and types of secondary schools had already been seriously questioned. In 1938, two researchers, Gray and Moshinsky, had published their findings of a survey which they had undertaken of more than 10,000 pupils in London aged between nine and twelve and a half and drawn from public elementary, central, private and secondary schools. Using intelligence tests, Gray and Moshinsky discovered that between 43 and 72 per cent of all central school pupils possessed superior ability to their counterparts in grammar schools. Again, of those in the elementary schools who had failed to be selected for central or secondary schools, between 9 and 22 per cent were capable of profiting by such an education. The overwhelming majority of sub-standard children who nevertheless obtained secondary education consisted of fee payers. Most disturbing of all was the finding that on the highest criterion of ability 45 per cent and on the lowest 59 per cent of the total number of gifted children in the school population, i.e. with a measured I.Q. of 130 or above, did not enjoy the opportunity of a higher education.[76]

By the outbreak of the Second World War then, selection played a crucial role in the distribution of secondary education. Hadow reorganization, under which distinctive primary and secondary schools were established, proceeded slowly and unevenly. But the sentiments expressed in the Norwood Report still prevailed. Politically, there was little pressure for change by the Labour Party and neither the teachers' unions nor local authorities were vocal in demanding any departure from the existing system.

The concept of those who were able to profit from selective secondary education had been clarified by the rise of mental testing and the number of free places offered continued to grow. Economically, the country could now afford to provide more education. By Autumn, 1938, almost 90 per cent of admissions to secondary grammar schools were awarded to special or free places and eleven authorities made provision for all vacancies in their schools to be filled by this category of pupil.[77] Inequalities of opportunity in education, as in other spheres of life, were taken for granted. Changes in society wrought by the war and the promises of the 1944 Education Act called for a restructuring of the system. Tawney's analysis of 1922 and 1924 was still relevant. Primary and secondary education were stages in a single process through which all normal children should pass, and should not be regarded as different systems of education. The two nations were represented by, on the one hand, the grammar schools and on the other, the elementary schools from which 'the cream of intelligence had been skimmed off by scholarships'. What was required was full time, universal, free secondary education for all up to the age of sixteen.[78] How far such a system was feasible, the form it would take and the need to re-interpret the conventional notion of secondary education remained to be decided.

NOTES

1. Bromsgrove Grammar School. H. Millington to Charity Commissioners, 20 July 1899, PRO Ed. 27/5327.
2. Report of the Board of Education for the year 1911-12 (1913), p. 20.
3. London County Council. Report of the Education Committee on the New Scholarship Scheme, 7 February, 1905, p. 3. EO/PS/3/1, GLRO. These findings bear remarkable similarity to those given in a recent study, M. Rutter et al, *Fifteen Thousand Hours* (1979) pp. 177-8.
4. Report of the Board of Education for the year 1911-12 (1913), p. 27.
5. Board of Education, Circular 569. Examination of Candidates from Public Elementary Schools for Free Places in Secondary Schools, 9 July 1907.

6. B. Simon, 'Classification and Streaming, A Study of Grouping in English Schools 1860-1960', in P. Nash (ed.), *History and Education* (1970), p. 120.
7. Board of Education, Pamphlet No. 50. *Some Account of the Recent Development of Secondary Schools* (1927), p. 11.
8. Lancashire Education Committee. Scholarships Sub-Committee. Report of Committee, 2 December 1918. Minute Book, 1916-25, ESM 2 Lancashire RO.
9. London County Council. Higher Education Sub-Committee. Junior County Scholarship Examination. Memorandum by the Chief Examiner, 27 January 1916. EO/PS/3/36 GLRO
10. London County Council. Education Committee. Extract from minutes of the Committee, 20 December 1916. March 1917, pp. 1-3, EO/PS/3/1.'GLRO.
11. Board of Education Annual Report and Statistics. *Education in 1938* (1939), Table 43, pp. 138-9.
12. Spurling Hey, Director of Education for Manchester, wrote, 'There are probably more suitable pupils demanding further education and failing to get it than at any time since the State assumed responsibility for education'. Spurling Hey, *Central Schools* (1924), p. 17.
13. Board of Education, Pamphlet No. 63. *Memorandum on Examinations for Scholarships and Free Places in Secondary Schools* (1928).
14. J. Synge, 'The Selective Function and British Rural Education', *British Journal of Educational Studies*, Vol. XXIII, No. 2, June 1975, p. 142.
15. Lindsey, Lincolnshire. Scholarships Sub-Committee, 21 July 1923, p. 121, Lincolnshire Archives Office.
16. East Riding of Yorkshire Education Committee. Minutes, 9 January 1933, p. 157, Humberside County Record Office.
17. Report of the Board of Education for the year 1911-12 (1913), p. 18.
18. In 1935, the East Riding Education Committee awarded £5 for a school uniform, £9 for lodgings. East Riding of Yorkshire Education Committee Minutes, 1 October 1935, p. 143, Humberside County Record Office.
19. D. W. Dean, 'The Difficulties of a Labour Educational Policy: The Failure of the Trevelyan Bill, 1929-31', *British Journal of Educational Studies*, Vol. XVII, No. 3, October 1969, pp. 290-3.
20. Board of Education, *Report of the Departmental Committee on Scholarships and Free Places* (1920). Note by Miss E. A. Conway, R. F. Cholmeley, F. W. Goldstone and R. Richardson, M.P., pp. 52-3.
21. For a fuller account of the historical background, see P. E. Vernon, *Intelligence and Attainment Tests* (1960), Ch. 1, pp. 9-26.
22. The influence of Spearman's work is succinctly stated in R. Thomson, *The Pelican History of Psychology* (1968), pp. 186-9.
23. L. M. Terman, *The Measurement of Intelligence* (1919), p. iii.
24. P. B. Ballard, *Group Tests of Intelligence* (Second edition 1923), pp. 145-7. Ballard devoted a whole chapter to examinations in his autobiography, *Things I Cannot Forget* (1937), pp. 194-211.
25. C. Burt, *The Distribution and Relations of Educational Abilities* (1917).
26. G. H. Thomson, The Northumberland Mental Tests, *British Journal of Psychology,* Vol. XII, December 1921, pp. 201-2.
27. E. H. Pelham to Selby-Bigge, 16 January, 1922, PRO Ed. 24/1644.
28. Board of Education, Regulations for Secondary Schools. Section 5. Entrance Tests.
29. Board of Education, *Report of the Consultative Committee on Psychological Tests of Educable Capacity and their possible use in the public system of education* (1924), p. xi.
30. Memorandum A. Entrance and Scholarship Examinations for Secondary

Schools in Leeds, Durham, Wiltshire, Surrey and Plymouth. E.D.M. 24 January 1923, PRO Ed. 22/127.

31. Entrance, Free Place and Scholarship Examinations conducted by Local Authorities. W. C. Fletcher, 19 August 1924, PRO Ed. 22/128.

32. City of Sheffield Education Committee. *Report by the Director of Education on the Preliminary and Final Examinations for Entrance to Secondary and Intermediate Schools,* (1929), p. 22.

33. F. H. Spencer had been an HMI since 1912. In 1922, as Divisional Inspector for Lancashire, he applied for and was appointed to the post of Chief Inspector for the London Education Committee. He held the post for eleven years. F. H. Spencer, *An Inspector's Testament* (1938), p. 278.

34. Wallis, writing in 1931, deplored the lack of any university research department in examining and added: 'Let me be frank, it is my privilege to produce annually many lists in order of merit which are held to determine the relative ability of children. These lists. . . . are not identical with the lists which would be produced at any other time by myself or would have been produced at that time by some other examiner.' B. C. Wallis, *The Measurement of Ability in Children* (1931), p. 20.

35. Minutes of Conference on Junior County Scholarships held on Friday 20 March, 1925, EO/PS/3/36, GLRO.

36. London County Council Education Committee. Higher Education Sub-Committee, 27 October 1927. EO/PS/3/37, GLRO.

37. London County Council Education Committee. Junior County Scholarship Examination – Intelligence Test. Report of the Committee of Officers. G. H. Gaber, 24 January 1933. EO PS 3/30, GLRO.

38. Silkin's draft memorandum, 24 January 1933. EO PS 3/35, GLRO.

39. Board of Education, Pamphlet No. 63. *Memorandum on Examinations for Scholarships and Free Places in Secondary Schools* (1928), pp. 54-5.

40. P. B. Ballard, 'The Special Place Examination' in M. Sadler (ed.), *Essays on Examinations* (1936), p. 116.

41. Kent Education Committee, *An Investigation of the Free Place Scholarship Examination* (1926) by Andrew Bell, p. 8.

42. Lancashire Education Committee. Scholarships Sub-Committee. Report of the Committee, 7 May, 1927. Minute Book, 1925-34, ESM3, Lancashire RO.

43. West Riding of Yorkshire County Council Education Committee. *Report on the Examination for County Minor Scholarships.* (1932). Thomson's Report (p.14ff) shows that a new Moray House Test was employed which had been tentatively standardized on about 200 children in another area.

44. C. W. Valentine, *The Reliability of Examinations* (1932), p. 98. This differs from Sutherland's calculations, that by 1936 only 34 out of 146 county and borough councils in England and Wales used intelligence tests in their Special Place examinations. G. Sutherland, 'The Magic of Measurement, Mental Testing and English Education, 1900-1940', *Transactions of the Royal Historical Society,* 5th Series, Vol. 27 (1977), p. 146.

45. County Borough of Northampton Education Committee. Schools Examinations, 8 December 1934. ML 1801, Northamptonshire RO.

46. Valentine, op. cit., pp. 163-4.

47. M. Jones to C. P. Trevelyan, 11 September, 1929, PRO Ed. 24/1651.

48. R. H. Tawney, 'Special Places in Secondary Schools'. This was written in response to an official paper on the subject dated 25 May 1934. EO/PS/3/30. GLRO.

49. Report of the Board of Education for the year 1911-12 (1913), p. 27.

50. Board of Education Pamphlet No. 63 (1928), p. 55 and Supplement (1936), p.8

In 1933, the Board instigated an enquiry into the free place examination. Experiments were devised for testing over 10,000 elementary school children and various authorities were chosen for this purpose. As a result, some 250 points came up for discussion including age allowance, weighting of subjects, age of entry, prognostic value of a single test, the possibility of assessing temperament, distribution of intelligence, school records, effects of special coaching, elimination of subjective judgment in the examiner and the meaning of 'fitness for secondary education'. Board of Education, M. to I. S. 585 (1934). See also Board of Education. Report of Conference of Secondary Inspectors. Malvern, 17-18 July, 1934, PRO Ed 22/138.

51. City of Sheffield. *Reports on Examinations for Free Places in Secondary Schools* (1920), p. 2.
52. City of Sheffield, *Report by the Director of Education, July 1929* (1929), p. 4. The remuneration to examiners in East Yorkshire remained at 6d. per script from 1924 to 1937.
53. Essex Education Committee. *Report of a Sub-Committee on the Selection of Children for Secondary Education* (1944), p. 7.
54. County Borough of Northampton Education Committee. Memorandum on Primary School Examinations, 1923, 30 September 1923, ML 1575 Northamptonshire RO.
55. Board of Education, Pamphlet No. 63 (1928), p. 13.
56. Joint Advisory Committee of the Association of Education Committees and the National Union of Teachers, *Examinations in Public Elementary Schools* (1930), p. 42.
57. 'Entrance, Free Place and Scholarship Examinations Conducted by Local Authorities.' W. C. Fletcher, 19 August 1924, PRO Ed. 22/128.
58. Ibid.
59. Board of Education, *Report of the Consultative Committee on the Primary School* (1931), p. 126.
60. West Riding of Yorkshire County Council, Education Committee. *Report on the Examination for County Minor Scholarships* (1932), p. 5.
61. 'Entrance, Free Place and Scholarship Examinations Conducted by Local Authorities', W. C. Fletcher, 19 August 1924, PRO Ed. 22/128.
62. Ibid.
63. Kent Education Committee, *An Investigation of the Free Place Scholarship Examination* (1926) by A. Bell, pp. 5-6.
64. PRO Ed. 22/128.
65. Report of Sir G. Balfour on the County Scholarship Examinations for 1920-1. Minutes of the Staffordshire Education Committee, 23 July 1921, p. 97.
66. PRO Ed. 22/128.
67. Lindsey, Lincolnshire, Scholarships Sub-Committee, 19 January 1912, p. 13, Lincolnshire Archives Office.
68. Board of Education, *Report of the Consultative Committee on Psychological Tests of Educable Capacity* (1924), p. 116.
69. A typical example was the popular *Evans Entrance Examinations for Scholarships* booklets. These contained a selection of questions from local education authorities' examination papers in English, arithmetic and intelligence tests. Editions date from 1935 to 1969, with slight changes in title.
70. P. B. Ballard, 'The Special Place Examination' in M. Sadler (ed.), *Essays on Examinations* (1936), p. 111.
71. Board of Education, *Handbook of Suggestions for the Consideration of Teachers and Others Concerned in the Work of the Public Elementary Schools* (1937), pp. 31-2.

72. Board of Education, Pamphlet No. 63 (1936 Supplement), pp. 4-5.
73. The consideration of psychological testing at 11 + by various members of the Spens Committee is reported by Joan Simon, 'The Shaping of the Spens Report on Secondary Education 1933-38: An Inside View. Part II', *British Journal of Educational Studies,* Vol. XXV, No. 2, June 1977, p. 174.
74. J. L. Brereton, *The Case for Examinations* (1944), p. 186.
75. Board of Education, *Curriculum and Examinations in Secondary Schools* (1943), p. 15 fn.
76. J. L. Gray and P. Moshinsky, 'Ability and Opportunity in English Education', in L. Hogben (ed.) *Political Arithmetic. A Symposium of Population Studies* (1938), p. 367.
77. Board of Education, *Education in 1938* (1939), p. 64.
78. R. H. Tawney, *Secondary Education For All* (1922). A succinct summary of the main arguments is given in Tawney's *Education, the Socialist Policy* (1924), pp. 31-6.

CHAPTER 9

Secondary Education for All: The End of Selection?

Even before the 1944 Education Act had been conceived, the question of selection was being re-examined in the context of secondary education as a whole. The distinguished educationist, Sir Fred Clarke, writing in 1940 summed up the mood of the time as follows:

> There is widespread dissatisfaction with the present form of selective examination at 11 + and, very significantly, a growing conviction that what is of primary importance is not so much reconstruction of the machinery of selection to fulfil its present purpose, as a complete reconsideration of the question as to what selection is to be *for*. In other words, the question 'Who is to be taught what by whom and how?' must be in respect of the whole child population, and with especial point and precision at the beginning of adolescence.[1]

In theory, the 1944 Act made possible a complete change in the system. That education should be organized in three stages, with secondary education being available according to the age, ability and aptitude of each child, thus allowing for equality of opportunity[2], required a reshaping of existing institutions. In practice, ministerial and other official pronouncements favoured the continuation of the separate schooling recommended by Hadow, Spens and Norwood. For example, the Ministry's pamphlet *The Nation's Schools* (1945), whilst declaring that 'fundamentally we have to select schools for children and not children for schools',[3] nevertheless assumed that the three types of secondary schools would remain.

Modern and technical schools were developed alongside existing

225

grammar schools. The abolition of fee payers in grammar schools if anything increased the pressure of numbers at the entrance stage. The raising of the school leaving age to 15 in 1947 also generated a demand for longer secondary courses. With superior facilities, well-qualified staff and offering an education to the age of 18, with entrance to examinations and subsequent careers which were not available to those attending the other schools, the grammar schools were inundated with applicants. Another factor which exacerbated the situation was the fast-increasing school population. Between 1945 and 1964, this rose from 5 million to more than 7 million. In 1951, the Ministry of Education complained that 'with reorganization not yet complete, the implications of the 1944 Act are lost upon many parents. Authorities are subjected to strong pressure to admit children who are unsuited to a grammar school course to what may appear to parents in some cases to be the only true secondary school available.'[4] The Act was silent on the point of how allocation to schools should be made.[5] Selection tests therefore continued to flourish within local authorities and in some cases were expanded in their thoroughness.[6] The London County Council for example, which had resisted the use of intelligence tests in their entrance examination, now introduced them. The persistence of standardized tests reflected teachers' lack of skill in using other methods.[7] Indeed, encouragement to continue with such procedures was provided by post-war researchers such as W. E. Emmett, who showed that correlations with grammar school success of about 0.8 could be obtained by the use of the Moray House battery of tests.[8]

The White Paper on Educational Reconstruction (1943) had recommended that selection should be made by means of 'record cards supplemented, if necessary, by intelligence tests', a judgment endorsed by Norwood. Whilst the restricted notion of secondary education prevailed, local authorities who wished for change found it difficult. As early as July 1946, Barrow-in-Furness Education Committee conceived of secondary education as being 'diagnostic and comprehensive'. It reported,

> The aim is a noble one but at the moment we are ill-equipped to achieve it. We are not likely to get for some time the schools, equipment and staff we need; we are lamentably ignorant of the technique of our craft and the principles underlying it; and there

is the refuse of the old system – ideological and administrative – to clear away.[9]

Some moves were made to break away from existing practices. The results of experiments at Lincoln, where pupils were selected for secondary schools without a written examination, were published in 1945.[10] A large scale investigation at Dundee, where admission to post-primary courses was determined by teachers' estimates of pupils' attainments and ability, was carried out by D. M. McIntosh. Its main conclusion, which received wide publicity, was that 'on no account should the results of one test or examination be used to select pupils for secondary courses of instruction'.[11]

However, a new examination at 16 which had replaced the School Certificate in grammar schools in 1951, the Ordinary Level General Certificate of Education, was fixed at a higher standard than the former examination. It followed that the academic calibre of pupils should be correspondingly high. As the majority of Modern school pupils left before taking this examination, it was difficult to assure parents of the existence of parity of esteem between the secondary schools.[12]

In the early 1950s, the confidence so far expressed in the reliability of standardized tests of intelligence was undermined.[13] The major cause of this shift arose from investigations by sociologists which demonstrated that the intelligence quotient correlated positively with social surroundings, even when non-verbal tests were used. A survey carried out by Floud, Halsey and Martin in 1952 in Middlesborough and South-West Hertfordshire showed that although manual workers formed 85 per cent of the population in Middlesborough and up to 65 per cent in South-West Hertfordshire, their sons took no more than 45 to 50 per cent of the annual places at grammar schools. The Early Leaving Report of the Central Advisory Council for Education, published in 1954, on a basis of a 10 per cent sample of all grammar schools in England for the year 1946-7, found that 25 per cent of places were allocated to the children of professional and managerial parents, a figure disproportionately large compared with other groups. This clearly showed the lack of equality of opportunity for children of equal ability.[14]

Added to this were the doubts expressed by psychologists themselves on the reliability of the results of intelligence tests. In January 1952, Professor P. E. Vernon raised considerable public interest[15] when he claimed that the average rise in I.Q. which was possible from a limited amount of instruction in the technique of answering test questions was as much as 14 points.[16] Hertfordshire became the first authority to abandon the use of intelligence tests in selecting children for admission to grammar schools. Nevertheless, five years later, despite changes in procedure and the availability of more grammar school places, Floud and Halsey reported that class chances had deteriorated for working class boys and improved for the sons of the professional and white-collar groups.[17]

The findings of the National Foundation for Educational Research, a body whose primary object is to assist local education authorities in solving their problems, raised further questions. Their First Interim Report on Allocation of Primary School Leavers to Courses of Secondary Education (1950), failed to find a single satisfactory test which could be applied for allocation to grammar and other schools.[18] A follow-up two years later reported two main weaknesses in local authorities' procedures: the fact that objective tests were susceptible to coaching and the difficulty of making fine discriminations between those children whose marks were close to the border line for grammar school entry.[19] By 1957, Sir Edward Boyle, the Conservative Minister for Education, agreed with Opposition M.P.s that 'the present system of selection causes a great deal of anxiety in many quarters, and it would be both foolish and wrong simply to remain content with it'.[20] In the same year, an inquiry carried out by the British Psychological Society concluded that 'Psychologists should frankly acknowledge that completely accurate classification of children, either by level or type of ability, is not possible at 11 years'.[21]

The argument put forward in 1926 by Kenneth Lindsay that the country could not afford educational waste was particularly true in post-war Britain where on economic grounds alone, a more skilled and better educated workforce was required. By 1963, the Newsom Report Half Our Future could claim, 'Intellectual talent is not a fixed quantity with which we have to work, but available talent can be modified by social policy and educational approaches' (p. 8). And in the Foreword to the Report, Boyle agreed that 'all children should have an equal opportunity of acquiring intelligence and of developing talents and abilities to the full'.[22]

Organizational factors still played a dominant part in determining who was selected for different types of secondary schools. A longitudinal study of more than 3,000 primary school children by J. W. B. Douglas, Director of the Medical Research Council at the London School of Economics, published under the title *The Home and the School* (1964), provided useful statistical information. Regional differences in the provision of grammar school places in no way reflected real differences in the ability of the children. In some authorities, grammar school places were given to more than 30 per cent of children, in others to less than 10 per cent. Whilst this situation existed, the best selection procedures would fail to make use of available talent. Many mothers were dissatisfied with the results of selection, which met only two-thirds of their demands for grammar school places. Again, as in other reports, the findings underlined environmental influences upon achievement.[23]

Besides regional variations, the internal organization of primary schools was found to be affecting pupils' performance. Competition for grammar school places became keener after 1944 when the distinction between fee and non-fee payers was abolished. It encouraged schools to prepare well those pupils likely to be successful at the 11 + examination. Streaming, as we have already seen in the previous chapter, operated in primary schools. This tendency was now reinforced and subsequent studies, such as Brian Jackson's *Streaming: an education system in miniature* (1964), examined the self-fulfilling prophecy and the different levels of teacher expectation which this process entailed.[24] Barker Lunn, in a study of streaming practices in over 2,200 primary schools begun in 1963, distinguished five main and two minor types of organization. 65 per cent of schools adopted 'homogeneous streaming' based on ability or attainment. It was suggested from the evidence that such streaming penalized boys and the younger children of a year group. Also the fact of a child being in anything but the top stream lowered parental expectations and aspirations for a grammar school place.[25] The claim of selective tests to forecast accurately the ability of pupils to benefit by a grammar school education was increasingly challenged: the debate now moved to a consideration of a form of common secondary school which would obviate the need for prior selection.

Comprehensive Schooling and Selection

The six years which spanned the Labour Government's period in office after the war (1945-51) produced no national policy which altered the basis of selection. The initiative in this matter was taken at local level, especially in Labour-controlled areas. The London County Council and South West Middlesex[26] were the earliest authorities in England to set up comprehensive schools.[27] In September 1954, the first school of its type in new buildings, Kidbrooke in London, was opened and by January 1966 there were 77 secondary schools of this order. The Council denied that it was aiming at grammar school education for all. The distinctive characteristics of the new school were described thus:

> A comprehensive school is not merely unselective: it is a school which caters for pupils of all levels of ability apart from handicapped pupils needing special education. The term is hardly justifiable unless there are in fact within it sufficient numbers of pupils in all parts of the ability range to call for and to justify proper provision for them... It is sometimes asked of a particular comprehensive school of moderate size how it differs from a successful secondary modern school of similar size.... the former sets out to provide for all abilities, the latter assumes previous selection elsewhere.[28]

Political opposition to the London Plan was complemented by teacher resistance which was not confined to the established grammar schools. Despite this, experiments in different types of secondary school were made. Multilateral schools, which would have housed the three separate streams of secondary education under one roof, were no longer part of official Labour Party policy from 1948.[29] Some authorities established bilaterals, which were a combination of either grammar and technical or technical and modern schools, and in Leicestershire, junior non-selective high schools were built alongside fully and partly comprehensive and existing grammar schools.[30] The Labour Party's attitude on the comprehensive issue was neither enthusiastic nor clear. As recently as 1963, Harold Wilson announced that grammar schools would be abolished 'over his dead body'.[31] In that year, as little as 4.6 per cent of secondary schooling was either partly or fully comprehensive. Only one English county borough, Bradford, had so reorganized its secondary education that no allocation procedure was required.[32] With the 1964 General Election, the issues of selection and segregation in education were for the first time prominently featured by the Labour Party. Electorally, as one political scientist has observed, the presentation of the tripartite system as being socially inegalitarian had not been popular with the electors. Now, it was decided to emphasize the ideological, rather than the social justice of comprehensive education, stressing the economic advantages of a system which did not fail to capture talent on the point of entry to secondary education.[33] This approach fitted in well with criticisms of the selection procedures voiced by psychologists and sociologists already described, and a Labour Government was returned, pledged to implement its promises.

Circular 10/65 issued by the Department of Education and Science in July 1965 to local authorities, set out six forms of comprehensive reorganization which would be acceptable. Four of these patterns which still exist are as follows. The type most advocated was the all-through school, 11 to 18, as in London. A second alternative was a two-tier system, in which pupils attended junior or lower schools and transferred at 13 or 14, as in Leicestershire.[34] A third possibility was for common schooling to 16, followed by sixth form colleges for those staying on, as in Hampshire and Surrey. The fourth plan involved the founding of middle schools, which catered for primary and secondary pupils of from 7 or 8 to 12 or 13 years as a first stage, transferring to upper schools thereafter, as in the West Riding of Yorkshire. Local authorities were to submit their plans for reorganization within a year.

The response to the Circular was mixed. Teachers already in comprehensive schools were on the whole more in favour of the spread of the system than those still outside it. Local education committees, representing a range of political interests, reacted in very different ways. A number wished to retain their selective grammar schools and submitted plans which they did not seriously believe would be accepted. Pressure groups of parents and teachers, such as the Campaign for Comprehensive Education (C.C.E.) and the Programme for Reform in Secondary Education (P.R.I.S.E.), stimulated debate on the future of comprehensive education and disseminated information on ways in which the schools were coping.

The organized vocal expression of parents in educational matters was a new phenomenon from the 1950s[35] and in no other field were parental aspirations (called by the Roman Catholic Archbishop of Liverpool, George Beck, 'the revolt of the Mums')[36] so clearly enunciated as in that relating to the 11 + examinations. The Confederation for the Advancement of State Education (C.A.S.E.), which took an active interest in selection, operated on a regional basis: the Cambridge Association, for example, undertook a survey in 1963 which was published under the title *Cambridge Parents on the Eleven Plus.*[37] Handbooks were also produced for parents by various organizations in response to the demand for fuller information on assessment procedures.[38]

With the return of a Labour Government in 1966 for a further four years, the adoption of comprehensive education was encouraged. The most significant change during this time was the number of authorities who had abolished their allocation procedures. Whilst there were only two in 1964, the number had grown to 26 in 1968. In these years, nearly two-thirds of all authorities had made major changes in their allocation procedures. By 1969, out of the 131 authorities who still retained selection, 104 said that they had plans to abolish allocation altogether.[39] In fact, reorganization subsequently proceeded at a slower pace than was anticipated. With the return to power of a Conservative Government in 1970 and in spite of the withdrawal of Circular 10/65, reorganization continued and by the mid-1970s, half the children of secondary school age in England attended comprehensives. Where grammar schools existed, selection tests continued to be given. But whether schools were selective or otherwise, no standard procedures were employed between authorities in forwarding information from primary schools to the secondary stage of education. A recent report has shown that although the use of verbal reasoning tests for allocating pupils to selective schools in the 1970s was declining, paradoxically, there was an increase in testing by secondary schools.[40]

The allocation of pupils between schools poses problems of choice. In the Inner London Education Authority, schools aim at obtaining a balanced intake of ability. If a school is oversubscribed in a child's particular ability band, this factor may affect his or her chances of acceptance.[41] Within a comprehensive school, the problem of differences between children remain. A Report issued by the Department of Education and Science in 1977 warned that in comprehensive schools, the identification and progress of gifted pupils might suffer.[42] Another difficulty has been the multiplicity of ages of transfer, especially since the advent of the middle school.

The use of attainment tests both in English and arithmetic continued to decline throughout the 1960s and 1970s, but there was little change in the employment of verbal reasoning, i.e. intelligence tests.[43]

However, the issues surrounding selection are still far from settled. There is a school of thought amongst present-day sociologists of education which claims that the comprehensive school reproduces the inequalities formerly found in the tripartite system.[44] Disagreement exists, especially between American writers, on the main influences on children's behaviour and attainment. Jensen (1969) stresses hereditary factors as the most important; Jencks on the other hand attributes success to random factors. The debate on the 'heritability' of I.Q. has received wide publicity by Professor Kamin's book *The Science and Politics of I.Q.* (1974), which advanced the view that I.Q. tests have served as an instrument of oppression against the poor.[45] In an introduction to the English edition of the book, however, Liam Hudson warns that this debate 'may be a dangerous distraction, channelling our energy away from impending social crises, rather than focusing our attention on the educational reforms that could help to avert them'.[46] Two neo-Marxist economists, Bowles and Gintis, have examined the role of I.Q. in the reproduction of social inequality. Their conclusion, which does not touch on the heredity-environment debate, is that I.Q. legitimates the hierarchical division of labour, dividing strata against one another in order to maintain the inferior status of minority groups.[47]

Nevertheless, there is a body of opinion which challenges some of these assumptions. The three *Black Papers,* which were educational pamphlets published between 1969 and 1975, contained essays written by educationists and others holding right-wing views. In the third set, the case for segregation and the upholding of standards is made by Iris Murdoch in an essay 'Socialism and Selection':

> The presence of clever children makes the others feel inferior, the less clever are just as likely to retard the clever as the latter are to inspire the former, a mixed class is likely to contain a group of thoroughly bored children. Mixed-ability teaching works best with small classes of docile pupils with roughly similar backgrounds, but demands very exceptional teachers

when these conditions are not satisfied. To be concerned about the fate of the clever child is not to be indifferent to the fate of the less clever. The latter, just as much as the former, needs specialized teaching and it is unreasonable to expect teachers to be universal geniuses, who can teach every sort of child. 'Streaming', in the sense of selective attention, must occur somewhere, and is it not better to do this on some general rational basis, rather than leaving it to the unfortunate teacher to 'stream' the class, which will often mean in practice placating the noisiest group?[48]

Expressed in a different way, a National Foundation for Educational Research report on allocation procedures for secondary education concluded that more than administrative changes are required:

Our current concern for equality and dissatisfaction with aspects of our educational system will prove fully fruitful only if they lead us to concentrate at both primary and secondary levels upon the social context of learning and upon the ways in which educational experience can be organised so that pupils learn to come to terms with their genuine weaknesses and to exploit their strengths.[49]

The establishment of the Department of Education and Science's Assessment of Performance Unit in 1974 has revived interest in testing performance in schools. Local authorities too are making use of tests to monitor the curricula in their own schools and, in the words of an official document, 'will often wish to place their own standards in a national context.'[50] In the Government Green Paper *Education in Schools: A Consultative Document* (1977), the point was made that with a mobile population, there needs to be a standard minimum similarity of curriculum across the country which could be secured by establishing a common 'core' curriculum.[51]

A report on comprehensive education in 1977 showed the extent to which selection still remained. Between 1975 and 1976, the total number of pupils in maintained grammar schools fell by only one per cent. Over 500 grammar schools remained and four per cent of comprehensives were officially selective. There had been a rise in the number of selective places local authorities were buying at private schools and only 26 out of the 75 local education authorities which remained to be reorganized had received requests to report plans for their remaining schools. Selection, it concluded, was therefore far from being on the retreat in Britain's secondary schools and could well be making a comeback.[52]

It was natural that Conservative-led local authorities were reluctant to lose their selective schools. Eleven years after Circular 10/65 had been issued, seven local authorities had not abolished their grammar schools or introduced comprehensive education. In 1976, one of these authorities, the Borough of Tameside, Greater Manchester, was challenged in the High Court by the Secretary of State for Education;[53] the local authority was successful and selective schools remained. One result of the case was that the law was changed. A new Education Act came into force in 1976 requiring local authorities to have regard to the general principle that secondary education should be provided only in schools where the arrangements for the admission of pupils are not based (wholly or partly) on selection by reference to ability or aptitude.[54] Under Section 2(4) of the Act, authorities had to submit proposals for establishing comprehensive schools. Since then, the Tameside authority has been involved in further litigation, with the Court finding once more in its favour.[55] In a more recent case, in October 1978 *(North Yorkshire County Council v. Secretary of State)* it was decided that local authorities were obliged to provide comprehensive schools of a kind favoured by central government.[56] Political interest in the selection process continues to be strong. The Conservative Manifesto for the 1979 General Election pledged the repeal of the 1976 Education Act, restoring powers to local authorities for the arrangement of secondary provision, the partial restoration of selective schools and streaming in secondary schools. Almost immediately after the Election, the Conservative Government promulgated a short Education Bill in line with their election promises. Since the Bill's successful passage through Parliament, local authorities were free to decide whether to retain the remaining 292 grammar schools. A second and more substantial Bill was promised later in the Parliamentary session which would help children from poor homes to win places at leading schools.

By May 1979, 44 of the 97 local education authorities had reorganized on comprehensive lines, with a number due to complete their schemes.[57] A recent Conservative Party statement on education indicates that a variety of approaches to comprehensive schools must be adopted.[58] It devotes some space to discussing the basis of selection, whether geographically or by ability. Selection is a live issue today, involving many of the principles and arguments with which the Endowed Schools Commissioners were concerned over a century ago.

*   *   *   *   *   *

The language in which selection has been debated has in the course of time become more sophisticated but fundamentally the central issue has remained the same. Given that schools should ensure that each pupil's talents are realized, it follows that those with special gifts and abilities should be adequately catered for. In other words, social justice for all must be reflected in schools and in their organization. Whether this can best be achieved by educating in separate institutions, as advocated in the past, or by offering a common curriculum but with special facilities for gifted pupils within a comprehensive system, is a matter on which there is as yet no consensus. Although there is no simple solution to hand, it is suggested here that administrators and politicians could with benefit refer to the evidence about selection for secondary education which has accumulated since the nineteenth century.

NOTES

1. F. Clarke, *Education and Social Change* (1940), p. 45.
2. See H. Silver (ed.), *Equal Opportunity in Education* (1973), pp. xxi-xxxiii.
3. Ministry of Education, Pamphlet No. 1 *The Nation's Schools* (1945), p. 13. For a criticism of the Ministry's attitudes see D. W. Oates, *The New Secondary Schools and the Selection of their Pupils* (1946), pp. 49-60.
4. Ministry of Education Annual Report for 1951, p. 11.
5. H. Davies, *The Boys' Grammar School, Today and Tomorrow* (1945), p.viii.
6. See, for example, the account of the selection procedures for the Wigan Education Committee, R. Edwards, *Classification for Secondary Education* (1951).
7. A Consultative Committee of the National Union of Teachers recommended in 1949 that standardised intelligence tests should be taken by all children in the 10-11 age groups in each area three times in the course of their last year at the primary school. National Union of Teachers, *Transfer From Primary to Secondary Schools* (1949), p. 37.
8. P. E. Vernon (ed.), *Secondary School Selection, A British Psychological Society Inquiry* (1957), pp. 26-7.
9. Barrow-in-Furness Education Committee, *Classification for Secondary Education* (1946), pp. 5-6.

10. A. Sutcliffe and J. W. Canham, *Selection for Secondary Education Without a Written Examination* (1945), pp. 18-25.
11. D. M. McIntosh, *Promotion From Primary to Secondary Education* (1948), p. 135.
12. W. Taylor, *The Secondary Modern School* (1963), pp. 112-16.
13. For a typical example of the doubts expressed at this time on the effect of selection, see G. B. Jeffrey, 'The Criteria for Selection', *Studies in Education* (1954), pp. 32-57. An evaluation of the tests currently in use at this time is given in J. J. B. Dempster, *Selection for Secondary Education* (1954).
14. See E. Fraser, *Environment and the School* (1959), J. Floud, A. H. Halsey and F. Martin, *Social Class and Educational Opportunity* (1956).
15. Vernon's articles from the *Times Educational Supplement* (2 January and 1 February 1952) and subsequent responses were published as a pamphlet. *Intelligence Testing. Its Use in Selection for Secondary Education* (1952). The Times Publishing Co.
16. B. Simon, *Intelligence Testing and the Comprehensive School* (1953), p. 70. For a useful account of the debate, see D. V. Skeet, *The Child of Eleven* (1957), Ch. VI, Doubts and Criticisms, pp. 86-108.
17. J. Floud and A. H. Halsey, 'Social Class, Intelligence Tests and Selection for Secondary Schools', *British Journal of Sociology*, Vol. VIII, No. 1, March 1957, pp. 33-9.
18. A. F. Watts and P. Slater, *The Allocation of Primary School Leavers to Courses of Secondary Education. First Interim Report* (1950), pp. 20-7.
19. A. F. Watts, D. A. Pidgeon and A. Yates, *Secondary School Entrance Examinations. Second Interim Report* (1952), pp. 31-3.
20. *Hansard*, Ser. 5, Vol. DLXVIII, 5 April 1957, col. 759, quoted in I. G. K. Fenwick, *The Comprehensive School 1944-70* (1976), p. 112.
21. P. E. Vernon (ed.), *Secondary School Selection* (1957), p. 169.
22. Report of Central Advisory Council for Education (England), *Half Our Future* (1963), p. iv.
23. J. W. B. Douglas, *The Home and the School* (1967 edn.), p. 59.
24. B. Jackson, *Streaming. An Education in Miniature* (1964), pp. 124-6.
25. J. C. Barker Lunn, 'The Effects of Streaming and Other Forms of Grouping in Junior Schools. An Interim Report' *New Research in Education*, Vol. 1, 1967, p. 12: and *Streaming in the Primary School* (1970), p. 180.
26. See Middlesex County Council Education Committee, *The Comprehensive School* (1948).
27. Fenwick, op. cit., p. 45. In Wales, Anglesey became fully comprehensive in 1952.
28. Inner London Education Authority, *London Comprehensive Schools* (1966), p. 17.
29. O. Banks, *Parity and Prestige in English Secondary Education* (1955), p. 134.
30. W. H. G. Armytage, *Four Hundred Years of English Education* (1964), p. 242.
31. M. Kogan, *The Politics of Educational Change* (1978), p. 58.
32. National Foundation for Educational Research, *Local Authority Practices in the Allocation of Pupils to Secondary Schools* (1964), p. 24. A number of authorities were weighing up the alternative patterns of organizing secondary comprehensive education well before the Circular 10/65. One of the most detailed documents was that issued by the County Borough of Bolton, *A Report on the System or Systems of Secondary Education That Will Obviate The Eleven Plus Examination and Selection* (1964), pp. 1-6.
33. Parkinson, op. cit., p. 88.
34. See S. C. Mason, *The Leicestershire Experiment and Plan* (1964, third edn.), pp. 11-13.

35. D. Rubenstein and B. Simon, *The Evolution of the Comprehensive School 1922-1966* (1969), pp. 57-60.
36. Lowndes (1969) 2nd edn., op. cit., p. 296.
37. Cambridge Association for the Advancement of State Education, *A Report. 'Cambridge Parents on the "Eleven Plus"'*, (1965)
38. E.g. *Encyclopaedia Britannica* issued an 'Advisory Guide for Parents' entitled *Selection For Secondary Education* in 1964.
39. National Foundation for Educational Research, *Trends in Allocation Procedures* (1969), p. 19.
40. R. Sumner and K. Bradley, *Assessment for Transition. A Study of New Procedures* (1977), p. ii.
41. J. Stone and F. Taylor, *Low-Down on Secondary Transfer in Inner London in 1973* (1973).
42. Department of Education and Science, HMI Series: Matters for Discussion 4, *Gifted Children in Middle and Comprehensive Secondary Schools* (1977), p. 41.
43. The decline in the use of English tests was from 120 authorities in 1964 to 67 in 1968 and 34 in 1972. In mathematics, the decline was from 118 in 1964 to 62 in 1968 and 27 in 1972. On the other hand, verbal reasoning tests were used in 136 in 1964, 127 in 1968 and 105 in 1972. C. J. Hill, *Transfer at Eleven* (1972), pp. 12-13.
44. See for example the evidence of research, especially J. Ford, *Social Class and the Comprehensive School* (1969), pp. 40-1.
45. L. J. Kamin, *The Science and Politics of I.Q.* (1977) p. 16.
46. Ibid., p. 14.
47. S. Bowles and H. Gintis, 'I.Q. in the U.S. Class Structure', *Social Policy,* Vol. 3, 1972-3, pp. 65-96, reprinted in J. Karabel and A. H. Halsey (eds.) *Power and Ideology in Education* (1977), pp. 215-31.
48. Iris Murdoch, 'Socialism and Selection', *The Fight for Education. Black Paper 1975* (1975), p. 7.
49. National Foundation for Educational Research, *Procedures for the Allocation of Pupils in Secondary Education* (1963), p. 24.
50. Department of Education and Science, No. 93. Report on Education. *Assessing the Performance of Pupils* (1978), p. 4.
51. *Education in Schools. A Consultative Document* (1977), p. 11.
52. Campaign for Comprehensive Education and Programme for Reform in Secondary Education, *Comprehensive Education – Our Last Chance?* (1977).
53. K. Alexander and V. Williams, 'Judicial Review of Educational Policy: The Teachings of Tameside', *British Journal of Educational Studies,* Vol. XXVI, No. 3, October 1978, pp. 224-33.
54. G. Fowler, 'The Politics of Education' in G. Bernbaum (ed.), *Schooling in Decline* (1979), p. 71.
55. Secretary of State etc. v. Tameside Metropolitan Borough Council (1977), AC 1014.
56. *The Times,* 20 October 1978, p. 12.
57. *New Society,* 17 May 1979, p. 367.
58. N. St. John-Stevas, *Better Schools For All* (1977), pp. 21-2.

Glossary

Any attempt to describe the English education system in the nineteenth century raises difficulties of nomenclature. The distinction between elementary and secondary education was often unclear as, for example, in the case of endowed schools. For a deeper understanding the reader is referred to the following books: E. J. R. Eaglesham, *The Foundations of 20th Century Education in England* (Routledge & Kegan Paul, 1967), P. H. J. H. Gosden, *The Development of Educational Administration in England and Wales* (Blackwell, 1968), and K. Evans, *The Development and Structure of the English Educational System* (University of London Press, 1975).

Board

Schools Boards were brought into being by the 1870 Education Act to provide elementary education in localities where insufficient provision had been made by voluntary bodies. Ratepayers voted for representatives every three years. The Boards were superseded by local education authorities after the 1902 Education Act.

Elementary

Before 1870, the bulk of elementary education was provided by three societies, the National Society (1811) which promoted Anglican schooling, the British and Foreign Society (1814) which looked after the interests of Nonconformists, and the Catholic Poor School Committee (1847). In 1833 the State, for the first time, allocated money for the furtherance of elementary education.

From 1862, grants were given to schools under the Revised Code. Henceforth, a school's income depended on the proficiency of its pupils in the 3 Rs. Annual examinations were carried out at six levels, Standards I to VI, and children were tested from the age of six. From the time of the 1870 Education Act, there was a Dual System of elementary education, with both the State and the Churches providing elementary schooling.

Endowed

These schools, financed by pious founders, were originally intended to provide free to local inhabitants an education based on the elements of grammar. By the mid-nineteenth century, all except a few hundred were elementary in character.

The Taunton Report (1868) advocated three types of endowed school, based on the gradations of society.

> *First Grade* – Classics were the hall-mark, along with mathematics and science, for sons of fairly wealthy parents. The leaving age was eighteen or nineteen.
> *Second Grade* – Intended mainly for those entering professions, the curriculum included more useful subjects e.g. arithmetic, English and perhaps Latin. The leaving age was sixteen.
> *Third Grade* – These schools were attended by sons of small tradesmen and superior artisans and offered an education not dissimilar to a good elementary school, including, for example, drawing. The leaving age was sixteen.

The three grades of school were established after the passing of the 1869 Endowed Schools Act. Some of the first grade schools became public schools (q.v.). The third grade school tended to disappear as the century progressed.

Grammar

Originally endowed grammar schools (q.v.), the term was popularly adopted for the system of secondary schools created by the 1902 Education Act. The new local authorities were given the task of providing a four year course of education, the contents of which were stipulated by the Secondary Regulations of 1904.

Higher Grade

Under the terms of the 1870 Education Act, Schools Boards (q.v.) were limited to providing elementary education only. However, a number of Boards established post-Standard VI establishments called higher grade schools giving an education equivalent to many endowed schools. These schools were declared illegal in a court case in 1900 and eventually they were discontinued.

Public

Nine 'public' schools were identified by the 1864 Clarendon Commission. Their chief characteristics were a largely classical curriculum and pupils who boarded. Since the formation of the Headmasters' Conference in 1869, which consisted of the leading public schools, membership has automatically carried public school status.

Voluntary

Refers to the provision of schooling by religious interests (see Elementary Schools). From 1870 the dominance of Church schools diminished as the School Boards were able to offer superior facilities. Nevertheless, by 1900 voluntary schools still attracted 46 per cent of the total elementary school population.

Bibliography

A. Manuscript Sources

    (i)   Individuals
    (ii)   Institutions

B. Official Records – Printed

    (i)   *Annual Reports and Returns*
    (ii)   *Select and Departmental Committees*
    (iii)   *Royal Commissions*
    (iv)   *Ministry Publications:*
          (a) Boa·d of Education
          (b) Ministry of Education
          (c) Department of Education & Science Publications

C. Books

D. Articles and Pamphlets

A. Manuscript Sources

(i) *Individuals*

A. H. D. Acland Papers - Bodleian Library, Oxford
T. D. Acland Papers - Devon Record Office
Baines Papers – Leeds Archives Department
Beaconsfield Papers – Hughenden Manor, Bucks.
Cairns Papers – Public Record Office
Cranbrook Papers – Suffolk Record Office, Ipswich Branch
Gladstone Papers – British Library
Glynne-Gladstone Papers – St. Deiniol's Library, Hawarden
Goodwood Papers – West Sussex Record Office
Granville Papers – Public Record Office
Huxley Papers – Imperial College of Science, University of London
Iddesleigh Papers – British Library
Longley Papers – Lambeth Palace Library
Lyttelton Papers – Hereford and Worcester Record Office
Salisbury Papers – Hatfield House, Herts.
Solly Papers – British Library of Economics and Political Science, London
Trevelyan Papers – University of Newcastle-on-Tyne Library

(ii) *Institutions*

Greater London Record Office
Humberside Record Office
Incorporated Association of Headmasters, London
Lancashire Record Office
Northamptonshire Record Office
Northumberland Record Office
Public Record Office

B.   Official Records - Printed

(i) *Annual Reports and Returns*

Annual Reports of the Charity Commission, 1854-1900

Reports of the Endowed Schools Commissioners to the Lords of Committee of
    H.M. Privy Council on Education 1872, P.P. 1872, XXIV; 1875, P.P. 1875,
    XXVIII

House of Lords
Return of Scholarships and Schemes made and approved under the Endowed
    Schools Acts up to 3 December, 1880, Fortescue Return 1884, P.P. 1884, X

House of Commons
Return showing the extent and manner in which LEAs in England, Wales and
    Ireland applied funds to the purpose of Technical Education, 1899, P.P. 1899,
    LXXXIII

House of Commons
Return showing occupation of parents or winners of County Council Scholarships,
    1900, P.P. 1900, LXXXIII

House of Commons
Return for every County and County Borough possessing organisation for
    promoting Secondary Education, 1901 P.P. 1901, LVI

House of Commons
Return showing provision by LEAs to enable Public Elementary Scholars to go to
    Secondary Schools, 1906, P.P. 1906, LXXXIX

House of Commons
Summary of figures relating to state-aided Secondary Schools in England, 1907,
    P.P. 1907, LXII

(ii) *Select and Departmental Committees*

Report of the Select Committee on the Endowed Schools Bill, 1869, P.P. 1868-9,
    VIII

Report of the Select Committee on the Endowed Schools Act (1869), 1873, P.P.
    1873, VIII

Report of the Select Committee on School Board Elections (Voting), 1884, P.P. 1884-5, XI

Report of the Select Committee on the Charitable Trusts Act, 1884, P.P. 1884 IX

Report of the Select Committee on the Endowed Schools Act (1869) 1886, P.P. 1886 IX; 1887, P.P. 1887 IX

Report of the Select Committee on the Charity Commission, 1894, P.P. 1894, XI.

Report of the Departmental Committee appointed by the Treasury to inquire into the Charity Commission, 1895, P.P. 1895, LXXIV

(iii) *Royal Commissions*

Report of the Public Schools Commission (Clarendon) 1864, P.P. 1864, XX-XXI

Report of the Schools Inquiry Commission (Taunton) 1868, P.P. 1867-8, XXVIII

Report of the Technical Instruction Commission (Samuelson) 1884, P.P. 1884, XXIX-XLIX

Report of the Secondary Education Commission (Bryce), 1895, P.P. 1895, XLIII-XLIX

Report of the Civil Service Commission, 1913, P.P. 1912-13, XV-XVIII

(iv) *Ministry Publications:*
(a) *Board of Education*

Regulations for Secondary Schools, 1907, HMSO

Report of the Board of Education for 1911-12, HMSO

Departmental Committee on Scholarships and Free Places, 1920, HMSO

Regulations for Secondary Schools, England, 1922, HMSO

Report for the Year 1921-2, HMSO

Report of the Consultative Committee on Psychological Tests of Educable Capacity and their possible use in the public system of education, 1924, HMSO

Report of the Consultative Committee on The Education of the Adolescent (Hadow), 1926, HMSO

Educational Pamphlets, No. 50. Some Account of the Recent Development of Secondary Schools, 1927, HMSO

Educational Pamphlets, No. 63. Memorandum on Examinations for Scholarships and Free Places in Secondary Schools, 1928, HMSO

Report of the Consultative Committee on the Primary School (Hadow), 1931, HMSO

Educational Pamphlets, No. 63. Supplementary Memorandum on Examinations for Scholarships and Special Places in Secondary Schools, 1936, HMSO

Handbook of Suggestions, 1937, HMSO

Report of the Consultative Committee on Secondary Education (Spens), 1938, HMSO.

Educational Reconstruction. White Paper presented by the President of the Board of Education to Parliament, July, 1943, HMSO.

Report of the Secondary School Examinations Council (Norwood), Curriculum and Examinations in Secondary Schools, 1943, HMSO

Report of the Committee on the Public School and the General Education System (Fleming), 1944, HMSO

(b) *Ministry of Education*

Pamphlet No. 1. *The Nation's Schools. Their Plan and Purpose,* 1945, HMSO

Report of the Central Advisory Council for Education (England), *15-18* (Crowther), 1959, HMSO

Report of the Central Advisory Council for Education (England), *Half Our Future,* 1963, HMSO

(c) *Department of Education & Science*

Circular 10/65 on the Organization of Secondary Education, 1965, HMSO

Report of the Central Advisory Council for Education (England), *Children and Their Primary Schools* (Plowden), 1967, HMSO

HMI Series: Matters for Discussion 4. *Gifted Children in Middle and Comprehensive Secondary Schools,* 1977, HMSO

Department of Education and Science No. 93, Report on Education, *Assessing the Performance of Pupils,* 1978, HMSO

Education in Schools, A Consultative Document, 1977, HMSO

C. Books

Abbott, A. (1933) *Education for Industry and Commerce in England,* Oxford University Press

Adams, F. (1882) *History of the Elementary School Contest in England,* Chapman and Hall

Adamson, J. W. (1930) *English Education 1789-1902,* Cambridge University Press

Allen, B. M. (1933) *William Garnett: A Memoir,* Heffer, Cambridge

Allen, B. M. (1934) *Sir Robert Morant,* Macmillan

Altick, R. D. (1957) *The English Common Reader: A Social History of the Mass Reading Public 1800-1900,* University of Chicago Press

Anon. (1818) *A letter to Henry Brougham, Esq., M.P., for a Master of Arts of Queen's College, Oxford, upon the best method of restoring decayed Grammar Schools*, London.

Appleton, C. E. (1874) *The Endowment of Education. A paper read before the Oxford Political Economy Club, 28 November, 1874*, Oxford.

Arch, J. (1898) *Joseph Arch. The Story of his Life told by Himself*, Hutchinson.

Archer, R. L. (1921) *Secondary Education in the Nineteenth Century*, Cambridge University Press, reprinted Cass, 1966.

Armytage, W. H. G. (1951) *A. J. Mundella*, Benn

Armytage, W. H. G. (1964) *Four Hundred Years of English Education*, Cambridge University Press

Arnold, R. (1962) *The Whiston Matter*, Hart-Davis

Ashby, M. K. (1961) *Joseph Ashby of Tysoe 1859-1919*, Cambridge University Press

Ashton, T. S. (1933) *Economic and Social Investigation in Manchester 1833-1933*, Manchester University Press

Askwith, B. (1975) *The Lytteltons. A Family Chronicle of the Nineteenth Century*, Chatto and Windus

Ausubel, H. (1960) *In Hard Times*, Oxford University Press

Balfour, G. (1903) *The Educational Systems of Great Britain and Ireland*, Oxford University Press

Ballard, P. B. (1922) *Group Tests of Intelligence*, University of London Press

Ballard, P. B. (1936) 'The Special Place Examination', in Sadler M , (1936), q.v.

Ballard, P. B. (1937) *Things I Cannot Forget*, University of London Press

Banks, J. A. (1953) *Prosperity and Parenthood*, Routledge and Kegan Paul

Banks, O. (1955) *Parity and Prestige in English Education*, Routledge and Kegan Paul

Bantock, G. H. (1963) *Education in an Industrial Society*, Faber and Faber

Barker Lunn, J. C. (1970) *Streaming in the Primary School. A Longitudinal Study of Children in Streamed & Non-Streamed Junior Schools*, NFER, Slough

Barker, R. (1972) *Education and Politics 1900-1951. A Study of the Labour Party*, Oxford University Press

Barnard, H. C. (1971) *A History of English Education from 1760*, Seventh impression, University of London Press

Baron, G. and Howell, D. A. (1968) *Royal Commission on Local Government. Research Studies 6, School Management and Government*, HMSO

Barrow-in-Furness Education Committee (1946) *Classification for Secondary Education*, Barrow-in-Furness

Beale, D. (1869) *Reports issued by the Schools' Inquiry Commission on the Education of Girls*, David Nutt

Bechofer Roberts, C. E. (1929) *Philip Snowden, An Impartial Portrait,* Cassell

Beer, M. (1924) *History of British Socialism,* Vol. II, Bell

Bernbaum, G. (1967) *Social Change and the Schools 1918-1944,* Routledge and Kegan Paul

Bingham, J. H. (1949) *The Period of the Sheffield School Board,* J. W. Northend, Sheffield

Birchenough, C. (1938) *History of English Education,* University Tutorial Press

Birrell, A. (1937) *Things Past Redress,* Faber and Faber

Boase, F. (1892-1921) *Modern English Biography,* 6 Vols., Netherton and Worth, Truro

Bowles, S. and Gintis, H. (1977) 'I.Q. in the U.S. Class Structure', in Karabel J. and Halsey A. H. (eds.), *Power & Ideology in Education,* Oxford University Press

Brennan, E. J. T. (ed.) (1975) *Education for National Efficiency: The Contributions of Sidney and Beatrice Webb,* Athlone Press

Brererton, J. L. (1944) *The Case For Examinations,* Cambridge University Press

Briggs, A. (1952) *History of Birmingham,* Vol. II, Oxford University Press

Briggs, A. (1954) *Victorian People,* Odhams, Penguin edn. 1965

Briggs, A. (1963) *Victorian Cities,* Odhams, Penguin edn. 1968

Briggs, A. and Saville, J. (eds.) (1960) *Essays in Labour History,* Macmillan

Brockett, A. (1962) *Nonconformity in Exeter,* University of Exeter Press

Bruce, M. (1961) *The Coming of the Welfare State,* Batsford

Buckle, G. E. (1926) *The Life of Benjamin Disraeli,* Vol. 5, Murray

Buckley, L. R. (1964) *Selection for Secondary Education. Advisory Guide for Parents,* Encyclopaedia Britannica

Bunce, J. T. (1885) *History of the Corporation of Birmingham,* Vol. II, Cornish Bros., Birmingham

Burke, J. (ed.) (1976) *Osborn's Concise Law Dictionary,* 6th edn., Sweet and Maxwell

Butler, Lord (1971) *The Art of the Possible,* Hamish Hamilton

Cambridge Association for the Advancement of State Education (1965) *A Report. Cambridge Parents on the 'Eleven Plus'*

Campaign for Comprehensive Education and Programme for Reform in Secondary Education (1977) *Comprehensive Education – Our Last Chance?*

Campbell, F. (1956) *Eleven Plus and All That,* Watts

Cardwell, D. S. L. (1957) *The Organisation of Science in England,* Heinemann

Carlisle, N. (1818) *Concise Description of the Endowed Grammar Schools in England and Wales,* 2 Vols., Baldwin, Gradock and Joy

Clarke, F. (1940) *Education and Social Change. An English Interpretation,* The Sheldon Press

Clarke, M. L. (1959) *Classical Education in Britain.1500-1900,* Cambridge University Press

Clementi, M. (1896) *St. Paul's, and the Charity Commissioners,* Bell and Sons

Cole, G. D. H. and Postgate, R. (1945) *The Common People, 1746-1938,* Revised edn., Methuen

Cole, G. D. H. (1927) *A Short History of the British Working Class Movement Vol. II, 1848-1900,* Allen and Unwin

Cole, G. D. H. (1948) *History of the British Working-Class Movement 1789-1947,* Allen and Unwin

Cole, G. D. H. (1956) *A History of Socialist Thought,* Vol. III, Macmillan

Cole, M. (1961) *The Story of Fabian Socialism,* Heinemann

The Compact Dictionary of National Biography, (1975), Oxford University Press

Conisbee, L. R. (1964) *Bedford Modern School, Its Origins and Growth,* Bedford Modern School, Bedford

Connell, W. F. (1950) *The Educational Thought and Influence of Matthew Arnold,* Routledge and Kegan Paul

Cotgrove, S. (1958) *Technical Education and Social Change,* Routledge and Kegan Paul

Coulton, G. G. (1923) *A Victorian Schoolmaster. Henry Hart of Sedbergh,* Bell

County Borough of Bolton, (1964) *A Report on the System or Systems of Secondary Education That Will Obviate The Eleven Plus Examination and Selection,* Bolton

Cox, M. (1975) *A History of Sir John Dean's Grammar School, Northwich,* Manchester University Press

Cruickshank, M. (1963) *Church and State in English Education,* Macmillan

Cullen, M. J. (1975) *The Statistical Movement in Early Victorian Britain,* Harvester Press, Sussex

Curtis, S. J. (1948) *A History of Education in Great Britain,* University Tutorial Press

Dale, A. W. (1899) *Life of R. W. Dale,* Hodder and Stoughton

Dark, S. (1929) *Archbishop Davidson and the English Church,* P. Allen and Co.

Davies, H. (1945) *The Boys' Grammar School. Today and Tomorrow,* Methuen

Day, E. S. (1902) *An Old Westminster Endowment,* Hugh Rees

Dempster, J. J. B. (1954) *Selection for Secondary Education,* Methuen

Dent, H. C. (1949) *Secondary Education For All. Origins and Development in England,* Routledge and Kegan Paul

Dent, R. K. (1860) *Old and New Birmingham,* Houghton and Hammond, Birmingham

Dobbs, A. E. (1919) *Education and Social Movements 1700-1850,* Longmans Green

Douglas, J. W. B. (1964) *The Home and the School,* MacGibbon and Kee, Panther edn. 1976

Douglas-Smith, A. E. (1965) *The City of London School,* 2nd edn., Blackwell, Oxford

Eaglesham, E. (1956) *From School Board to Local Authority,* Routledge and Kegan Paul

Earle, F. M. (1936) *Tests of Ability For Secondary School Courses,* University of London Press

Edmonds, E. L. (1962) *The School Inspector,* Routledge and Kegan Paul

Edwards, F. W. (1885) *Technical Education. Its Rise and Progress,* Longmans

Edwards, R. (1951) *Classification for Secondary Education,* Wigan Education Committee

Essex Education Committee (1932) *Board of Education Circular 1421,* Chelmsford, Essex

Essex Education Committee, (1944) *Report of a Sub-Committee on the Selection of Children for Secondary Education,* Chelmsford, Essex

Fabian Tract 70 (1896) *Report on the Fabian Party,* London

Fabian Tract 106 (1897) *The Education Muddle and the Way Out,* London

Fenwick, I. G. K. (1976) *The Comprehensive School 1944-1970. The Politics of Secondary School Reorganization,* Methuen

Fisher, H. A. L. (1941) *An Unfinished Biography,* Oxford University Press

Ford, J. (1969) *Social Class and the Comprehensive School,* Routledge and Kegan Paul

Fortescue, Earl (1864) *Public Schools for the Middle Classes,* Longmans

Fowler, G. (1979) 'The Politics of Education', in Bernbaum G. (ed.), *Schooling in Decline,* Macmillan

Fox, L. (1967) *A County Grammar School. A History of Ashby-de-la-Zouche Grammar School through Four Centuries 1567-1967,* Oxford University Press

Fraser, E. (1959) *Home Environment and the School,* University of London Press

Garvin, J. L. (1932) *The Life of Joseph Chamberlain,* Vol. I, Macmillan

Gibbon, G. and Bell, R. W. (1939) *History of the London County Council 1889-1939,* Macmillan

Girouard, M. (1978) *Life in the English Country House. A Social and Architectural History,* Yale University Press, New Haven, Yale, and London

Godber, J. (1973) *The Harpur Trust 1952-1973,* The Harpur Trust, Bedford

Gordon P. and Lawton, D. (1978) *Curriculum Change in the Nineteenth & Twentieth Centuries,* Hodder and Stoughton

Gordon, P. and White, J. (1979) *Philosophers as Educational Reformers,* Routledge and Kegan Paul

Gosden, P. H. J. H. (1970) 'Technical Instruction Committees', in History of Education Society, *Studies in the Government and Control of Education Since 1860*, Methuen

Gourlay, A. B. (1951) *A History of Sherborne School*, Warren and Son, Winchester

Graham, J. A. and Pythian, B. A. (1965) *The Manchester Grammar School 1515-1965*, Manchester University Press

Graves, J. (1943) *Policy and Progress in Secondary Education 1902-1942*, Nelson

Gray, I. E. and Potter, W. E. (1950) *Ipswich School 1400-1950*, W. E. Harrison, Ipswich

Gray, J. L. and Moshinsky, P. (1938) 'Ability and Opportunity in English Education', in Hogben, L. (ed.), *Political Arithmetic: A Symposium of Population Studies*, Allen and Unwin

Green, J. L. (1920) *Life of the Rt. Hon. J. Collins*, Longmans Green

Gregg, P. (1962) *A Social and Economic History of Britain 1760-1960*, Harrap

Grier, L. (1952) *Achievement in Education. The Work of M. E. Sadler 1885-1935*, Constable

Griffith, G. (1864) *The Endowed Schools of England and Ireland. Their Past, Present and Future*, Stourbridge

Hadow, W. H. (1923) *Citizenship*, Oxford University Press

Halifax, Earl of (1957) *Fullness of Days*, Collins

Haldane, Viscount (1927) *The Next Step in National Education Being the Report of a Committee*, University of London Press

Halévy, E. (1939) *History of the English People. Epilogue 1895-1905*, Book 2, Penguin

Hamer, D. A. (1977) *The Politics of Electoral Pressure*, Harvester Press, Sussex

Hansome, M. (1931) *World Workers' Educational Movements*, Columbia University Press

Harrison, J. F. C. (1961) *Living and Learning 1790-1960*, Routledge and Kegan Paul

Heaseman, K. (1962) *Evangelicals in Action. An Appraisal of their Work in the Victorian Era*, Cape

Henthorn, F. (1959) *The History of Brigg Grammar School*, The Grammar School, Brigg, Lincs.

Hill, C. J. (1972) *Transfer at Eleven*, NFER, Slough

Hill, C. P. (1951) *The History of Bristol Grammar School*, Pitman

Hinder, E. F. (1883) *The Schoolmaster in the Gutter*, E. Stock

Hobhouse, A. (1880) *The Dead Hand*, Chatto and Windus

Hobhouse, L. T. and Hammond, J. L. (1905) *Lord Hobhouse. A Memoir*, Arnold

Hodgen, M. T. (1925) *Workers Education in England and the United States*, Kegan Paul

Hodgson, S. (1941) *Lord Halifax, An Appreciation,* Christophers

Hogan, J. F. (1893) *Life of Robert Lowe,* Ward and Downey

Horn, P. (1978) *Education in Rural England 1800-1914,* Gill and Macmillan

How, F. D. (1904) *Six Great Schoolmasters,* Methuen

Howard R. (Rev.) (1870) *A Plea for the Establishment of Additional Public Schools in Yorkshire for the Upper and Middle Classes,* London

Howe, E. M. (1896) *The Organisation of Secondary Education. An Address to the Liverpool Philomathic Society,* Liverpool

Hurt, J. (1971) *Education in Evolution. Church, State, Society and Popular Education, 1800-1870,* Hart-Davis, Paladin edn. 1972

Hutton, T. W. (1952) *King Edward Schools, Birmingham 1552-1952,* Blackwell, Oxford

Huxley, L. (ed.) (1912) *Thoughts on Education Chosen from the Writings of Matthew Arnold,* Smith, Elder and Co.

Inglis, K. S. (1963) *Churches and the Working Classes in Victorian England,* Routledge and Kegan Paul

Inner London Education Authority (1966) *London Comprehensive Schools*

Jackson, B. (1964) *Streaming. An Education System in Miniature,* Routledge and Kegan Paul

Jackson, B. and Marsden, D. (1962) *Education and the Working Class,* Routledge and Kegan Paul

Jeffrey, G. B. (1956) 'The Criteria for Selection', in *Studies in Education,* Evans Bros. for University of London Institute of Education

Johnson, L. G. (1959) *The Social Evolution of Industrial Britain,* Liverpool University Press

Joint Advisory Committee of the Association of Education Committees and The National Union of Teachers (1930) *Examinations in Public Elementary Schools*

Jones, M. G. (1938) *The Charity Movement. A Study of Eighteenth Century Puritanism in Action,* Cambridge University Press, reprinted Cass 1964

Judges, A. V. (1952) *Pioneers of English Education,* Faber and Faber

Kamin, L. J. (1974) *The Science and Politics of I.Q.,* Lawrence Erlbaum Associates, USA, Penguin Education edn. 1977

Kamm, J. (1965) *Hope Deferred. Girls' Education in English History,* Methuen

Kazamias, A. M. (1966) *Politics, Society and Secondary Education in England,* University of Pennsylvania Press, Philadelphia

Kekewich, G. W. (1920) *The Education Department and After,* Constable

Kelly, T. (1962) *A History of Adult Education in Great Britain from the Middle Ages to the Twentieth Century,* Liverpool University Press

Kennedy, A. L. (1953) *Salisbury. Portrait of a Statesman,* Murray

Kenny, C. S. (1880) *Endowed Charities. The True Principle of Legislation with regard to Property given for Charitable or other Public Uses,* Reeves and Turner

Kent Education Committee (1926) *An Investigation of the Free Place Scholarship Examination, 1926,* Maidstone, Kent.

Kerchensteiner, G. (1914) *The Schools and the Nation,* Macmillan

Kirk, K. E. (1937) *The Story of the Woodard Schools,* Hodder and Stoughton

Kitson Clark, G. (1962) *The Making of Victorian England,* Methuen

Kogan, M. (1978) *The Politics of Educational Change,* Fontana Collins

Lang, A. (1890) *Life, Letters and Diaries of the First Earl of Iddesleigh,* 2 Vols., Blackwood

Lawson, J. (1962) *The Endowed Grammar Schools of East Yorkshire,* East Yorkshire Local History Society

Lawson, J. (1963) *A History of Hull Grammar School against its Local Background,* Oxford University Press

Lawson, J. and Silver, H. (1973) *A Social History of Education in England,* Methuen

Lee, J. B. (Rev.) (1885) *Middle Class Education and the Working of the Endowed Schools Act,* Rivingtons

Lawson, W. R. (1908) *John Bull and His Schools,* Blackwood

Leese, J. (1950) *Personalities and Power in English Education,* Arnold

Legge, J. G. (1929) *The Rising Tide,* Blackwell, Oxford

Lempiere, W. (1924) *A History of the Girls School of Christ's Hospital, London, Hoddesdon and Hertford,* Cambridge University Press

Lester, D. N. R. (1962) *The History of Batley Grammar School 1612-1962,* Printed by J. S. Newcome and Son, Batley

Lester, L.V. (1896) *Memoir of Hugo Daniel Harper D. D.,* Longmans Green

Lester Smith, W. O. (1945) *To Whom Do The Schools Belong?* Blackwell, Oxford

Lilley, A. L. (1906) *Sir Joshua Fitch,* Arnold

Lindsay, K. (1926) *Social Progress and Educational Waste,* Routledge

Lowe, R. (1868) *Middle Class Education: Endowment or Free Trade,* London

Lowndes, G. A. N. (1937) *The Silent Social Revolution. An Account of Expansion of Public Education in England and Wales 1895-1965,* 2nd edn., 1969, Oxford University Press

Lynd, H. M. (1945) *England in the 1880s,* Oxford University Press

Lyttelton, Lord (1853) *Thoughts on National Education,* Murray

Lyttelton, Lord (1874) *A speech delivered in the House of Lords, 3 August 1874 on the Endowed Schools Amendment Bill,* Murray

McBriar, A. M. (1962) *Fabian Socialism and English Politics,* Cambridge University Press

McIntosh, D. M. (1948) *Promotion from Primary to Secondary Education*, University of London Press

McKenna, S. (1948) *Reginald McKenna. A Memoir*, Eyre and Spottiswoode

Maccoby, S. (1938) *English Radicalism 1853-1886*, Allen and Unwin

Maclure, S. (1970) *One Hundred Years of London Education 1870-1970*, Allen Lane, The Penguin Press

Mack, E. C. (1941) *Public Schools and British Opinion since 1860*, Columbia University Press

Magnus, P. (1954) *Gladstone,* Murray

Magnus, P. (1910) *Educational Aims and Efforts 1880-1910*, Longmans

Marsden, W. E. (1977) 'Education and Social Geography of Nineteenth Century Towns and Cities', in Reeder, D. A. (ed.) *Urban Education in the Nineteenth Century,* Taylor and Francis

Marshall, T. H. (1963) *Sociology at the Crossroads,* Heinemann

Mason, S. C. (1964) *The Leicestershire Experiment and Plan,* 3rd edn., Councils & Educational Press

May, D. M. (1960) *The History of Lymm Grammar School,* John Sherratt and Son, Altrincham

May, T. (1975) *The History of Harrow County School for Boys,* Harrow County School for Boys, Middx.

'Members of the XIII' (1891) *Thirteen Essays in Education,* Percival and Co.

Merson, A. D. (1975) *Earls Colne Grammar School, Essex. A History,* Earls Colne Grammar School, Essex.

Miall, A. (1884) *Life of Edward Miall,* Macmillan

Middlesex County Council Education Committee (1948) *The Comprehensive Secondary School,* Middlesex County Hall

Montmorency, J. E. G. (1902) *State Intervention in English Education,* C.U.P.

Montmorency, J. E. G. (1904) *The Progress of Education in England,* Knight and Co.

Morley, J. (1874) *The Struggle for National Education,* Chapman and Hall

Morley, J. (1905) *Life of Gladstone,* 2 Vols., Macmillan

Morris, A. J. A. (1977) *C. P. Trevelyan 1870-1958. Portrait of a Radical,* Blackstaff Press

Mowat, C. L. (1961) *The Charity Organisation Society 1869-1913, Its Ideas and Work,* Methuen

Muirhead, J. H. (1909) *Nine Famous Birmingham Men,* Cornish Brothers, Birmingham

Murdoch, I. (1975) 'Socialism and Selection', in *Black Paper 1975: The Fight For Freedom,* Dent

Murray, A. L. (1952) *The Royal Grammar School, Lancaster,* Heffer, Cambridge

National Education League (1872) *Religious Instruction in Board Schools. Report of a Debate in the Birmingham School Board, 8 May, 1872,* Birmingham

National Foundation for Educational Research (1963) *Procedures for the Allocation of Pupils in Secondary Education,* NFER, Slough

National Foundation for Educational Research (1964) *Local Authority Practices in the Allocation of Pupils to Secondary Schools,* NFER, Slough

National Foundation for Educational Research (1969) *Trends in Allocation Procedures,* NFER, Slough

National Union of Teachers (1949) *Transfer from Primary to Secondary Schools. Report of A Consultative Committee appointed by the Executive of the National Union of Teachers,* Evans Bros.

Newsome, D. (1961) *Godliness and Good Learning. Four Studies on a Victorian Ideal,* Murray

Norwood, C. (1929) *The English Tradition of Education,* Murray

Norwood, C. and Hope, A. (eds.) (1904) *The Higher Education of Boys in England,* Murray

Oates, D. W. (1946) *The New Secondary Schools and the Selection of their Pupils,* Harrap

Ogg, D. (1947) *Herbert Fisher. A Short Biography,* Arnold

Oldham, J. B. (1952) *A History of Shrewsbury School 1552-1952,* Blackwell, Oxford

Otter, J. (1925) *Life of Nathaniel Woodard,* Lane

Owen, H. (1875 edn.) *Manual for School Board Elections,* Knight and Co.

Parkin, G. R. (1898) *Life and Letters of Edward Thring,* 2 Vols., Macmillan

Parkinson, M. (1970) *The Labour Party and the Organization of Secondary Education 1918-65,* Routledge and Kegan Paul

Percival, A. (1969) *The Origins of the Headmasters' Conference,* Murray

Percy, E. (1958) *Some Memories,* Eyre and Spottiswoode

Pinchbeck, I. and Hewitt, M. (1969) *Children in English Society, Vol. I. From Tudor Times to the Eighteenth Century,* Routledge and Kegan Paul

Philpott, H. B. (1904) *London At School. The Story of the London School Board,* T. Fisher Unwin

Pillans, J. (1861) *On the Relative Importance of Mathematics and Classics in the Higher Instruction,* Edinburgh

Pollard, H. M. (1957) *Pioneers of Popular Education,* Harvard University Press

Pollard, S. (1959) *A History of Labour in Sheffield,* Liverpool University Press

Pound, W. (Rev.) (1886) *Remarks Upon English Education in the Nineteenth Century,* Rivingtons, Oxford

Pritchard, F. C. (1949) *Methodist Secondary Education,* Epworth Press

Rawnsley, W. F. (1926) *Edward Thring,* Kegan Paul

Reid, T. Wemyss (1888) *Life of the Rt. Hon. W. E. Forster,* Chapman and Hall

Reid, T. Wemyss (1899) *Memoirs and Correspondence of Lyon Playfair,* Cassell

Report of the Cambridge Conference on Secondary Education (1896) Cambridge University Press

Report of the Oxford Conference on Secondary Education (1893) Oxford University Press

Richter, M. (1964) *The Politics of Conscience. T. H. Green and His Age,* Weidenfeld and Nicolson

Roach, J. (1971) *Public Examinations in England 1850-1900,* Cambridge University Press

Roberts, B. C. (1958) *The Trades Union Congress 1868-1921,* Allen and Unwin

Rubenstein, D. and Simon, B. (1969) *The Evolution of the Comprehensive School 1926-1966,* Routledge and Kegan Paul

Rutter, M. et al (1979) *Fifteen Thousand Hours. Secondary Schools and their Effects on Children,* Open Books

St. John-Stevas, N., (1977) *Better Schools For All. A Conservative Approach to the Problems of the Comprehensive School,* Conservative Political Centre

Sadleir, M. (1949) *Michael Ernest Sadler,* Constable

Sadler, M. (1911) *Syllabus of a Course on a History of Education in England,* University of Manchester Press

Sadler, M. (ed.) (1936) *International Institute Examinations Enquiry. Essays on Examinations,* Macmillan

Sandford, E. G. (ed.) (1906) *Life of William Temple,* 2 Vols., Macmillan

Sargeaunt, J. (ed.) (1925) *A History of Bedford School,* T. Fisher Unwin

Saunders, H. W. (1932) *A History of Norwich Grammar School,* Jarrold and Sons, Norwich

Saville, J. (ed.) (1954) *Democracy and the Labour Movement,* Lawrence and Wishart

de Schweinitz, K. (1943) *England's Road to Social Security,* University of Pennsylvania

Selby-Bigge, L. A., Sir, (1927) *The Board of Uducation,* 2nd edn. 1934, Putnam

Sharpless, I. (1892) *English Education in the Elementary and Secondary Schools,* P. Appleton, New York

Sheffield Education Committee (1920) *Reports on Examinations for Free Places in Secondary Schools, 1920,* Sheffield

Sheffield Education Committee (1929) *Report of the Director of Education on the*

Preliminary and Final Examinations for Entrance to Secondary and Intermediate Schools, Sheffield

Sheridan, L. A. and Delany, V. T. H. (1961) *The Cy-Près Doctrine,* Sweet and Maxwell

Silver, H. (1965) *The Concept of Popular Education,* MacGibbon and Kee

Silver, H. (ed.) (1973) *Equal Opportunity in Education. A Reader in Social Class and Educational Opportunity,* Methuen

Simon, B. (1953) *Intelligence Testing and the Comprehensive School,* Lawrence and Wishart

Simon, B. (1960) *Studies in the History of Education 1780-1870,* Lawrence and Wishart

Simon, B. (1965) *Education and the Labour Movement 1870-1920,* Lawrence and Wishart

Simon, B. (1970) 'Classification and Streaming: A Study of Grouping in English Schools, 1860-1960', in Nash, P., (ed.), *History and Education,* Random House, New York

Simon, B. (1974) *The Politics of Educational Reform 1920-1940,* Lawrence and Wishart

Skeet, D. V. (1957) *The Child of Eleven. A Brief Survey of Transfer Tests Between Primary and Secondary Schools,* University of London Press

Skrine, J. H. (1899) *A Memory of Edward Thring,* Macmillan

Smith, F. (1931) *A History of English Elementary Education,* University of London Press

Snowden, Philip, Viscount (1934) *An Autobiography,* 2 Vols., Ivor Nicholson and Watson

Spalding, T. A. (1900) *The Work of the London School Board,* P. S. King and Son

Spencer, F. H. (1938) *An Inspector's Testament,* English Universities Press

Spender, J. A. (1932) *The Life of the Rt. Hon. Sir Henry Campbell-Bannerman,* 2 Vols., Hodder and Stoughton

Springall, L. M. (1936) *Labouring Life in Norfolk Villages 1834-1913,* Allen and Unwin

Staunton, H. (1865) *The Great Schools of England,* Straham and Co.

Stewart, W. A. C. (1953) *Quakers and Education,* Epworth Press

Stone, J. and Taylor, F. (1973) *Low-Down on Secondary Transfer in Inner London in 1973,* n.p.

Stone, L. (1965) *The Crisis of the Aristocracy 1558-1641,* Oxford University Press

Sumner R., and Bradley, K. (1977) *Assessment in Transition. An NFER Report,* NFER, Slough

Sutcliffe, A. and Canham, J. W. (1945) *Selection for Secondary Education Without a Written Examination,* Murray

Sutherland, G. (ed.) (1973) *Arnold on Education,* Penguin

Sutherland, G. (1973) *Policy-Making in Elementary Education 1870-1895,* Oxford University Press

Tarver, J. C. (1898) *Essays on Secondary Education,* Constable

Tawney, R. H. (1922) *Secondary Education For All,* Allen and Unwin

Tawney, R. H. (1924) *Education. The Socialist Policy,* Independent Labour Party

Tawney, R. H. (1932) *The New Children's Charter,* Workers' Education Association

Taylor, W. (1963) *The Secondary Modern School,* Faber and Faber

Temple-Patterson, A. (1954) *Radical Leicester 1780-1850,* Leicester University Press

Terman, L. M. (1919) *The Measurement of Intelligence,* Harrap

Terrill, R. (1974) *R. H. Tawney and His Times,* Andre Deutsch

Thompson, D. (1950) *England in the Nineteenth Century,* Penguin

Thompson, E. P. (1963) *The Making of the English Working Classes,* Gollancz

Thompson, F. M. L. (1963) *English Landed Society in the Nineteenth Century,* Heinemann

Thomson, R. (1968) *The Pelican History of Psychology,* Penguin

Times Publishing Co. (1952) *Intelligence Testing. Its Use in Selection for Secondary Education*

Tompson, R. S. (1971) *Classics or Charity? The Dilemma of the 18th Century Grammar School,* Manchester University Press

Trevelyan, G. M. (1947) *British History in the Nineteenth Century and After,* Longmans

Tripp, C. L. (1935) *Queen Elizabeth's School, Barnet,* Heffer, Cambridge

Tropp, A. (1957) *The School Teachers,* Heinemann

Valentine, C. W. (1932) *The Reliability of Examinations. An Enquiry,* University of London Press

Vernon, P. E. (ed.) (1957) *Secondary School Selection. A British Psychological Society Inquiry,* Methuen

Vernon, P. E. (1960) *Intelligence and Attainment Tests,* University of London Press

Wallis, B. C. (1931) *The Measurement of Ability in Children,* Oxford University Press

Walpole, S. (1904) *The History of Twenty Five Years,* Vol. II, Longmans Green

Ward, W. R. (1965) *Victorian Oxford,* Cass

Watts, A. F., Pidgeon, D. A. and Yates, A. (1952) *Secondary School Entrance Examinations. Second Interim Report,* NFER, Slough

Watts. A. F. and Slater P. (1950) *The Allocation of Primary School Leavers to Courses of Secondary Education. First Interim Report,* NFER, Slough

Wearmouth, R. F. (1937) *Methodism and the Working Class Movements of England 1800-1850,* Epworth Press

Webb, S. (1891) *The London Programme,* Swan and Sonnenschein

Webb, S. (1904) *London Education,* Longmans

Webb, B., (Drake, B., and Cole, M. (eds.)) (1948) *Our Partnership,* Longmans

Webb, R. K. (1955) *The British Working Class Reader 1790-1848,* Allen and Unwin

West Riding of Yorkshire. County Council Education Committee (1932) *Report on the Examination for County Minor Scholarships,* Wakefield

Whiston, R. (Rev.) (1849) *Cathedral Trusts and Their Fulfilment,* John Oliver

Wilkinson, R. (1964) *The Prefects: British Leadership and the Public School Tradition,* Oxford University Press

Willson, A. N. (1972) *A History of Collyer's School,* Arnold

Wilmot, D. (1910) *A Short History of the Grammar School in Macclesfield,* Claye, Brown and Claye, Macclesfield

Yeaxlee, B. A. (1921) *Working Out the Fisher Act,* Oxford University Press

Young, A. F. and Ashton, E. T. (1963) *British Social Work in the Nineteenth Century,* Routledge and Kegan Paul

Young, G. M. (1953) *Victorian England: Portrait of an Age,* Oxford University Press

Yoxall, J. H. (1896) *Secondary Education,* A. Brown and Sons

D. Articles and Pamphlets

Alexander, K. and Williams, V., 'Judicial Review of Educational Policy: The Teaching of Tameside', *British Journal of Educational Studies,* Vol. 26, No. 3, October 1978

Alsobrook D., 'The Reform of the Endowed Schools: The Work of the Northamptonshire Educational Society 1854-1874', *History of Education,* Vol. 2, No. 1., 1973

Arnold, M., 'A French Eton or Middle-Class Education and the State', *Macmillan's Magazine,* 1863-4

Bailey, C., 'John William Mackail OM', *Proceedings of the British Academy,* Vol. 31, 1947

Balls, F. E., 'The Endowed Schools Act 1869 and the Development of the English Grammar School in the Nineteenth Century – I', *Durham Research Review,* Vol. 5, No. 19 September, 1967

Barker Lunn, J. C., 'The Effects of Streaming and Other Forms of Grouping in Junior Schools: Interim Report'. *New Research in Education,* Vol. 1, June 1967

Dean, D. W., 'The Difficulties of a Labour Educational Policy: The Failure of the

Trevelyan Bill, 1929-31', *British Journal of Educational Studies,* Vol. 17, No. 3, October 1969

Dean, D.W., 'H.A.L. Fisher, Reconstruction and the Development of the 1918 Education Act', *British Journal of Educational Studies,* Vol. 18, No. 3, October 1970

Floud, J. and Halsey A.H. (1957), 'Intelligence Tests, Social Class and Selection for Secondary Schools', *British Journal of Sociology,* Vol. 8, 1957

Gomez, F.C., 'The Endowed Schools Act, 1869 – A Middle Class Conspiracy? The South-West Lancashire Evidence', *Journal of Educational Administration,* Vol. 6, No. 1, June 1974

Gorst, J.E. (Sir), 'Prospects of Education in England,' *North American Review,* October 1896

Higginson, J.H., 'Evolution of "Secondary Education" ', *British Journal of Educational Studies,* Vol. 20, No. 2, June 1972

Hyndman, M., 'Multilateralism and the Spens Report: Evidence from the Archives', *British Journal of Educational Studies,* Vol. 24, No. 3, October 1976

MacNamara, T.J., 'The State and Secondary Education', *Independent Review,* May 1905

Robertson, A.B., 'Children, Teachers and Society: The Over-Pressure Controversy, 1880-1886', *British Journal of Educational Studies,* Vol. 20, No. 3, October 1972

Sharp, F.R., 'The Origin and Early Development of Local Authority Scholarships', *History of Education,* Vol. 3, No. 1, January 1974

Simon, J., 'The Shaping of the Spens Report on Secondary Education 1933-38: An Inside View: Part II', *British Journal of Educational Studies,* Vol. 25, No. 2, June 1977

Stansky, P., 'Lyttelton and Thring: A Study in Nineteenth Century Education', *Victorian Studies,* Vol. 5, No. 3, March 1962

Sutherland, G., 'The Magic of Measurement, Mental Testing and English Education, 1900-40', *Transactions of the Royal Historical Society,* 5th Series, Vo!. 27, 1977

Synge, J., 'The Selective Function and British Rural Education', *British Journal of Educational Studies,* Vol. 23, No. 2, June 1975

Thomson, G.H., 'The Northumberland Mental Tests', *British Journal of Psychology,* Vol. 12, December 1921

Index